A HISTORY OF FRAMLINGHAM

From Saxon times to 1977.

BY

MURIEL L. KILVERT

With all good wishes
Muriel L Kilvert.

BOLTON & PRICE LTD.
1995

ISBN 0 9527364 0 3

A History of Framlingham

*This book is copyright in all countries which
are signatories to the Berne Convention*

First Edition 1995

BOLTON & PRICE LTD.
201 Spring Road, Ipswich, Suffolk

PRINTED BY PLANAGRAPHIC
Farthing Road, Ipswich

Framlingham, Suffolk

FOREWORD

The guide books tell us that Framlingham is steeped in history, and so it is. Even a cursory glance at the curtain wall of the castle or the Norfolk tombs in the Parish Church will confirm that impression.

This town has a rich story which needs to be told, from the earliest days of its settlement up to the present day. Muriel Kilvert tells that story in this chronicle in which she weaves the history of Framlingham into the history of the kingdom. Most local history gives particular detail to the tapestry of national events. The Civil War, for instance, had an immediate and lasting impact on Framlingham. Just occasionally (and most excitingly), Framlingham stood at the centre of the national stage. When Mary Tudor rallied her supporters at the Castle, where she proclaimed herself queen, and rode out to London to claim her throne, the eyes of the whole nation were turned upon Framlingham.

In this book Muriel Kilvert gives details of the impact of the nation on Framlingham and of Framlingham on the nation and we thank her for it.

Richard Willcock, Rector of St. Michael's Church, Framlingham, Suffolk.

Framlingham, Suffolk

Framlingham, Suffolk

ACKNOWLEDGEMENTS

A very great number of the local inhabitants of Framlingham have given me much encouragement and help in my endeavours to write a history of the town. Notable among them are:

Janet Adcook	Ipswich Building Society
Dorothy and Peter Allen	Arthur and Constance Kirby
Barclays Bank	Phillip Lanman (Photographs)
George Barker	Peter Northeast (Wills)
Nancy Bowen	Lloyds Bank
John Bridges	Noel Mander
John Bush	Mark & Diana Meynell
Paul & Monica Briscoe	Midland Bank
Reg and Marjorie Finbow	Margaret Murrell
Bob Gillett	G.J. Pankhurst (Brickmaking)
Harold Hammond	Charles Seeley (Castle Bookshop)
Diana Howard	John Symonds
Emma Hebblethwaite	Tony & Janet Webb
Ipswich Record Office	Richard Willcock

My most grateful thanks to them, and especially to Reg Finbow who has drawn the road maps of the town and the many delightful illustrations. Bob Gillett, who has painstakingly put me right with syntax, and Emma Hebblethwaite who has proof read the manuscript, but above all my thanks go to Stella Sills who has supported me throughout and has expertly and cheerfully typed and retyped my script, so that I present this history as a joint effort between us.

I should also like to thank Brian Bolton of Bolton & Price Ltd. who has most expertly collated the text and illustrations, and presented this work in its present form.

CONTENTS

Section 1.0 ....Introduction.

Section 1.1 ....The Saxon period until c. 1100 A.D.

Section 2.0 ....Framlingham dominated by the occupants of the Castle, c.1100 until 1635, the sale of the castle.

Section 3.0 ....Framlingham from 1624 when Richard Golty came to Framlingham as Curate and kept a tithe account book (still extant).

Section 3.1 ....Framlingham from 1724, marked by the Surveyor's comprehensive report, the establishment of small businesses, and the knocking down of the Market House.

Section 4.0. ....Framlingham from 1832, an account of the Great Reform Act and George Brooke Keer's bankruptcy, and the coming of the railway - the age of development for the town.

Section 4.1 ....Framlingham from 1863 following the death of Prince Albert, the plans for the Memorial College and the extension of the town.

Section 5.0. ....Framlingham from 1901, the death of Queen Victoria, the first World War, and the coming of mass-made goods, surfaced roads and improved street lighting.

Section 5.1. ....Framlingham from 1930 following the end of World War 1, the inter-war years, the coming of cars and bicycles; the Second World War, educational developments and piped water for the town.

Section 5.2. ....Framlingham from 1950, conservation in Framlingham, to 1977, the Queen's Silver Jubilee including the extension of the town and its dependence on prepackaged goods.

FORMAT
After the five main sections, an alphabetical **subject list** and notes on **families** follow:

SUBJECTS		FAMILIES	
Banking	Maltings	Brooke Keer	Lanman
Brickmaking	Mills	Buckmaster	Larner
Buildings	Non-conformity	Clarke	Maulden
Castle	Parish Council	Corrance	Mayhew
Charities	Printing	Fruer	Mills
Church	Railway	Garrard	Porter
Education	Roads	Golty	Potter
Fairs	Services	Green	Sampson
Farming	Tanneries	Hitcham	Self
Fire Brigade	Trades	Kinnell	Thompson
Inns	-	Lambert	Walne & Manby

Section 1.0

INTRODUCTION

Several books printed by private subscription in the eighteenth century (among them Hawes & Loder's *'History of Framlingham'*, and John Kirby's *'The Suffolk Traveller'*) have given a detailed account of Framlingham during the times of the earlier Earls and Dukes of Norfolk, who resided in the castle, owned a great deer park, and managed the demesne lands through their Stewards, One of these Stewards was Robert Hawes, the author, who lived in Framlingham, and was Steward from 1712 to 1731 for Pembroke Hall Cambridge, but there are no modern accounts of Framlingham.

The following extract from the *Domesday Heritage* sums up the early history of Framlingham.

> **Framlingham, Suffolk.**
>
> **This is a charming little town with neat streets, prosperous houses and sloping market place and far less important than its *Domesday* self must have been. From the outside St.Michael's is as tranquil as its surroundings. The chancel tells another story, crowded with the sixteenth-century tombs of the Howards of Norfolk, a mausoleum of vanity and bloodshed.**
>
> **Nearby is Framlingham Castle, a tall, irregular circle of grey stone. A castle stood here in Saxon times, perhaps as early as the sixth century. King Edmund, it is said, sought protection within its walls from the Danes, but was driven forth and murdered in the forests which covered much of this region.**
>
> **John Evelyn in his *Discourse of Forest Trees (1664)* praised Framlingham for its magnificent oaks, the finest 'perhaps in the world'. And the seventeenth-century warship *Royal Sovereign,* the flagship of King Charles II's navy, was built of Framlingham oak.**
>
> **Roger Bigot's manor had grown substantially since the Conquest. His total of 19 ploughs indicates that a large area had been cleared for crops, a sign of a prosperous community. Framlingham suffered less in the transition from Saxon to Norman rule than many neighbouring settlements. But why there were so many goats - well above the local average is one of the many minor curiosities of *Domesday*.**
>
> **The Bigot family (especially Roger's son, the scheming and ruthless Hugh) became warlords of Suffolk. Subsequent castle owners continued to fall foul of royalty. The Howards, Dukes of Norfolk, who took possession late in the fifteenth century, had a disastrous history, from the first duke, who backed the losing side in the Battle of Bosworth, to the fifth, beheaded for plotting to free Mary Queen of Scots.**
>
> **Edward VI held his first court here at Framlingham Castle and his sister Mary proclaimed herself queen while rallying her forces against the armies of Lady Jane Grey. There is a legend that, during her stay, she 'gave birth to a monster, which ... she instantly destroyed' on a stone pointed out to eighteenth-century travellers. By then Framlingham had ceased to have any political or military importance. The inside of the castle was gutted and a workhouse, which still stands, was built within the walls. This picturesque shell and the proud tombs are all that remain of grandeur.**

A History of Framlingham — Section 1.0 — INTRODUCTION

This book attempts to follow the significant changes which this historically important little market town underwent through the ages, starting with its selection by the Saxons as a vantage point suitable as a fortified settlement.

The Normans appreciated this, and Section 2 suggests that the first owners of the area built a stone stronghold, and in about 1190 the second Earl of Norfolk built the castle whose curtain walls survive to today. During this occupation until 1524 the castle was dependent on the inhabitants of Framlingham, and they, living at subsistence level in their small dwellings, were dependent upon the wishes of the owners of the castle.

The third section traces both religious and civil combats of the seventeenth century that substantially affected the whole country, with the particular effects of these struggles as they concerned Framlingham; coupled with the additional changes brought about as a result of the sale of the castle by Theophilus Earl of Suffolk to Sir Robert Hitcham and his devising in 1636 these great estates upon Pembroke Hall, Cambridge. The effect of this was to release the local inhabitants from their dependence on the family in the castle, and to make Framlingham tantamount to a self-supporting open borough, to encourage education, and craftsmen, artisans and skilled workmen to settle in this natural market centre. The market played an important part in the lives of many who were stall holders, selling wares they had produced themselves. In 1666 the plague reached Framlingham and nearly a quarter of the population died within a year. House building, in Castle Street and Church Street replaced some of the cramped old dwellings and made provision for the newcomers who were attracted to the borough. Both individuals and the borough were self-supporting.

The fourth section recounts that Framlingham regained its local importance when in 1830 and 1832 respectively it was chosen as the legal and the political centre for its surrounding villages. Specialisation caused the development of a variety of small businesses creating many skilled craftsmen and women. Farmers were gradually changing from dairy to arable farming to supply the maltings and breweries which were brewing beer in bulk. (The largest of these failed in 1832 causing much distress and rearrangements within the town). Windmills were developed for milling wheat into flour and for the production of animal feeding stuffs.

In 1859 a branch railway came from Wickham Market to Framlingham, and industrial development took place along the line while a residential area developed on the south side of the river, near to the 1863 Prince Albert Memorial College for boys. The local shops sold not only goods produced by the owners but became outlets for mass produced goods such as bicycles and then cars, ploughs and tractors. Further changes followed the establishment in 1894 of the first Parish Council, supplanting the old local offices and taking responsibility for the administration of the town.

The fifth section takes account of the two world wars and the loss of many inhabitants, the presence of the 390th U.S.A. Bomber Group in the 1940s, the development of the public services, including the educational rearrangements and expansion, the surfacing of the roads, the increase of lighting, the improvement of the sewage and the supply of piped water. The loss of horse-drawn vehicles and the growth of the number of bicycles, cars and tractors, the changes in farming practices, and the reduction in the variety and number of shops and shop owners, mark the 1970's with developments of the prepackaged goods and the self service stores, of the radio and television expansion, and of the expansion of the town along the Saxmundham Road and off Brook Lane and along Mount Pleasant for many who work away from Framlingham, using it as a dormitory town.

Section 1.1

THE SAXON PERIOD UNTIL C.1100 A.D.

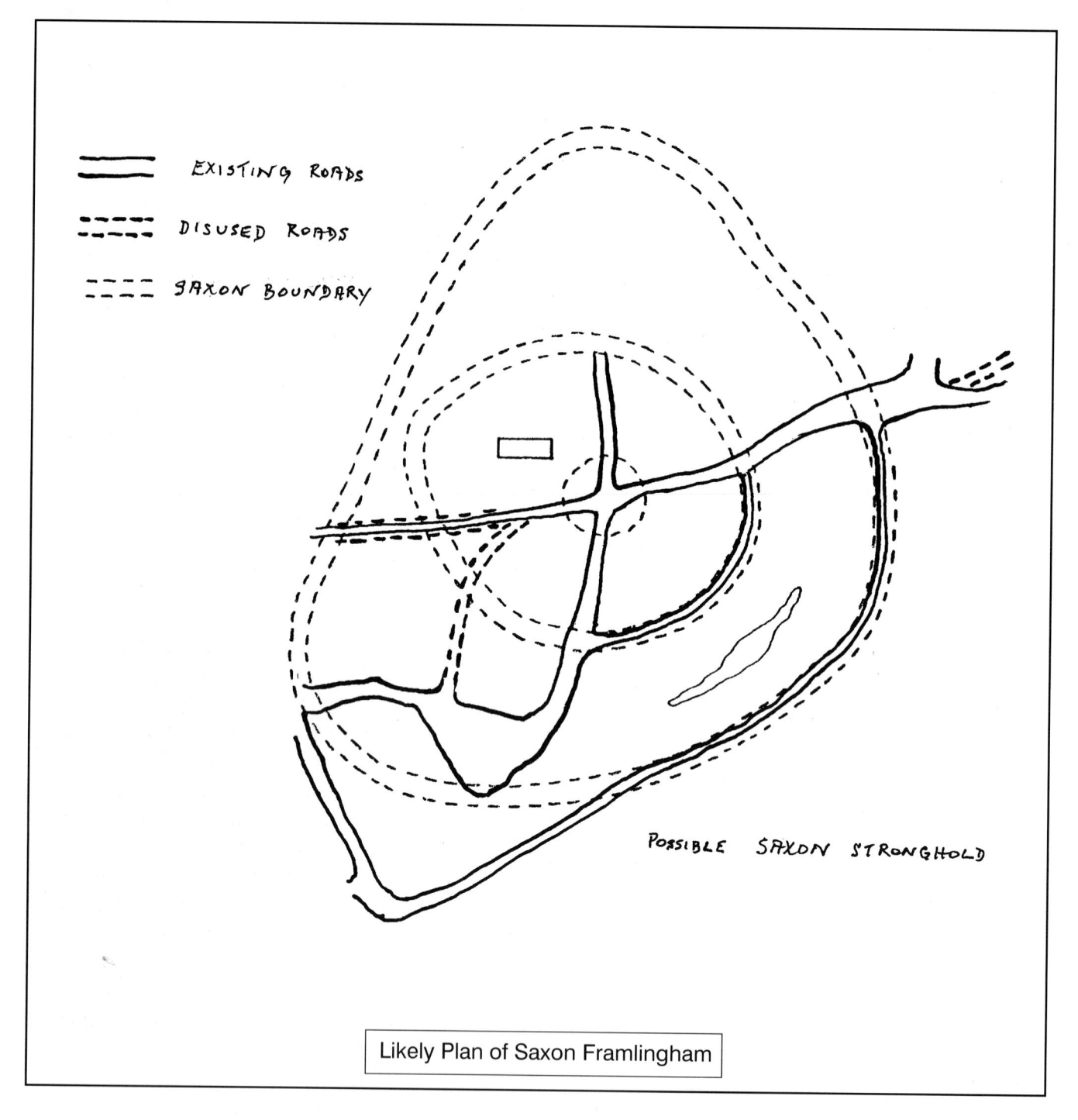

Likely Plan of Saxon Framlingham

The word Framlingham may derive from Fromus, the early name of the local river, now called the Ore; or it may come from the Saxon word 'friendling', and 'ham' meaning a house of strangers. Although the Saxons were likely to have been pagan until Pope Gregory sent St. Augustine to convert England to Christianity in the year 598, we do know that a great East Anglian King, King Raedwald, became a Christian c. 627. it is also supposed that he, or perhaps Uffa the First, or Titulus, may have built the wooden Saxon castle at Framlingham between 571 and 624. We also believe that Edmund, the last Saxon monarch, who was crowned King of East Anglia, aged 14, on 25th December 856, took refuge in the castle when pursued by the Danes led by Hingwar and Hubba c. 868/870, and that a battle took place in defence of the castle. King Edmund fled West, and was defeated and martyred in Hoxne in 870, whereupon the Danes made intermittent use of the castle until they departed these shores.

From the *Great Survey, or Little Domesday*, we learn that the castle and the Saxon church were again in the hands of the Saxons in Edward the Confessor's reign, for Aelmer/Ailmarus the Thane held the castle from sometime between 1041 and 1065.

> "Aelmer, a thane, held FRAMLINGHAM. Now R(oger) Bigot holds (it) [from Earl Hugh]. Then 24 villagers, now 32; then 16 smallholders, now 28. Then 5 ploughs in lordship, now 3; then 20 men's ploughs, now 16. Woodland, 100 pigs; meadow, 16 acres. Then 2 cobs, now 3; then 4 cattle, now 7; then 40 pigs, now 10; then 20 sheep, now 40; always 60 goats; now 3 beehives. Value then; £16; now £36.
>
> In the same (Framlingham) Munulf held, half under the patronage of Aelmer and half under (that) of Malet's predecessor; 1 carucate of land and 40 acres as a manor. Always 4 villagers; 12 smallholders; 2 ploughs in lordship; 2½ men's ploughs. Woodland, 100 pigs; meadow, 6 acres. 8 cattle, 20 pigs, 60 sheep, 40 goats, 4 beehives. Value always 40s. William Malet was in possession. Under him, 6 whole free men and 4 half (free) men; 30 acres of land. Always 1 plough. Meadow, 1 acre. They are in the assessment of 40s. In the same (Framlingham) 1 free man under patronage; 40 acres, 1 villager who dwells in *Ethereg*, 3 smallholders. Meadow, 1 acre. 1 plough. Woodland, 4 pigs. Value 8s. In the same (Framlingham) 3 free men under patronage; 56 acres. Always 3 ploughs. Meadow, 2 acres; woodland, 4 pigs. Value 17s. 1 church, 60 acres. 1 villager; 4 smallholders. 2 ploughs. Value 15s. In length 14 furlongs, and 12 in. width; 20d in tax. [St] Etheldreda's [had] the jurisdiction but (Earl) Hugh's predecessor had it from him."

This Saxon castle may well have stood at the confluence of the east/west and north/south roads, for the road pattern, as seen from the air in the accompanying photograph, indicates clearly parts of two concentric circles, which may have had as the centre the area now dominated by the *"Castle Inn"*, with Castle Street running off towards the Badingham Road to the north east, while Church Street leads to the river, and the Rectory driveway leading to the Meres to the west. This would indicate that the original Saxon castle, or wooden stockade known to have existed in Framlingham would have occupied this central position and been defended by a double moat which presently may be traced as Double Street (the inner) and Fore Street with Riverside (the outer moat). When these concentric arcs are extended into circles, it will be noted that they pass through existing ponds and join with existing moats (See diagram) and as an Archaeological officer to the Ordnance Survey suggests, "The Bigods, who were granted the tenancy of the castle by William I, would quickly have realised that with changing methods of warfare this arrangement would be untenable. This would indicate that the original Saxon Castle or wooden stockade known to have existed would have to be replaced with a stone curtain wall, and the township would have to be erased and placed further away in order to provide a 'No man's land' across which any attackers would have to come. In Saxon times, there were two approaches to the Castle, one from the Meres, which were tidal, and the other on the opposite side leading out on to the Badingham Road. When the Bigods put their plan into effect and wiped out what might be called 'Old Framlingham', they established 'New Framlingham' on the high ground to the south. The first thing they did was to erect a Church, and drive a new path from a new exit from the Castle straight across the old burial ground. This is the present Castle Path, which is, so to speak, modern. Thus 'Old Framlingham' was demolished, including the Saxon Church which is probably under the present car park, and 'New Framlingham' was started."

Section 2.0

FRAMLINGHAM 1100 - 1635

The fortunes of Framlingham fluctuated with the relationships of the Earls and Dukes, the inhabitants in the castle, with the sovereign of the time.

William the Conqueror (1066-1087) and his son William II (1087-1100) recognised the importance of the stronghold in Framlingham with its proximity to the sea, and kept the castle for themselves, only leasing it while giving the surrounding manors first to Ralph Guader and then to Hugh de Abrincis, who later became a monk and died in 1101. When Henry I (1100- 1135) came to the throne, the castle was given to Roger de Bigod with the surrounding 117 manors and nine plough lands in Framlingham. They passed to Roger's brother Hugh whom Henry created Earl. Hugh built a 'strong castle' in Framlingham. Times were uncertain during the reign of Stephen (1135-1154) and his wife, Matilda, daughter of Henry I. Hugh de Bigod at first supported Stephen who created him Earl of the Angles, but with many others, following the civil war and Stephen's defeat in 1141, he transferred his allegiance to Matilda who was not popular in England, and retired to France. On the death of Stephen, Matilda's son Henry II (1154- 1189) was proclaimed King, and did much to restore order in the kingdom by compelling Flemish auxiliaries to leave England, by recalling Stephen's grants of royal lands and by demolishing many of the recently built castles. He confirmed Hugh de Bigod in his estates but in the next year Hugh rebelled against him, and in 1174 Henry II received the surrender of the castle and ordered its destruction. In 1177 Hugh joined Crusaders and on his return, aged 78, he died. Roger, his son, created second Earl of Norfolk, succeeded to the castle and lands. He may be considered as the builder c.1190 of the fine curtain wall castle that stands on its mound today. Framlingham and its castle was the seat of the Earls and Dukes of Norfolk, heads of one of the most powerful families in the land. For long periods Framlingham castle contained the treasury of all the family estates and was a centre of trade. Medieval court rolls and bailiffs accounts show a turnover of about £2,000 per annum for commodities such as herrings, beer, cereals, pottery and iron for tools. With this background it may be seen that the people of Framlingham were there to serve the castle as stewards, officials, agricultural workers and servants and that the castle depended upon them for its wellbeing; for instance, deer were kept in the large park, flour was milled in the six-sail mill that probably stood by the mill bridge to the south of the town, and a Norman church was built.

When Henry II's eldest surviving son, Richard I (1189-1199), came to the throne, he confirmed Roger as Earl of Norfolk and made him Steward of his Household. John (1199-1216), the fourth son of Henry II, had a contentious reign. Until 1204 he was in dispute with Prince Arthur, grandson of Henry II, who claimed the throne, and during these years lost Normandy. He was in contention with Pope Innocent III over the election of the Archbishop of Canterbury. Then he came into conflict with the Barons, who, led by Stephen Langton, the Pope's choice of Archbishop (opposed by King John) were demanding rights and liberties for the citizens of the realm. Roger Bigod was one of the barons who met at Bury St. Edmunds and swore on the High Altar of that important abbey that they would compel John to grant their demands and put a seal to a charter. This *Magna Carta*, conceding rights to the church, to the feudal tenants, to traders and to freemen was indeed signed by King John at Runnymede in 1215 but was followed by ravages of the north of England and East Anglia by the King with his mercenary troops. Framlingham castle surrendered to him on 12th March 1216 shortly before his death in Newark castle. His young son Henry III (1216-1272), a minor, was subject to the Earl of Pembroke who as 'Governor of the King and the Kingdom' ruled the kingdom well. Roger Bigod was reinstated in the castle, where he died in 1220, leaving his estates to his young son, a minor, Hugh, who in turn died in 1225 and was succeeded by his son Hugh, the fourth Earl, who had entertained Henry III at the castle in 1235.

The steady government of England ended in 1230 when the King married Eleanor of Provence, who encouraged many Frenchmen to the country, a number of whom, marrying English heiresses, were given important offices in church and state. The country drifted away from recognised English government to a state of near anarchy and embarked on an expensive war to regain her French possessions. The King was again at variance with the Barons on account of his lavish expenditure, the unsuccessful war with France, his extreme partiality for foreigners and the heavy taxation and the oppressive extortions of the Court of Rome; but even so, Roger Bigod, Chief Justice of England, entertained him at the castle in 1248 and 1256 and assisted in the rebuilding of Westminster Abbey (where on the wall of the north choir aisle his arms are displayed). At the Provisions of Oxford an attempt was made to devolve powers of government from the King to the Barons, which led to the gradual formation of the Commons House of Parliament, but following the death of Simon de Montfort, the chief instigator, authority was restored to the King so long as he kept the regulations laid down in the *Magna Carta*.

In 1270 Hugh Bigod died and was succeeded by his brother, Roger. In 1272 Henry III died and was followed by his son Edward I (1272-1307) who was entertained at the castle on 9th and 10th April 1277. Roger in 1285 claimed to have rights including a warren in Framlingham and was granted a license for both the holding of a fair on the vigil of St. Michael and on the four following days and for a weekly market to be held on Sundays, Tuesdays and Fridays. In 1297 Earl Roger, Marshal of England, was involved with Humphrey Bohun, Earl of Hereford, High Constable, and others in refusing to supply troops for Edward I, who wished to invade Flanders. This cost him much money, some being supplied by his clerical and affluent brother, John, who demanded repayment. Roger was incensed by this so by a special instrument of 12th April 1301/2 made Edward I his heir and granted him all his castles, manors and lands and his titles on condition that he paid his debts and would regrant the earldom of Norfolk, the marshalship, castles and lands to the use of himself and his wife Alice and to any heirs should they occur. Roger died without issue in 1305/6 and the earldom of Norfolk and marshalship of England reverted to the King. Alice his wife lived for a further three years and then the whole estate passed to Edward II(1307-1327) who appointed John de Hastings esq. Steward of the castle during the life of Alice. In 1312 Edward appointed his half brother Thomas Plantagenet Brotherton, the fifth son of Edward I, to the castle and lands with the title Earl of Norfolk with a grant for the earl marshalship of England for him and his heirs male. During his stay at the castle in 1313 a licence was granted for a second annual fair to be held on Mondays, Tuesdays and Wednesdays in Whitsun week. Thomas de Brotherton was nominated as one of the three members of the regency for the minor Edward III (1327-1377).

During Edward III's reign the Black Death of 1349 almost halved the population and changed the balance of power between landlords and farm workers whose rarity value increased their wages. Many farm 'cots' were left empty and derelict. Mention should be made of the three essential principles of government which were firmly established during this reign, namely the illegality of raising money without the consent of Parliament, the necessity that the two Houses of Parliament should concur before any alteration could be made in the law, and the rights of Commons to inquire into public abuses and to impeach counsellors.

On the death of Thomas de Brotherton in 1338 his widow, Mary, held for her lifetime the castle and manor of Framlingham, which was in 1362 conveyed to William Ufford, Earl of Suffolk, widower of the Lady Joan de Montecute, the daughter of Thomas and his first wife, Alice de Brotherton.

This William built the Church at Parham. He was styled in the Court Rolls of the manor as *'Gulielmus Comes Suffolciae Dominus de Framlingham et Eye'* and was a pious, much respected man. The Commons in Parliament selected him to represent to the Lords certain important matters of public welfare, but in 1382 he suddenly died as he was on his way to fulfil his mission. The castle and manor passed to Lady Margaret, Countess of Norfolk, the eldest daughter and surviving heiress of Thomas de Brotherton. In 1378 she was styled *'Margaretta Marischalla Comitissa Norfolciae'* and so created Duchess of Norfolk in her own right, with an award from the king of a revenue of forty marks per annum.

Living through Richard II's reign (1377-1399) she must have witnessed the Peasants' Revolt of 1381 which had the effect of weakening the landowners' demands of villeinage service, and she must have co-operated with the garrisoning of Framlingham castle in 1386 against a possible French invasion. She died on 24th March 1398/9.

In 1399 Thomas Lord Mowbray, husband of Elizabeth, the daughter of the Lady Margaret, succeeded to the castle. He had been constituted earl marshal of England by Richard II and in 1396/7 he had obtained the King's charter and confirmation to this office to the heirs male of his body. This entitled him to carry a golden truncheon enamelled with black, with the King's arms at the upper end and his own at the lower end. In 1395 he went on a successful embassy to the King of France to seek the hand of the daughter of Charles VI, Isabelle, who subsequently became Richard's queen, a union of which the Duke of Gloucester disapproved. This duke hatched a conspiracy with the Earl of Arundel and others of which Thomas Mowbray acquainted the King, and with him, by a trick, captured the duke, who died in custody in Calais. For these 'services' Richard II created Thomas Duke of Norfolk and gave him the forfeited Arundel lands, yet looked for an opportunity to exercise his authority over him. This came when Thomas and the Duke of Hereford (later Henry IV) prepared to fight a duel which was stopped by the King who banished the Duke of Norfolk for life and the Duke of Hereford for ten years, later commuted to four years. Thomas died in Venice in 1399, shortly after the death of Richard II who had been compelled to resign the crown when (charged with tyranny and misgovernment), he was a prisoner in the Tower.

Hereford, now Duke of Lancaster, grandson of Edward III was declared King Henry IV (1399-1413). The castle, its manor and the Hundred of Loes passed to Elizabeth, the dowager duchess, who agreed with Henry IV to exchange this property, so near to the sea, for estates in Buckinghamshire, Leicestershire and Derbyshire. The King granted the castle to Sir Thomas Erpingham of Norfolk who managed it until his death in 1403, when the King restored the castle to the son of Thomas Mowbray Thomas, who had married the Lady Constance, one of the King's nieces. Thomas using the title earl marshal, Nottingham, Lord of Mowbray, Segrave and the Gower held court for the manor 1403/4 and then joined forces with Henry Percy and Richard Scroop, the Archbishop of Canterbury, and others, enemies of the King, in order to avenge his father's death. They were in 1404 arrested and beheaded, so the castle was in the hands of the King until 1412 when he granted it to Thomas' brother, John. When Henry IV's son Henry V (1413-1422) came to the throne he confirmed the office of earl marshal on John Mowbray and was supported by him in his war with France until his death in 1422, when his son Henry VI (1422-1461) succeeded him. Following a petition to Parliament John Mowbray was in 1426 declared Duke of Norfolk and inherited the castle on coming of age in 1427. He with others of nobility in 1430 accompanied the young King to Paris and witnessed his coronation as King of France. John died in 1434 and his young son John as a minor had as his guardian until 1437 the Duke of Gloucester. John was confirmed as Duke of Norfolk in about 1445 and to escape the rivalries of the houses of York and Lancaster he broke his allegiance to the King by undertaking, without permission, a pilgrimage to Rome. On his return to England, in order to avoid forfeiture of his lands, he made over the castle to John Stafford,

Archbishop of Canterbury, Humphrey Stafford, Duke of Buckingham and others as feoffees in trust for himself and his heirs. By 1455 John was a supporter of the Yorkist cause, and having fought with them in 1460 and 1461, was rewarded by Edward IV (1461-1483) by being given honours including the appointment of the post of Justice Itinerant of all the forests south of the Trent, a post he held for less than a year, for he died in 1461 and was succeeded by his 17 year old son, John, created Earl of Surrey and Earl of Warren by Henry VI in 1450/51. He became earl marshal and presided at the summary trial and condemnation of Edmund Beaufort and other supporters of the red rose Lancastrians. It is likely that he resided in the castle of Framlingham and was responsible for the building of the present church of St. Michael during the years between 1483 and 1534.

Certainly he died in the castle (at the age of 31) in 1475, leaving his infant daughter Anne one of the richest ladies in the land. She was given in marriage in 1477, aged six, to the second son of Edward IV, Richard Duke of York.

Found at Framlingham Castle Suffolk.

The strife between the houses of York and Lancaster devolved into the widowed Queen Elizabeth's faction of New Nobility and the Old Nobility represented by the Dukes of Gloucester and Buckingham, who were responsible for imprisoning the brothers Edward V and Prince Richard, who died together in the Tower of London in 1483.

Richard III (1483-1485), brother of the Yorkist Edward IV, was well received in the country. He created John Lord Howard, a cousin of Anne Mowbray and the new owner of the castle of Framlingham, the first Howard Duke of Norfolk. In Edward IV's reign in 1470 he had been made admiral and was later installed a Knight of the Garter. Richard III appointed him on 28th June 1483 earl marshal and conferred on him the titles Duke of Norfolk and Lord Admiral of England, Ireland and Acquitain for life; it was he who carried the imperial crown at the coronation of Richard III and joined him at the fatal battle of Bosworth where they both died.

Henry VII (1485-1509) the grandson of Edward III and husband of Elizabeth of York, daughter of Edward IV, claimed the throne and caused the late John, Duke of Norfolk, and his son, Thomas, Earl of Surrey, to be attainted by Act of Parliament and the earl to be committed to the Tower. He granted the castle of Framlingham and estates in Suffolk to John de Vere, Earl of Oxford who had supported him at the battle of Bosworth. In 1490 Henry VII restored the Castle and lands to Thomas Howard, Earl of Surrey, whom the King had heard had behaved gallantly, though for the Lancastarians, on the field of battle and honourably as a prisoner.

Shortly after the earl's release from the Tower he supported Henry VII against an uprising of rebel lords in the north and was made chief captain of the vanguard; the King left him in charge in the north making him Lieutenant General from the Trent northwards and warden of the east and middle marches of England against Scotland, where he kept the peace over a ten year period.

The King made him treasurer of England and of his privy Council and one of his executors, and his son Henry VIII (1509-1547) continued this trust in him confirming him in all his offices and additionally making him high marshal of England. While Henry VIII was fighting in France the earl was again left in charge of the country. He thwarted a Scots invasion by a mighty and terrible victory at Flodden field where the King of the Scots was killed with his two bishops, 400 knights and about 17,000 other men. Thomas, Earl of Surrey, brought King James' body south and left it at the Charter House 'to await the King's pleasure'. For this great triumph and skill of arms Thomas was created the second Howard Duke of Norfolk. In the absence of the king 'he remained as protector and defender to minister justice and to see good rule and government in the realm'. He continued on 'active service' and as a privy councillor until he was 80 years of age, when he repaired to his castle in Framlingham and 'kept a very noble and an honourable house unto the hour of his death on 21st May 1524'.

Thomas, the eldest son, became the third Duke of Norfolk and was created earl marshal in 1534 as well as Lord High Admiral and Knight of the Garter. It was he who, as Lord High Steward, presided over the trial of his niece, Anne Boleyn, before he was appointed Lieutenant General of all the King's forces north of the Trent, and in 1542 Captain General of the army in the north. This third duke did not live in Framlingham castle but built a palace at Kenninghall, Norfolk, taking the fine tapestries and valuables from the castle to furnish his new home. He also caused the chancel of St. Michael's Church to be razed (photograph next page) and a new and wider chancel to be built to house his family's sarcophagae which held the remains of those removed from Thetford Priory; but he did not live to see its completion, for he was falsely attainted and sent to the tower, and only escaped execution by the death of Henry VIII on the night before the date for his execution. His son, the poet, the Earl of Surrey, similarly attainted, was executed on the day before the death of the King.

Edward VI (1547-1553) son of Henry VIII and Jane Seymour succeeded his father and reigned for six years; the first two under the protectorship of Lord Hertford, the Duke of Somerset, and a Council of 16, and under the influence of Archbishop Cranmer who was pursuing further Protestant reforms such as the removal of images and paintings from churches, and requiring the English liturgy and not the Roman Catholic Mass book to be used. In 1549 the first Act of Uniformity enforced the use of the first prayer book of Edward VI and granted complete liberty for the general use of the Bible in English.

When in 1553 Edward VI fell dangerously ill he was persuaded to sign a declaration naming the Lady Jane Grey, the great grand-daughter of Henry VI and daughter of the Earl of Suffolk, his successor in preference to his half sisters Mary and Elizabeth. However, Mary (1553-1558) daughter of Henry VIII and Catherine of Aragon, was recognised by the people to have the right of succession, and although Lady Jane was proclaimed Queen, Mary was popularly proclaimed Queen while she was in Framlingham Castle surrounded by about 13,000 supporters with whom she subsequently marched to London. In 1553 she was crowned and soon released the third Duke of Norfolk from the Tower and restored him his lands and Framlingham Castle, appointing him Lord Lieutenant of the counties of Norfolk and Suffolk. Parliament repealed his act of attainder and within two weeks he presided as Lord High Steward at the trial of his bitter enemy John Dudley, Duke of Northumberland, who was decapitated. He marched against Sir Thomas Wyatt who led a rebellion against the projected marriage of Queen Mary with the powerful Roman Catholic Philip, King of Spain, for the people, fearing his potential power in England and the possibility of the Inquisition reaching these shores, rose in arms against the Queen. Thomas suffered the first defeat of his life. He was an eighty-year-old weakened man, and when his troops deserted he left public office and retired to his seat at Kenninghall, where he died on 25th August 1554. He left 56 manors, 37 advowsons and considerable estates which had accrued to him from his father by his two marriages the first to Anne, the third daughter of Edward IV, and then to Elizabeth, daughter of Edward Stafford, the Earl of Buckingham, by whom he had two sons, Henry, the Earl of Surrey, Knight of the Garter, the poet of renown who had been executed in 1547, and Thomas who became the fourth Duke of Norfolk, succeeding to the title at 17 years of age as a page and ward of Philip and Queen Mary until 1557/8 when he was described as '*Thomae, Dux Norfolciae Comes Mareschallus Angliae Filius et haeres Henrici Comitis Surriae Filii et Hoeredis Apparentis Thomae Ducis Norfolciae, post complevit aetatem viginti et unius annorum*', and was supported by them at his first Manorial Court held in Framingham Castle in 1559.

St. Michael's Church

Queen Mary's reign was not favoured. Sir Thomas Wyatt, who had had popular support was executed with Lady Jane Grey, her husband, father and uncle, with over one hundred commoners. The country was in an uproar as Mary, trying to restore the pope's authority, caused upwards of 280 Protestants to be burnt at the stake in different towns. Those to suffer included Archbishop Cranmer with Bishops Latimer and Ridley in Oxford. Furthermore, Calais, England's last foothold in France, was lost.

So it was that Elizabeth (1558-1603), the daughter of Henry VIII and Anne Boleyn, was proclaimed Queen amidst much enthusiasm. Thomas the fourth Duke of Norfolk as a young man had been taught by John Fox, and earned degrees at Oxford and Cambridge. He welcomed Elizabeth's title to the crown. He was invested by her with the Order of the Garter, then in 1567 with the much valued French Order of St.Michael. He was one of three commissioners to examine at York the charges against the captive Queen Mary of Scotland for whom he developed an attachment which caused his downfall, and in 1572 his execution. In his early years he added to the wealth of the family through his three marriages; the first to Mary Fitzalan, co-heiress of the 14th Earl of Arundel; the second to Margaret Audley, sole heiress to Lord Audley of Waldon, and the third to Elizabeth Dacre, widow of Lord Dacre, who had three daughters. Thomas had three sons, Philip by his first wife and Thomas and William by his second wife. These three boys each married a Dacre girl, so securing the property for the Norfolk family. After the death of his third wife, Thomas, who had become the leader of the Roman Catholic party in England, planned to marry Mary Queen of Scots, lead a rising of Roman Catholics and, joined by a Spanish army, de-throne Elizabeth; but this plot was in 1572 discovered by Lord Cecil. Thomas was tried and executed in June of that year.

The eldest son, Philip, had the estates restored to him in 1573, but as a leading Roman Catholic was brought before the Star Chamber and confined in 'a secluded apartment [in] Beauchamp's Tower' where he died in October 1595. This Philip was canonized as a martyr by the Roman Catholic Church. In 1559 Queen Elizabeth restored the Protestant religion through the second Act of Uniformity, which required that the second prayer book of Edward VI should be used in all churches and that everyone, on pain of a shilling fine, should attend the Church of England. Roman Catholics who refused were known as recusants and imprisoned. Framlingham Castle was used for this purpose.

Parliament also passed the second Act of Supremacy declaring that no foreign potentate should exercise any power or authority in England and that the sovereign was the supreme head of the Church.

Queen Elizabeth's long and eventful reign ended in 1603, when James I (1603-1625), King of Scotland and great grandson of Henry VII, son of Mary Queen of Scots and Lord Darnley, came to the throne. In 1604 he restored the castle and lands to Henry Lord Howard, appointing him to be his Privy Counsellor and constituting him Warden of the Cinque Ports and Constable of Dover Castle. In the next year Henry was advanced to baron as Lord Howard and Marnhill, Earl of Northampton, and then earl marshal of England, and, in 1605, Knight of the Garter. He died a bachelor in 1614, leaving the castle to his nephew, Thomas Lord Howard who often commanded Queen Elizabeth's fleets and in 1588 was knighted following his part in the rout of the Spanish armada. In 1597/8 he became Earl of Suffolk. With Lord Mounteagle in 1605 he searched the Houses of Parliament and discovered the 36 barrels of gun-powder, an exposure which resulted in the apprehension of Guy Vaux and the other conspirators. In 1614 he was appointed second Treasurer of England, it was he who built Audley End mansion at a cost of £200,000 and removed there from Kenninghall, with other treasures, the famous tapestry depicting Hercules. When Chancellor of Cambridge University, with the Revd. Samuel Harsnet (Master of Pembroke College) Vice Chancellor, he entertained James I at a cost of £5,000. He died on 28th May 1626. He was twice married, first to Mary Dacre (see above) and then to Catherine co-heiress of Sir Henry Knevit, to whom his son, Theophilus, was born. In 1626 Theophilus succeeded to Framlingham Castle and its lands, which in 1635 he sold to Sir Robert Hitcham (See Section 3.0).

Section 3.0

FRAMLINGHAM, 1624 - 1724

17th Century

In order to appreciate the changes experienced by the inhabitants of Framlingham in the early seventeenth century, it is useful to note the contrast between the splendid events the town witnessed up to the mid sixteenth century - such as the funeral in 1524 of Thomas, second Duke of Norfolk, the hero of Flodden field, and the last Duke to make Framlingham Castle his home, with the conditions that prevailed in 1624 when the young Richard Golty became curate of St.Michael's Church, Framlingham.

The funeral procession of 1524, numbering over 2,000 persons and stretching over about two miles, was resplendent with Heralds, Kings of Arms, the Duke's Standard-bearer, Knights, Esquires and Gentlemen of his household besides the chief mourners: Dukes, Earls and Lords, Knights and gentlemen in black, according to their degree, accompanied by horses caparisoned with escutcheons of the Duke's arms beaten in oil with fine gold. The procession wended its way from Framlinghan to Thetford, pausing in Hoxne, where the Bishop of Norwich met them in his *pontificalibus*, and stopping the night in Diss. Two days later, 300 priests sang the Requiem Mass in Thetford Abbey, where the Duke was laid to rest. Costs for this funeral amounted to £1,340. All seemed so fitting and secure. Thomas, the son and third Duke of Norfolk, was to build himself a Palace at Kenninghall, in Norfolk, and to remove from Framlingham Castle the treasures such as the Arras story of Hercules tapestries. The castle was allowed to fall into disrepair.

There was one reprieve for Framlingham in 1553 when Mary, Henry VIII's daughter, chose to establish herself in the protection of the Castle. While she was there all around became bustle and busyness, for she was proclaimed Queen of England and flew the Royal Standard from the Castle walls, surrounded by about 13,000 of her subjects.

The absence of nobility in the castle had led to Framlingham becoming less important. This was reflected in the appointment, by the Earl of Suffolk, of Richard Golty to the living of St Michael's, following the death of Thomas Dove in 1630. Unlike his predecessor, Richard Golty was relatively unknown. He had, for six years served as curate to the well-known Thomas Dove, who had held this rich and important living *in commendum* since 1584, while Bishop of Peterborough and close spiritual adviser to Queen Elizabeth. The appointment of Richard Golty, coupled with the experiences of Pembroke Hall and its members, throw into relief the religious and political confusions of the time, which directly affected the incumbents of this living. Richard Golty was a student at Pembroke Hall when the Royalist, High Church Laudian Matthew Wren was its President. Richard Golty subscribed to these positions, and continued to uphold his beliefs while a number of his parishioners became non-conformist and supporters of the Commonwealth faction. Notable among them was one of his churchwardens, a leading and respected figure in Framlingham, one Nicholas Danforth, whose non-conformity led him, on the death of his wife and one child, to take ship with his five remaining children and to set sail for New England, where he became a leader and a Selectman.

Richard Golty's Laudian convictions did not preclude him from marrying, in 1627, Deborah Ward, the daughter of Samuel Ward, one of the chief Puritan preachers of Ipswich, who later suffered imprisonment for his beliefs and preaching. Samuel Ward, so well-known and respected among the non-conformists, received a £20 legacy from the professed Churchman, Sir Robert Hitcham, who stipulated in this same Will that his almsmen and women should all be practising church people.

The change of ownership of the castle coincided with the second great disruption for Framlingham, the influence of the Commonwealth. Many changes were experienced in East Anglia and the country during the troubled years of 1633 to 1640, culminating in the assembly of the Long Parliament in 1640. In 1641, episcopacy was abolished, and in 1642, the Civil War broke out. On the whole, East Anglia declared for Parliament, and sequestrations of Anglican clergy followed. Suffolk became an ecclestical province divided into 14 precincts, and committees were appointed in each precinct to institute ministers whose beliefs accorded with those of the Westminster Assembly of Divines.

Richard Golty, staunch in his loyalties, would not sign the Oath of Allegiance to the Commonwealth, and in 1650 was sequestrated from his parish. Pembroke Hall, now patrons of the living, appointed to the post Henry Sampson, a brilliant young non-conformist graduate and Fellow of the College, though still only 21 years old. Henry Sampson had gone up to Pembroke Hall in 1646 just two years after the Earl of Manchester had caused the ejection of a number of the Fellows of the Colleges for 'offending the privileges of Parliament' and had established the prominent Presbyterian divine Richard Vines as Master, with Henry Sampson's own tutor, William Moses, as his lieutenant. William Moses, a lawyer, also played a conspicuous part in gaining the rights bequeathed to Pembroke Hall by securing an ordinance from Cromwell which settled in favour of the College the long dispute over Sir Robert Hitcham's Will. Strangely, Sir Robert Hitcham had been advised by Matthew Wren to buy the castle, William Moses had secured the bequest, and Matthew Wren, on his release from prison after the restoration of the monarchy, supervised the implementation of the Will, building a part of the college and the cloisters, emblazoned with the Hitcham arms, which was consecrated in 1667.

Henry Sampson combined his care of the parish of St.Michael's not only with his responsibilities in 1654 as a Commissioner for one of the 14 precincts of East Anglia, but also with his duties at Pembroke Hall as Junior Bursar and lecturer in Greek and Philosophy. His brother-in-law, Jonathan Grew, also a Pembroke graduate, and a strong non-conformist, was appointed as his assistant in Framlingham. During the ten years of Henry Sampson's administration, teaching and preaching, non-conformity in Framlingham was strengthened. He laid the foundation stone of an independent chapel built in College Road (Horn Hill) in 1651. The Baptist congregation that had practised clandestinely in Lincoln's Barn (to the southwest of the parish) was gradually assimilated into his congregation. But circumstances were reversed in 1660 when Henry Sampson would not conform, and was removed from the living.

Richard Golty, after writing his humble petition to the Right Honourable Peers of the Realm of England assembled in parliament, was re-instated as Rector in 1660, and remained there until his death in 1678. Nathaniel Coga, his successor, (as became the practice) was Master and Senior Fellow of Pembroke Hall. He served until his death in 1693, and was replaced in 1694 by Marcus Anthony, who was responsible for the fine wall which skirts the south side of the churchyard dividing

Churchyard Wall

it from the Guildhall property, and for the three-decker pulpit, and for substituting box pews for the sixteenth century carved pews, and possibly for the *trompe l'oeil* glory in the chancel arch. (See Church).

On account of the absence of a resident Lord of the Manor, Framlingham became tantamount to an open borough. Opportunities were taken by enterprising craftsmen, artisans and enthusiastic entrepreneurs to set up family businesses in this natural market centre, with its great reputation from its earlier days of importance, that had earned it three market days a week and two fairs a year.

The powers given to the churchwardens and overseers of the poor by the Act of 1601 had strengthened the control of these elected members of the parish in the absence of the Lord of the Manor in the castle. They had become yet more important during the Long Rebellion, since manors could no longer collect dues for reliefs, wardships, marriages and the like. Bailiffs were appointed to collect rents, and the old feudal method, practised in Framlingham where the 'coliarholders', those who paid two and a half pence annually for every acre, and who also bore the office of collectors of the Lord's Rents - without payment - were abolished. Something of the time-honoured system of dividing tenants into groups remained for Freeholders and Burgenholders, those who lived within the Borough and paid five pence for each house, and persisted even until 1844, as did Copyholders *Magnae Tenorae*, whose payments on admission to the property, however, were now assessed by the Land Steward.

The third great disruption for Framlingham was the plague which reached Framlingham in 1666. The effect was serious: one hundred and eleven people died within four months, 19 in July, 43 in August, 21 in September and 28 in October - 150 during the year - perhaps more. The figure is uncertain because there was much confusion and distress at the time. It is likely that interments of the plague victims were made in the Glebe pightle to the North of the Church. It is also very likely that, because of the plague, a number of the older and smaller houses in and around the market area were destroyed, and that this may partly account for the building of a number of the smaller two-storeyed, timber-framed and thatched houses on the south side of present day Castle Street, with their gardens reaching the north side of Double Street (Bow Street). In 1632 John Edwards had been heavily penalised with a fine of £5 for disregarding a law in use from 1589 to 1775 that stipulated that four acres of land had to accompany any new cottage. It seems unlikely that each house in the row in Castle Street had this amount of land!

Double Street in the seventeenth century had the Town House on its north side, and the house of the burgenholder, John Sea, on the south side, flanked by the *Bull Inn*, and a cottage. The gardens of these houses reached Back Lane (see road plan), and their water supply was from wells in the road that are still evident.

According to the 1674 Hearth Tax, 142 households were recorded, and from this we may conjecture that there may have been approximately 860 inhabitants, in spite of the decimation of the population in 1666. Most occupations, apart from the innkeepers and the four bootmakers, were linked with farming and accompanying trades. Households were for the most part self-supporting. For example, only one baker is listed, and drapers are not included in the early lists (see Trades). Later, shop-keepers prospered as demand increased. We learn that by 1703 the two drapers, Francis Kilderbee and Samuel Wightman, and the apothecary, John Sheppard, were each 'worth' £600. Responsibility was taken for the paupers, with accommodation for the aged and infirm in the Town House in Double Street (Bow Street), while work and clothing were provided. Marriages took place between families of equal standing and the new recognisable strata in this society developed. In 1705, only five families earned the privileged Esquire after their names. The families that prospered shouldered the responsibilities of administration, becoming Over-seers of the Poor, Surveyors, Churchwardens and Feoffees of the Town.

The look of Framlingham in the seventeenth century may be imagined from contemporary documents, amongst them the extant Tithe Account Book kept by Richard Golty from 1628 to 1678. In this book he enters all his parishioners, with the tithes they owe, and he arranges these entries for those persons within and without the Borough, under such headings as 'Dwellers in the plumpe of howsen next the market and the back lane adjoyning to that', and again, ' the plumpe of howsen next the market and churchyard to the milbridge' and 'Outdwellers in the subburbes'. From Richard Golty's Tithe Account Book we learn that the 'borough' of Framlingham was bounded by the Mere, the river Ore, the Tun Ditch and the old Saxon ditch, which runs behind the houses in Fore Street, once Back Lane, and present day Castle Street, earlier Swan Lane. (See road plan). Not only may we count his parishioners, but we can begin to see where they lived and what their standing in Framlingham may have been, and in the extended town, which was surrounded by a number of small mixed farms, and one or two gracious farmsteads such as D'Urbans Farm in Apsey Green, and Red House Farm in the same area, Nicholas Danforth's property in New Street, and Edward's Farm in Coles Green. These farms, we learn, were cultivated for the most part by the owners or tenants living on the property. Cattle, particularly, and sheep played a more important part in the seventeenth century than in the present day. Most farms grew wheat and barley, some also grew oats and flax. Few farms listed horses, but a number kept bees, and of course chickens, and often a pig.

From Richard Golty's lists we can place the houses with their inhabitants. For example, Thomas Clark, a burgenholder and chandler and father of Richard Clark, was entered in Richard Golty's book under the heading 'Next the churchyard down to the bridge'. It would seem that he owned the Guildhall of St. Mary the Virgin on the Market Hill. From Richard Clark's Will of 1701, we learn that he left to his daughter Mary 'the hall, hall chamber, the shop, the shop chamber, the buttery and kitchen chamber, the clothes, and brewhouse and a little bottle house, the barn, cart house, and orchards abutting on the meer to the west, on Parsonage Hill to the north and to the south of the last-mentioned piece, and the yards, gardens and orchards from the pump to the Parsonage Barn'. These details greatly assist us in establishing the look of the north side of the Market Hill. The whole area West of Church Lane to the river was therefore open, and belonged to Richard Clark, who later built the little house with the initials R.B.C. 1681 - Richard and Bridget Clark, now No. 19 Market Hill.

We know of seven inns to the north and east of the Market Place; the *Griffin*, the *Lyon*, the *White Hart*, the *Black Swan*, the *Crown*, the *Duck and Mallard*, and the *Queen's Head*.

The Crown Inn

The *Griffin* stood in Griffin Close, a sizeable property that belonged to Richard Porter. This property, presently occupied by Bridges & Garrards and Carley & Webb, was then a site on which were three dwellings, reaching to Back Lane/Fore Street. (See Griffin). The *Griffin Inn* was flanked by the *Crown Inn* on its south side. This inn, two storeyed, timber-framed and thatched, was possibly built to accommodate the visitors to Framlingham at the disturbed times following the death of Edward VI and Mary's sojourn in the Castle. The main road to London went through this inn, vehicles from London approaching up Fairfield Road from the East, and those from Norwich entering from the Market Hill. (See Crown).

The north side of the *Griffin Inn* was flanked by the *Lyon Inn*, which once had a finely carved corner-post. It stood on the corner of White Hart Lane. Between this lane and Swan Lane (now Castle Street) stood the *White Hart Inn*, then three dwelling houses, and to the north, a large and important property, the *King's Head Inn*, later to become the *Black Swan* (hence Swan Lane).

It is possible that the Market House, pulled down in 1788, stood near to the *Crown Inn*. It was a two-storey building, dominating the Market Place, possibly known as the Market Cross, for early documents mention Crosse Street. Then to the south of the Market Place came the *Duck & Mallard Inn*, and the *Blue Boar*, later to become the *Queen's Head*, with its walkway through to Back Lane (even earlier known as Lurke Lane). The south side of the Market also had Samuel Wightman's three burgens, which included a butcher's shop, a tannery, and his house, along with several notable houses, with properties reaching to the River Ore. Until the early years of this century a sizeable barn survived on what is now the site for the new Co-operative building, with other rural buildings. Across the river in Well Close Square stood the sizeable brewery run by John, then Stephen, Welton. This brewery supplied the *Black Swan* in Church Street and the nearby *White Horse Inn*, owned in 1632 by Nicholas Sheen, a Churchwarden.

The perspective of Framlingham changed in the latter years of the seventeenth century - the outlook becoming positive, purposeful and expansionist. The numbers of houses within the town grew, its boundaries were extended, the population and the number of trades increased. (See Trades). The building development included carrying out the stipulations in Sir Robert Hitcham's will. Twelve single-storeyed dwellings were built for churchgoing almsmen and women, beyond the River Ore in New Road. They were built in 1654, of bricks and tiles from the demolished buildings within the castle.

The Hitcham Almshouses

The readery was built on the north side of Castle Street (Swan Lane) for the Reader to the almsfolk, and next to it on the east side, Moat House, which probably incorporated sound beams and panels from the castle buildings. Michael Baldry, later to become the second headmaster of the Sir Robert Hitcham School, built his house to the west of the Readery. These two houses were subsequently incorporated into one to improve the Readery. The houses on the north side of Castle Street were the subject of a dispute at a later date, for it was claimed that they were built on land stolen from castle property. Houses were built in Double Street (Bow Street) with their gardens reaching to Back Lane (Fore Street).

A start was made in the 1670s on building the Poor House within the castle walls, using bricks as specified in Sir Robert Hitcham's will. The building was completed in 1729, when the two-storey central 84 ft. range was built on the site of the Great Hall, of flint and stone from the demolished castle.

The Poor House, Framlingham Castle.

1703 saw the building of the eight two-storey almshouses on Feak's pightle, six provided by Thomas Mills, and two by William Mayhew, almshouses of which Robert Hawes, comparing them with the Hitcham almshouses wrote 'the wheelwright's Almshouses as far exceeds the Knight's in magnificence, as the Knight exceeded the wheelwright in quality'.
(See photograph next page).

The year 1703 was also the year of the great storm, when much of Southwold was devastated and trees and crops in Framlingham suffered from the salt carried on the wind from the sea. Unwanted stone, flint and materials from the castle were sent to rebuild Southwold.

The Mills Almshouses

Hitcham   Mills

While the early part of the seventeenth century was dominated by the non-conformist and High Church rivalries, the latter part of the century was threatened with the revival of Roman Catholicism. James II's fervent determination to relax the Penal Laws against Roman Catholics aroused much opposition from the Anglican majority of the holders of public office and from the landowning inhabitants who dominated both Houses of Parliament. Louis XIV of France had aspirations of ascendancy and dominance that led him to give fiscal assistance to Charles II and the Roman Catholic James II as they strove to govern the country without the control of the estranged elected Parliament. This led to an alert, questioning body of opinion among the citizens, jealous of their rights and responsibilities. The dynamism of the enterprising craftsmen and businessmen who were setting up in Framlingham was given a boost following 1685, when Louis XIV revoked the Edict of Nantes. The flight of some 200,000 industrious, intolerant and hard working skilled Huguenot refugees leaving France, many of whom settled in England, was a further influence for the 'self-help' attitude that was most apparent in Framlingham and gaining ground in the country. Abraham Javelleau, a peruke maker, was among those who prospered in Framlingham.

The country became divided into Whigs and Tories. Framlingham reflected the national mood with its keen and growing body of non-conformists, who built themselves their first chapel in 1651 and, in 1717, the fine chapel in Bridge Street. They were high-principled and fervent in their religious practices and way of life. For the most part they were of the protestant, parliamentary persuasion, and ready followers of the Whig trend, strong in East Anglia, and growing in popularity in the country, especially following the accession of George I and the Jacobite rebellion of 1715, with the collapse of the Tory party. St.Michael's Church gave only limited leadership, for it was in the hands of ageing Rectors. Richard Golty was 64 years old when he returned to Framlingham in 1660, and typical of the disgruntled Tory clergy. He continued, in failing health, until his death in 1678, and was followed by three elderly Masters of Pembroke Hall in succession from 1678 to 1705, each of whom died in office. We learn from the audit of 1687 that the Church was in poor repair, especially the chancel aisles, which had been hurriedly built. They were started by the Dukes of Norfolk to accommodate their tombs and completed by Edward VI while Thomas Duke of Norfolk was a prisoner in the Tower. Church funds were scarce. The problem was referred to the Master of Pembroke Hall who, accepting responsibility for the aisles to the chancel, spread the cost of repairs between the beneficiaries of Sir Robert Hitcham's will, Framlingham, Coggeshall, Debenham and his College.

Division of the expenses of repairing
the isles in Framlingham Church Suffolk

Framl: Account Audit 1687

Mem.   That the isle on the South Side of the Chancel of the parish of Framlingham (in which Sir Robert Hitcham lyes buried) had so far ran to decay - the charges for Timber, Lead and other Materials, with the workmanship in repairing the same did amount to £82. 17s. 4d.

Whereupon the Master and Fellows of Pembroke Hall as Trustees for the Estate of the Said Sir Robert Hitcham (by and with consent of the three Towns here undernamed) did make this order following viz

That whereas the 2 Isles on each side of the Chancel aforesaid are distinct from the Chancel itself, and supposed to have been built at first by some of the Dukes of Norfolk for burying places for the owners of that Estate; they the above said Trustees did upon that consideration allot to all the Enjoyers of that Estate, their respective shares in the above said charges of repairs; according to their several proportions; in manner following

Viz	That the Town of Framlingham should pay for their proportion	£30.	0.	0.
	Coxall	15.	0.	0.
	Debenham	15.	0.	0.
	that the College would allow	22.	17.	4.
		£82.	17.	4.

(Coxall contraction for Coggeshall)

Section 3.1

FRAMLINGHAM 1724 - 1832

18th Century

The extant 1724 *Surveyor's Report for Framlingham* was presented to the Town at their General Meeting on Easter Tuesday (30th March) 1725 and confirmed at the next Quarter Session. The Report is most comprehensive; owners are entered alphabetically with their tenants and their payments listed in three columns. The first column shows the surveyor's tax rate, the second (which is rather sparse) a comparative 1724/25 rate, and the third the Poor Rate Tax. The document sets out 'to be a standing Rule and Direction (there being none at present) to make all the Town Rates be hereafter for the Church, poor, surveyors and constables with Liberty, nevertheless, to excuse such poor people from paying to future Rates as the said parishioners shall think necessary...'

The total of the Surveyor's Rate of 1724 amounted to £175.17s.6d., while the Poor Rate Tax amounted to £155.7s.9d. Additionally, eight people were to pay a King's Tax ranging in amounts from £2 to £89. Many properties are listed by name, and the tax payers' list shows 26 professions or trades (See Trades). It is possible to place many of the houses and shops in Church Street, Castle Street, Double Street, Market Hill and Bridge Street. Framlingham was developing the shape of the Town as we know it today, for the population had increased from about 860 in 1674 to about 1,460 in 1724, and it is apparent that many new houses were being built, though, strangely, there is no mention of builders, brickmakers, nor bricklayers among the lists of trades.

The precise information of the 1724 Survey was followed in 1729 by Robert Hawes' (the Steward in the Castle) new feoffment for the Town Lands, which were vested in the Rector, Christopher Selby, and a group of trusted citizens. They saw fit in that year to buy the 'Sick House', a farm on a hill to the S.E. of the town, reached via Infirmary Lane from Back Lane (Fore Street). From other sources we know of the Fruer family, the builders and bricklayers who in the mid - 1700s built two houses on the North side of Double Street and two houses in Back Lane. They also developed part of the Welton's Brewery site between Well Close Square and Riverside (see plan, Families: Fruer) and built a number of houses in Horn Hill (College Road) as well as the Primitive Methodists Temperance Hall which was built in 1842.

The people of Suffolk, and noticeably those of Framlingham, still appear to be particularly confused and indignant by the Act of Parliament in 1750 decreeing that 2nd September should be accepted as 14th September, in order to correct the Julian calendar and bring England into line with the Gregorian calendar that had operated on the continent since 1582! Furthermore, no longer would 25th March (the date reckoned to be the date of our Lord's conception, called Lady Day) be the start of the new year. This hence forward would be 1st January. Reluctantly, most people accepted this change by 1752, apart from the Banking fraternity, who added 11 days from 25th March, so making the start of their year 5th April, the day still operating as the start of the tax year. There was particular confusion over the date of Michaelmas, one of the quarter days of the year, with the cry 'Give us back our 11 days!' This unease has persisted locally into this century.

The industrial Revolution, which made itself felt in the country during the second half of the C18, did not bear heavily on Framlingham, the centre of productive farming country; though farming methods changed and developed - dairy herds were reduced and more wheat and barley were grown, for example. Threshing machines were introduced and a large beer maltings was established by John Welton, South of the River Ore, in Well Close Square. Windmills were busy grinding wheat for flour. Two were situated South of the town, one near Well Close Square and another on land now known as Mount Pleasant, between Horn Hill and the road to Earl Soham, and there was a third North-East of the town at the crossing of Cold Hall Lane and the old road to Peasenhall.

Framlingham was changing. It was growing in numbers and in prosperity. In company with much of the country it was also growing in specialization. No longer did each household provide for itself. The 26 trades in the 1724 Surveyor's Report included four butchers, four grocers and chandlers, three drapers, an apothecary, tailors and cordwainers and eleven other shopkeepers. These permanent shops were gradually supplanting the need for the market stalls. In turn the diminishing numbers of stalls reduced the need for the large market cross which dominated the East side of the market area. This two-storey building had been deteriorating for some time. The

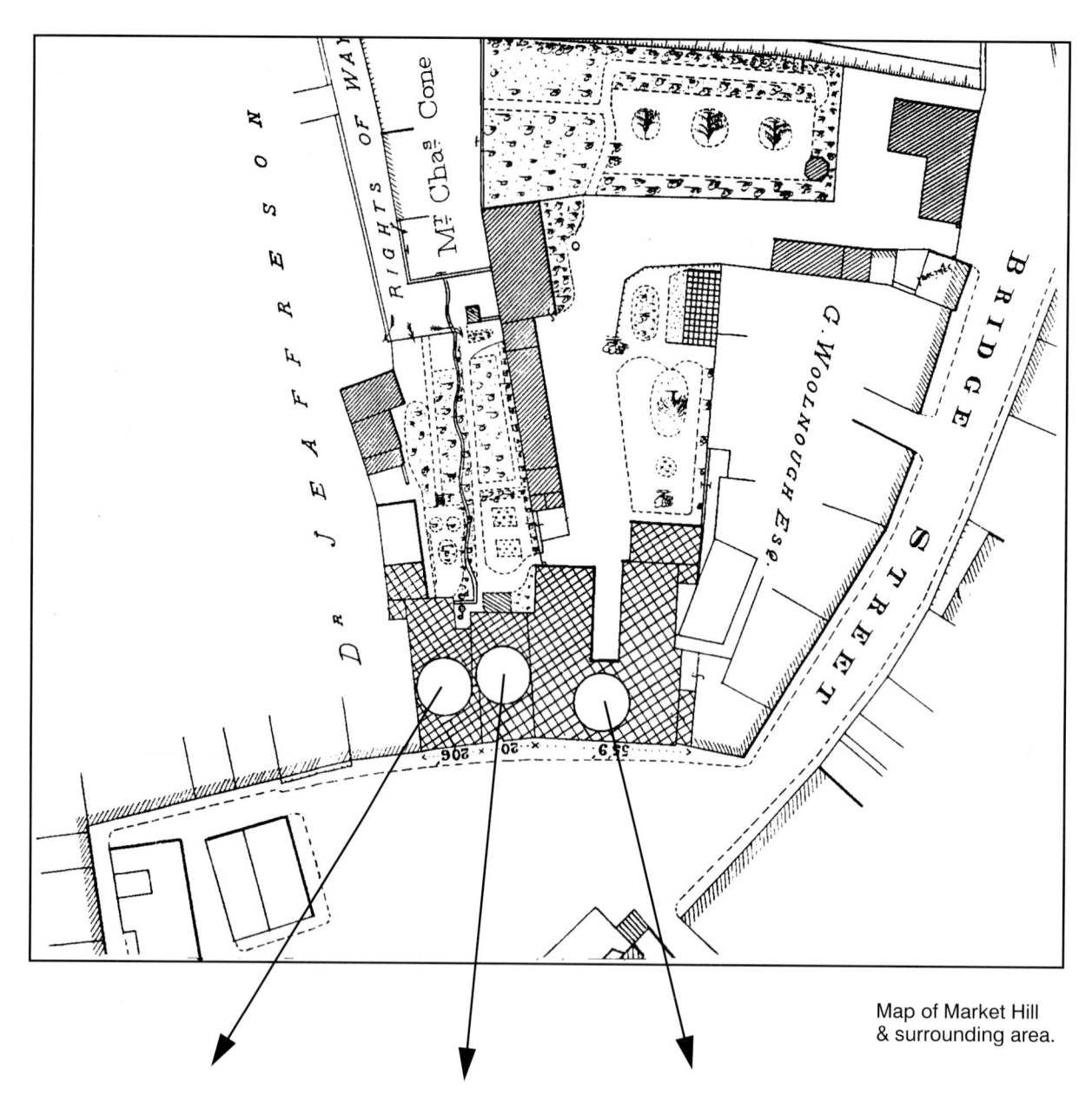

FRAMLINGHAM 1724 - 1832   Section 3.1   A History of Framlingham

Map of Market Hill
& surrounding area.

Framlingham Market Hill: The extensive trade premises of the late Mr. Hatsell Garrard.

low and ill-ventilated upper room was used as the schoolroom for the Sir Robert Hitcham school, provided for in the Will of 1635; but there were no arrangements for sanitation, so the boys used the outside walls of the building in full view of the distinguished properties of the area. In 1787, the Rector, William Wyatt, (who was also a Fellow of Pembroke Hall) and 15 leading citizens of the Town wrote to the Rev. Joseph Turner the 'Master or Keeper ... of Pembroke Hall' to ask for consideration of the problem of the market cross. They proposed that it be removed and a suitable school building be erected elsewhere 'with conveniences'. Permission was granted. The building was removed and a school was built at right angles to the Hitcham Almshouses in New Road. (See Education).

A further petition was made on 13th July, 1789, asking that shops occupied by Fynn Minter, the peruke-maker, and another used by George Cooper, and another lately occupied by Robert Hayward, 'with a certain cage there for confining disorderly persons, be granted a licence for the taking down of said shops and cage'. This petition, raised by the Rector, William Wyatt, and ten citizens, also requested that wool and implements for spinning should be provided for the poor and that a Sunday school should be provided for children. The Master and Fellows of Pembroke Hall approved that a Sunday School should be held in the School House on each Sunday, from 9 a.m. to Church time, and from 1 p.m. to Church time, and from then until 5 p.m., that a Master or Mistress be appointed and that the Creed, the Lord's Prayer, Collects and the Catechism be taught, and that only the Bible and the Book of Common Prayer be read. The art of writing should not be taught. It was supposed in this way, that 'children be inculcated into such sober, decent, quiet and respectable behaviour at all times'. Approval was also given for the supply of materials for the poor, but judgment of the College would be required for the dismantling of the shops, and for this no approval was received.

Framlingham, so near to the coast, was much concerned with the possibility of disruption, even invasion from France, and in 1798 established an Association for the Prosecution of Felons. A report on Framlingham in 1798 quoted in the Survey Report in 1959: 'In 1798 the town was 5,000 acres in extent and within the Hundred of Loes and a market had been established on Market Hill about which the tradesmen have good houses and convenient shops for the sale of wares and merchandise in the general line of trade; interspersed with several reputable inns'. Also in 1798 the 'Articles of Association' were entered into by the loyal inhabitants of this Town in case of invasion or public commotion. (List of the 77 signatories follows).

ARTICLES OF ASSOCIATION, 1798.

Entered into by the 77 Loyal Inhabitants of this Town:-

John Aldrich	John Fruer	Robert Paxman
Philip Aldrich	Samuel Fruer	Jasper Peirson
Josiah Bennington	John Goodwin	Rowe Pierce
Thomas Bennington	Jasper Goodwyn	Daniel Pipe
William Bloss jnr.	Samuel Goodwyn	Paul Read
George Blumfield	George Hayward	William Read
Thomas Boughton	Robert Horner	George Rowland
William Boughton	Abraham Hucklesby	John Say
Edward Bridges	Davie Keer	William Smith
John Bridges	G. B. Keer	John Stanford
Silvanus Bridges	Gissing Kersey	John Taylor
William Brown (Clerk)	Thomas Kersey	Miel Taylor
Thomas Buckingham	Stephen Leek	William Tebbenham
Richard Burman	James Leggatt	Abraham Thompson
William Burman	Nathaniel Leggatt	Thomas Thompson
Robert Carr jnr.	B. Luffingham	Crawin Till
Nathaniel Clubbe	William Mantle	John Turtill
Edward Clodd	Nathaniel Marsh	Leb. Tydeman
Robert Crane	John Measures	G. M. Underwood
John Daniels	Nathaniel Middleton	Daniel Walker
George Edwards	Fynn Minter	Robert Walker

George Edwards jnr.
John Edwards
William Edwards
John Folkard
William Wyatt (Rector) Treasurer

William Pain
James Pallant
William Palmer
James Paxman

William Warner
Jonathan Wightman
Samuel Wightman
John Woolnough
John Wright

They agreed to 'be ready to protect the Town and neighbourhood within four miles of its bounds'. It was agreed that there should be no political discussion, but that all should 'be Firm, Loyal and Faithful to our King & Country'. A Committee of 19 was formed with John Stanford Esq, as Captain, serving without pay, the Rector, William Wyatt, as Treasurer. The sum of £159 was raised locally for this force, and £125 was received from 'the Lord Mayor of London's Fund'. The Rev. W. Browne, of the Readery, was appointed Chaplain and Secretary, William Edwards was Lieutenant, G.B. Keer, Ensign. Fynn Minter and Edward Clodd the two drummers, with fifes who were supported by 10 musicians (for the Band) with 'most excellent instruments bought by themselves and partly by subscribers'.

The Ladies of the Town presented a pair of Colours which were solemnly consecrated. The motto of the force was 'Our King & Country'. The uniform was striking; it was made of blue cloth faced with black velvet and trimmed with silver, and with silver buttons. The hats were round bearskins with blue and white feathers. Four spears were provided for the four serjeants, and 28 pikes were deposited in the Church for the men.

None of the Dissenters in the Town offered his services for this force. This volunteer force was disbanded in 1801. It was truly said that 'the 1802 Peace of Amiens was a peace which everyone would be glad of, but which nobody would be proud of''. It was unlikely that the peace would last. By 1803 preparations were apparent for the war with Napoleon that lasted from 1805 to 1815. Framlingham mustered a larger force than before; John Shafto was its first Major, John Stanford was in command of the three companies of approximately 240 members, and its military band with drummers and fifers. The uniform this time was a red jacket faced with yellow, with 'white small clothes', felt caps and long black gaiters. They adopted the flag presented by the Ladies of Framlingham to the 'Blues' in 1798. These men were the forerunners of the second World War 'Home Guard', for they mustered occasionally, received £1 per annum and continued their normal local way of life.

Coachman

Colourful uniforms were later seen in the Borough when carriages drawn by a pair of horses were driven through the town with a post lad carrying a short riding whip, dressed in a scarlet jacket with a hunting cap, leather breeches and top boots and spurs, mounted on one of them. The Rector of Dennington, the Hon. Rev. Frederick Hotham, used to drive into Framlingham with coachman and footman dressed in blue livery with silver buttons, in a yellow and black carriage slung on broad leather straps. John Moseley Esq., of Great Glemham Hall, drove into Framlingham in a painted yellow carriage, while the Rev. George Turner of Kettleburgh had only a drab uniform for his liveried servants with his 'pair horse carriage', Dr. Field, of The Oaks, Framlingham, drove a yellow cabriole.

There is no record of Dr. John Kinnell's means of transport, but records reveal his concern for the people of Framlingham. He acted as Trustee for several young families whose fathers had died, and he bought two cottages and plots of land in the Saxmundham Road, built brick buildings to accommodate six families (see photograph) and altered an existing barn for a further two families. Moreover, following the first Reform Act of 1832, he arranged and funded a tea party in Double Street for the inhabitants of the Town, causing tables to be fixed on each side of Double Street.

A great tragedy which affected many people overcame Framlingham in 1832 (See George Brooke Keer). In the 1820s and 1830s probably the largest employer in the Town was George Brooke Keer. He and his son George Brooke Keer had built up a large and prosperous brewing business which occupied the whole area bounded by White Hart Lane/Crown & Anchor Lane, Back Lane/Fore Street, part of Bow Street/Double Street and part of Church Street. He had built for himself a lovely Georgian mansion on the Clark's land (described in Chapter 2) with a large garden, vinery and greenhouse, and his son lived in the newly built Manor House in Church Street, which had a sizeable garden and a tennis court. It flanked part of the brewery site. He had bought 21 public houses which were supplied from his brewery. In order to do this he had borrowed heavily, and additionally was subjected to heavy malt taxes by Customs and Excise. He could not meet his commitments, and in 1832 was declared a bankrupt, and, by order of the Commissioners acting under a fiat in bankruptcy, was compelled to sell his properties to cover his commitments. A public auction for 31 lots was held on the Bowling Green by the Castle on 21st June 1832 and conducted by William Butcher of Norwich, before a large concourse of people. The sale realised approximately £20,885. (See George Brooke Keer). Much of the brewery site was bought by Mr. Everett for Abraham Thompson, a builder and the son of the landlady, Amelia Thompson, of the *White Hart Hotel*.

The *White Hart* was bought by John Cobbold, who dispensed with Mrs. Thompson's services and changed the name of the premises and the adjacent lane to Crown & Anchor. Abraham Thompson was so incensed by this high-handed treatment that he built a three-storey brick building adjacent to the renamed *Crown & Anchor* and called it the *White Hart Inn*, and installed a hairdresser in the building. Abraham Thompson was a public spirited man, who built many of the houses in the new area South of the River Ore, known as the Freehold and Hermitage. His generosity to others caused him to become a bankrupt in his turn, and the George Brooke Keer site sold to him for £1,400 passed to Edward Lankester for £650.

The break-up of the Brooke-Keer empire necessitated a number of readjustments, among them the development of the north side of the Market Hill. Regrettably the fine Georgian Mansion was pulled down and its materials were dispersed. (See George Brooke Keer). The site became available for the building of the row of shops that stand on the previously well-ordered garden that stretched from Church Lane to the Unitarian Chapel. This Chapel had been served by Samuel Say Toms from 1773-1829. In 1823 the people of Framlingham, whether Church members or chapel-goers honoured him by the ringing of the Church bells and by presenting him with a silver tea set at a well-attended luncheon held in the *Crown Hotel*.

Malt House

In the early years of the nineteenth century several institutions were established, among them the Wesleyan Chapel in 1808 and the Independent Chapel in 1823 (see 'Non Conformity'). Many shops were established in Castle Street, Double Street, on the Market Hill and in Well Close Square. The 'parish pound', a wooden open pen for straying animals was built on the Badingham Road (on the 1841 Tithe Apportionment Plot 8281). Animals were redeemed by the owners from the Surveyor on payment of a fine that went towards the animals' care and repairs of the highways. The whipping-post and stocks which once stood on the Market Hill were removed to the Castle and recently used as a bearer for the head of the waterpipe from the Castle ditch along Church Road to the parish fire engine on the Market Hill.

Section 4.0

FRAMLINGHAM FROM 1832 - 1863

19th Century

The passing of the Great Reform Act of 1832 was a landmark for the country, and it marked a revival of the importance of Framlingham, which became one of the seven polling centres for the Eastern Division of the County and for 37 parishes within the Hundreds of Loes, Hoxne, Plomesgate and Thredling. This confirmed the standing of Framlingham in the area which had been selected in 1830 as the Framlingham New Division of Magisterial Jurisdiction for the villages in the same four Hundreds. The Boundary Act, with the Reform Act, both redistributed the seats of Parliament and widened the franchise. Framlingham already had 47 new Freeholders and 23 new voters which included 8 Copyholders with a payment value of £10 per annum or more, 14 Occupiers with £10 annual rents, and one leaseholder who paid a rent of £50 or more, according to the Act. Of the 70 persons eligible to vote, 66 exercised this right and 49 of these voted for R.N.Shawe Esq. of Kesgrave, 6 votes were split between him and Lord Henniker, and 11 between his Lordship and Sir Charles B. Vere of Nacton.

This first election following the Act, held on 17th & 18th December 1832, was reported to be run 'with great good humour and vivacity throughout the first day, and again next morning'. A booth with two compartments had been erected on the Market Hill; in each was a poll-clerk and two check clerks. At the close of the Poll, the Poll Books were conveyed to the High Sheriff of Suffolk, Joseph Burch Smyth Esq., by the Deputy Sheriff, Mr. William Edwards of Framlingham, and on 20th December the High Sheriff announced at Ipswich that the seven districts had polled 2,032 for Lord Henniker, 1,990 for R.N.Shawe Esq., and 1,787 for Sir Charles B. Vere. He declared the first two to be duly elected as independent representatives for East Suffolk.

One of the first Acts passed by this predominantly Whig Parliament was the Abolition of Slavery Act of 1833. This was a cause strongly supported by Mr. Thomas Cooper, a man born in Framlingham's Swan Lane, who was a missionary in Jamaica, and who gave evidence before a Committee of the House of Lords of the evil effect of slavery both on slaves and slave-holders. He spent the last twenty years of his life as Minister of the Old Meeting House, and in his old age even became friends with the Rector, the musical Rev. G. Attwood, who lent him his bath-chair.

The Educational Grant Act of 1833, which provided money for elementary education, was not itself applicable in Framlingham, but it was instrumental in concentrating thoughts on the future of local education, which were to bear fruit in the establishment of Framlingham College in 1865. At this time there were seven small fee-paying schools for boarders and day-pupils in Framlingham and William Hill's larger school in 42 Double Street as well as the Sir Robert Hitcham Boys' Free School in New Road and the Thomas Mills Charity School in Brook Lane. (See Education).

The 1830s were notable for the setting up of various societies within the Town. In c. 1835 a district parochial lending library was incorporated with a committee 'under the care and guidance of the Rev. W. Greenlaw, to induce the lower classes to read the S.P.C.K.'s books, and the number of applicants for such publications was numerous.' There were, already, two Book Societies, one established in 1825 under the auspices of the Rev. J.W. Darby, Secretary & Treasurer, patronised by the Ladies and Gentlemen in the Town and neighbourhood, and the other which had members who met in each other's houses once a month 'for the general diffusion of knowledge'. The Framlingham Horticultural Society, with a five shilling annual subscription, set up in 1834, attracted members from Glevering Hall, Glemham House and Great Glemham, and in that year held a competitive exhibition on the Bowling Green; six cottagers were awarded prizes for their fruit and vegetables.

Additionally, the Framlingham District Agricultural 'Hand in Hand' Society was founded in 1832, with John Moseley Esq. as President, in order to establish a body of farming opinion for the 37 parishes of the new polling district, with which to confront Parliament. The struggles for and against the duties on corn were of importance to the landowners in and around Framlingham, who made their views known in this way, while the poorer members of the community were finding crippling the high prices for bread, especially following the poor harvest of 1845. Concern was also being shown for the poor of the parish, and, in addition to the Lying-In Charity founded in 1826 the Penny Clothing Club was started in 1833. The Municipal Reform Act of 1835 provided that all members of Town Councils should be elected by the rate-payers, instead of being self-chosen, and that the Town Councils should publish their accounts, showing how the public money had been spent, thus giving more information and responsibility to the local population.

Pembroke Hall, very properly, arranged for the second tower to the right of the Castle entrance to be rebuilt after it fell one evening in September, 1833, but for some unknown reason this order was never undertaken. Remains of the tower may still be seen.

The Chartist movement in the country was reflected in Framlingham and in company with other boroughs two special constables were sworn in to keep the peace.

Another change that affected Framlingham was the Order of September 1835 of the Poor Law Commissioners, which made provision for 39 other parishes to form the Plomesgate Union: the aged poor were removed to the Parham Workhouse on the North Green with the Master, Mr.Girling, to make room within the workhouse in the Castle for the younger poor of the 39 parishes in the Plomesgate Union. This arrangement lasted until May 1837, when every pauper, man, woman and child was removed to the new Union House at Wickham Market. This freed the fine Poor House Building, now with the upper floor and the central staircase removed, and it became a handsome hall for other uses. The Rev. G. Attwood had a porch built in 1841. In 1847 the hall was used for the first monthly sitting of the Framlingham District of the County Court of Suffolk 'for the better recovery of small debts', a provision which continued until 1861, when the sittings were alternated between Framlingham and Saxmundham. Further regularisation occurred in 1837 with the Tithe Communication Act, after which all tithes were paid in money, based on the price of wheat over the past seven years. Framlingham was kept in touch with the outside world with letters arriving daily by 8 a.m. and being despatched at 6 p.m. Two Victorian Mainland Type Pillar Boxes of 1856/7 made by Andrew Hendy & Co. of Derby were bought and positioned one in Double Street and the other on the corner of College Road with Mount Pleasant. Also an omnibus leaving the Crown Inn to meet the London Steamers at Ipswich each Monday and Thursday, and coaches for Ipswich leaving the Crown & Anchor for Ipswich daily at 10.30, and for Norwich at 3.30 daily. Carriers left six of the Inns of the Town for London, Halesworth, Ipswich, Norwich and Woodbridge on stated days of the week.

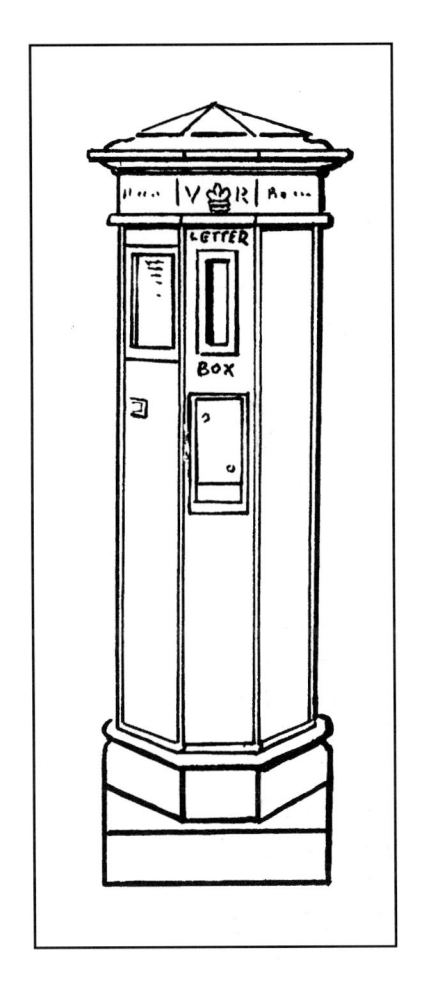

Circa 1838/9 Mr. Samuel Bloss, landlord of the *Crown & Anchor Inn* undertook to horse the coaches from Framlingham to Wickham Market, and from Framlingham to Peasenhall. He also put the Union coaches on the road; these coaches reached London in a day, and returned in two days' time. Before the establishment of Union coaches it had been necessary for a passenger for London to go to Wickham Market several days before the journey, to reserve, for one sovereign, a place on the coach; then again to walk the seven miles to Wickham Market to catch the coach on the appointed day. This was the case for inside and outside passengers, and a further 1s. was expected by the driver for looking after the luggage. S. Fruer worked up a company to guarantee connections between Framlingham, Ipswich, Halesworth and Norwich.

Fish Trap

Travelling by coach had its dangers: on one occasion a coach had just been re-horsed at the *Crown & Anchor Inn*, when the horses started off without the driver. Two or three female outside passengers were terrified and screamed, causing the horses to bolt down Fairfield Road, with the coach out of control. A brave man, one Henry Fuller, leapt at the head of one of the horses and stopped them, but not before being dragged some distance and being severely injured. A growing number of residents had their own horses, carriages and gigs. There was a certain affluence in the town, and the population turned its attention to entertainment. The bowling green was used by Gentlemen on Thursdays, and by Tradesmen on Wednesdays through the Summer, from May until October. In the Winter months there were lectures and whist playing parties. After the break up of the George Brooke Keer's brewing empire the tun-house was fitted up as a theatre, with boxes for the leading families, side seats in the gallery and a pit. The Barthrop family had come to Framlingham in 1735, and married into the Brooke Keer family, and it was they who were instrumental in encouraging Mr. Fred Atkins and his strolling players to make this theatre their headquarters and who patronised the theatre through the Winter months, and, with other leading families ensured an audience for the plays, which included pieces from Shakespeare as well as comedies, farces and dances, including the Highland Fling and the Hornpipe.

Mr. Atkins himself was a comic actor, and attired in a dressing-gown with a night cap, and holding a chamber candlestick with lighted candle, regularly brought down the house with his rendering of 'My grandfather was a most wonderful man'. In front of the stage, local men, under the leadership of Mr. Copping, formed an orchestra of strings, a clarionet and a serpent. The theatre lapsed into disuse in about 1874.

The year 1837 marked the start of Queen Victoria's long reign and 1840 saw her marriage to Prince Albert of Saxe-Coburg - events which were quietly celebrated in the town. 1837 was the year of the Civil Registration Act of 1st July, followed by the census of 1841, with provision for census registers to be completed every following ten years.

St. Michael's Church had suffered from an absentee Rector for 18 years from 1815 to 1833, because John Norcross would not accept the tithe payments. In his absence his curates, the Rev. E. Davies from 1815, and then the Rev. W. Greenlaw from 1832, had run the parish. (Mr. Norcross continued as Rector until 1833). In 1837 Pembroke Hall appointed the young and musical Rev. George

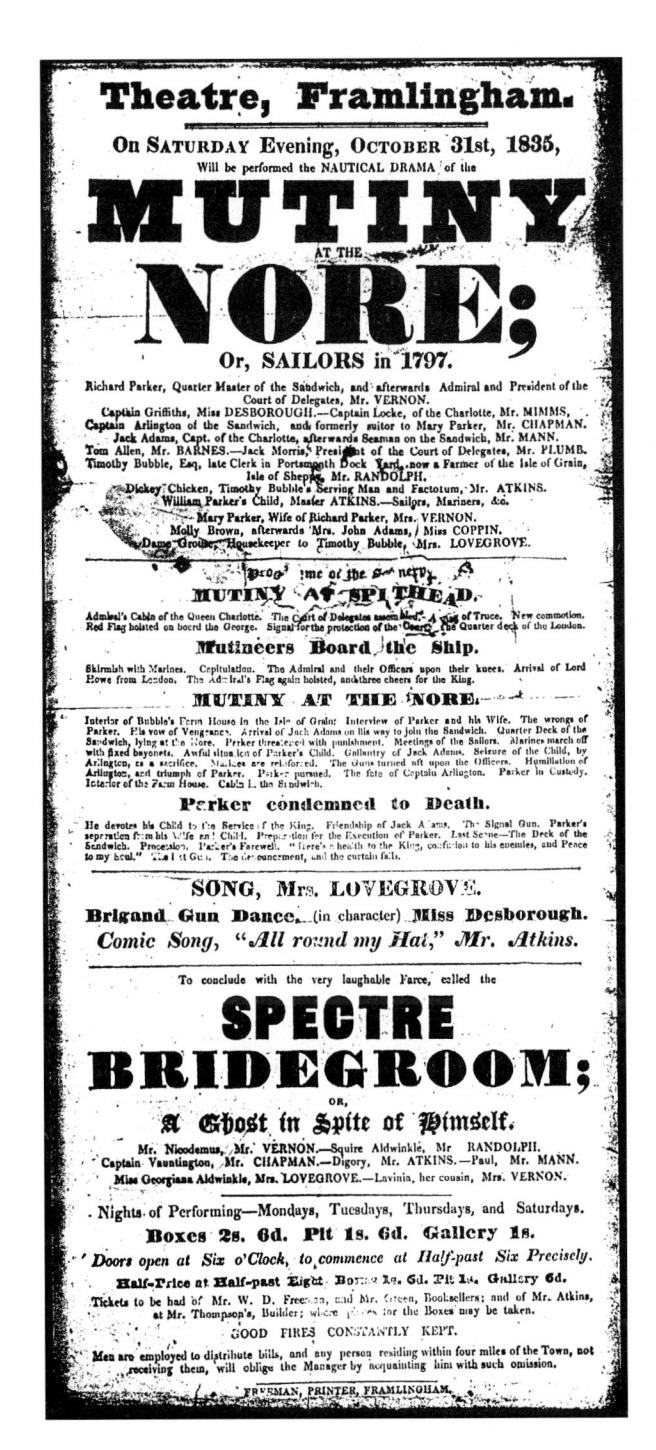

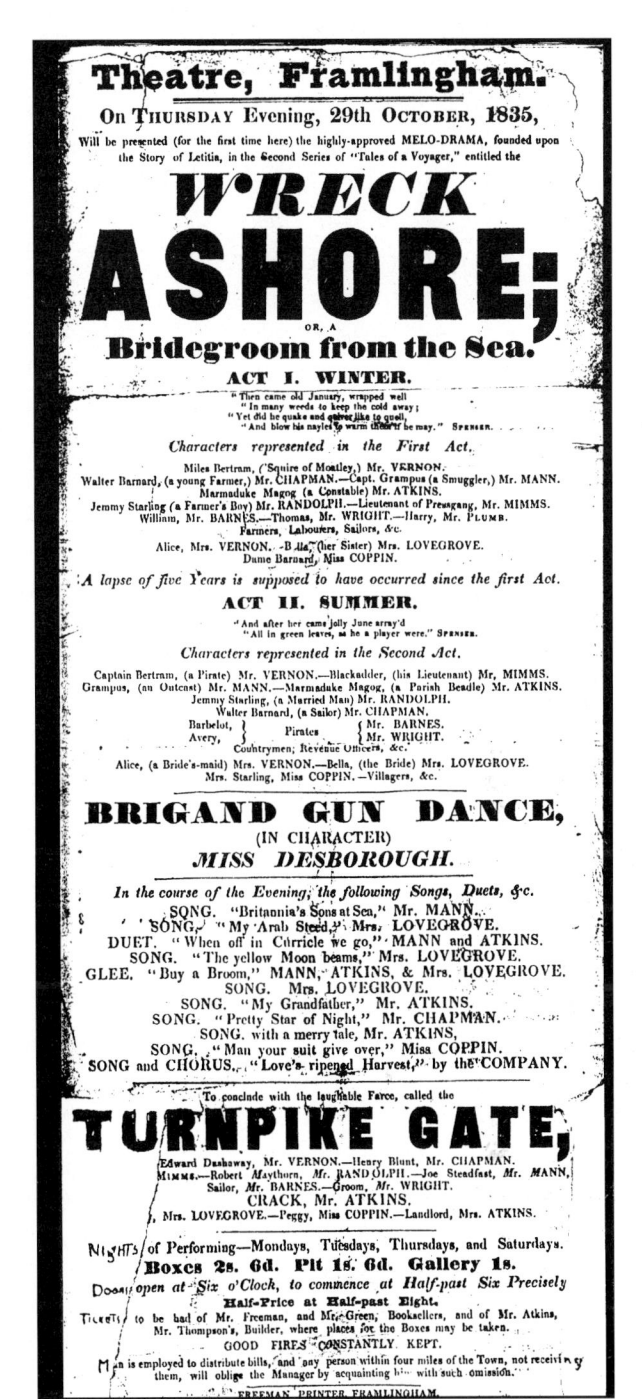

Theatre Bills

Attwood, who served the parish for nearly fifty years, until 1884. He was a Pembroke graduate, the son of the organist of St. Paul's Cathedral in London, and music thrived in the town during his ministry, with a certain Zebedee Tydeman, a professor of music, with his musical wife, giving lessons in Framlingham and the surrounding towns. An oratorio was performed in St. Michael's Church under his baton, when Sir George Smart came from London to play the notable organ. (See Church). Concerts were regularly given, and a harmonic society was formed.

The look of Framlingham was again altered to suit the current fashions. Captain Poole, who came to the town from London, bought Church House, one of the old Tudor houses in Church Street, and had a false Regency wooden front made for it by London craftsmen who came and attached this façade to the house.

In turn, 6 and 8 Church Street were given brick façades, along with several houses in Double Street, and Abraham Thompson built the three-storey *White Hart Inn* building in White Hart Lane/Crown & Anchor Lane as well as developing the Hermitage area of Framlingham, south of the River Ore. He built many of the lofty houses in the town, fulfilling his saying that 'there's plenty of room upwards'.

By the time of the Great Exhibition of 1851, Framlingham had its own industries such as coach building, with inventions carried out by Samuel Hart and his three sons. Mr. Hart took out a patent for lancewood springs to replace the solid block of lancewood, recognising that flexibility would be achieved by strips or leaves, the accepted method used in cars today. In the C19, because steel carried a heavy duty, cumbersome wooden springs were employed rather than steel leaves.

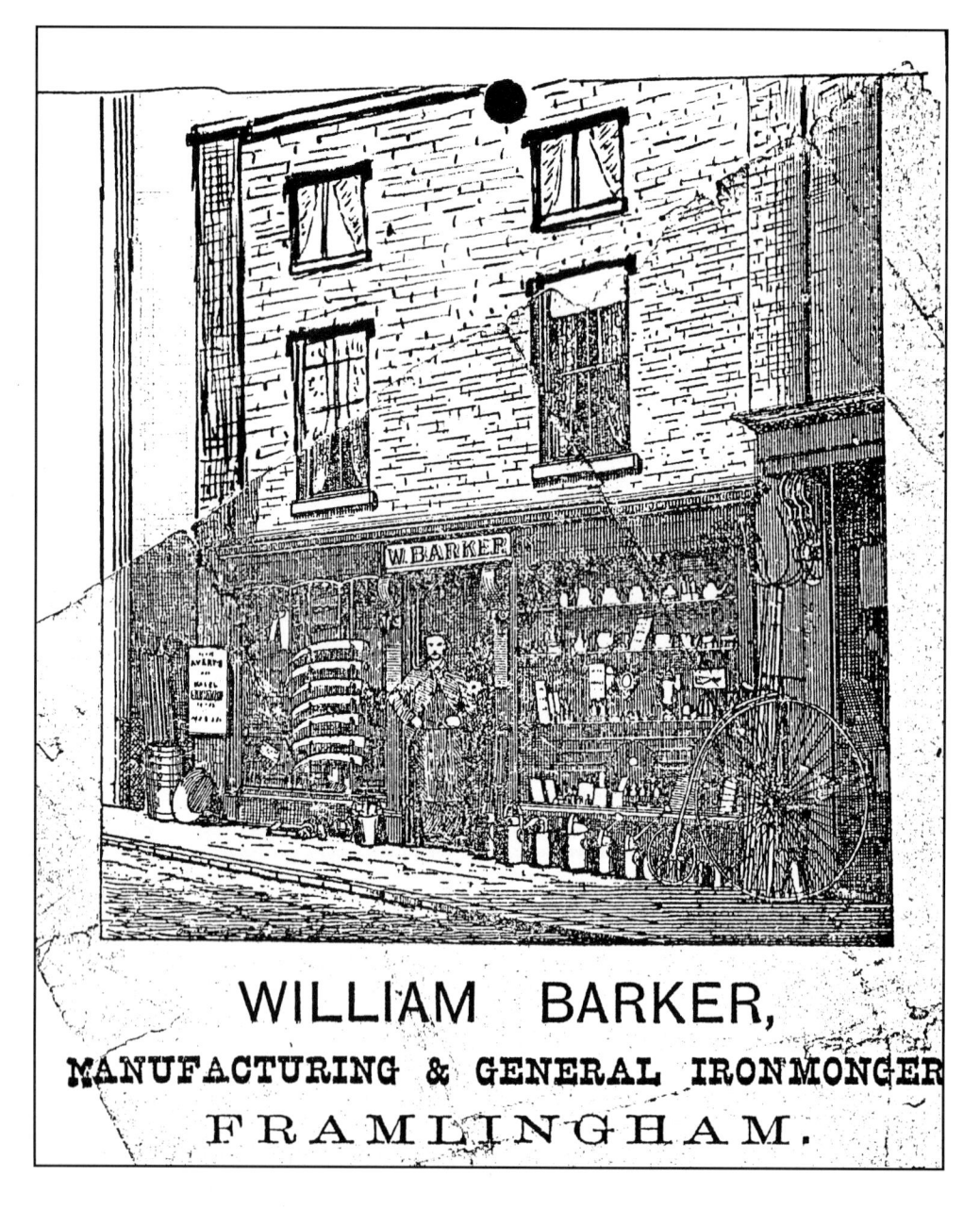

William Barker

Mr. Edgar Roe established his chemical manure works in Broadwater, called the East Suffolk Manure Works. Later, his son took out patents for a gravy and juice preserver; for a rosebud support for pastry, with a hole to let out the steam, and for a chimney pot of a particular design to cure smoky chimneys. From 1828 until 1850 the streets of Framlingham had been lit by oil lamps, but in 1850 Joseph Barker, one of Thomas Barker's great-grandsons, introduced gas and gas lighting to the borough, installing 43 lamps at a cost of 2s.6d. per lamp. These lamps were lit daily by Minter Damant who was paid 10d. per night. Joseph Barker's next venture for 1855-1857 was the laying of sewage pipes from Framlingham to the River Ore to the South of the borough. Later, in 1910, modern sewage works were established alongside the Kettleburgh Road. (See Services)

The increased activity of trades and industry in Framlingham was at first contained within the borough, in Castle Street, Double Street and Bridge Street (Millbridge Road); then there was movement in Well Close Square, especially from 1835, when the builder John Fruer developed the Welton Maltings, this site being divided into six properties. When Abraham Thompson built the two-coloured brick building for Henry Wells, now occupied by Clarke & Simpson, Mr. Jasper Peirson owned the southern tip where, in 1853, he erected the first steam flour mill for Edmund Kindred. A bakery in white bricks was built for Spencer Leek, near to the *White Horse Inn*, with a group of buildings that included the present *Wheelwright's Restaurant*, so called because of the bicycle shop and car hire business run by Mr. Walter Fairweather in the 1920s.

The 'Ancient House' near Well Close Square was extended and pargetted, and part of the Old Rectory near the Church was pulled down in 1833 and rebuilt.

In 1844, when Mr. Jesse Wightman was the Surveyor, it was decided to lower by 14 ft. the steep and unmanageable clay road over Holgate Hill, at a cost of £1,203.18s.5½d., for the horses could not manage the heavy loads in wet weather and the volume of traffic along this main artery from Framlingham to Wickham Market and Woodbridge had greatly increased. Mr. Wightman caused this work to be carried out without conferring with John Shafto Esq., J.P., who lived in a property abutting this road, at the top of the hill, an omission that cost him a refusal to his application to turn his beer house, the *King's Arms* on Riverside, into a licensed public house!

The Ancient House

The same year 1844 marked the year of the opening of the Oddfellows Lodge, called the 'Star of the East Lodge' which by 1878 had 198 benefit and 20 honorary members, with a surplus brotherhood-fund of £4,928.13s.2d. The Provident Benefit Society was also started, its funds in 1876 standing at £900.0s.0¾d. A Lodge of Freemasons opened in 1865.

From the 1851 Census returns, we learn that Framlingham had a population of 2,450 and no fewer than 58 trades and occupations undertaken by the heads of households, and about 60 when including the servants and minor trades of lodgers. This well-knit community, now stratified into employers and employed, had been attracting trade to the borough, and the traffic was becoming so heavy that rail transport was required. The Great Eastern Railway line ran from London to Lowestoft; it was decided to run a branch line from Wickham Market (Campsey Ash) to Framlingham. Completed and opened in 1859, this further stimulated both trade and demand in the community, and the end of the Kettleburgh Road near Framlingham (now called Station Road) was developed along the railway line as an industrial area.

The Rectory

The brick-making works, further along the Kettleburgh Road, started about 1845 and run by Mr. Peter Smith of Badingham, came into full production, firing 30,000 bricks at a time in each of the two kilns. They included bricks made in the daisy-rose decorative moulds, which may be seen on houses in Station Road. The Barrack Cottages, built of flint and brick between Horn Hill and the Earl Soham Road, were probably built around 1840 to accommodate the Dragoons who were billeted in the town to assist the Excise Officers in their drive against smuggling.

The Daisy Rose Design

Government control was playing an ever greater part in the affairs of the borough, and the Churchyard was to be closed against interments from 1st June 1856, by order of the Secretary of State. This order was followed by the election of a Burial Board, and the purchase of two acres of land on the outskirts of the town, about half way up Back Lane', once part of Muckhill Close. Iron folding gates were made and hung on white brick pillars and the new cemetery was opened on 1st June 1856.

There was a fear of a French invasion following the 1848 year of revolutions and 1850 saw the formation of the Volunteer Movement throughout the country, with the motto 'Defence not Defiance'. This was taken up by Framlingham on the day that the new branch line railway was opened for traffic, and a corps was formed. Subsequently it amalgamated with and formed part of the 2nd Battalion of the East Suffolk Volunteer Rifle Corps. By the 1870s it had its military brass band, and 75 members, with Mr. R. Garrard as Captain, Mr. G. Jones, 1st Lieutenant, and Mr. F. Ling 2nd Lieutenant. Their uniform was dark green with black accoutrements, with a dark green cap bearing a cap badge, in frosted silver, depicting the Gate Tower of the Castle. The Castle was their Headquarters; rifles were kept in the Library Tower, and ammunition was stored in a wall chamber nearby.

The Castle was a focal point for the Suffolk Agricultural Association's annual meeting on 4th July 1860, when at least 15,000 persons attended in the meadows on the South-East side and the admission fees reached £273.14s.6d. from the sale of 5,929 tickets.

Barrack Cottages

The death of the Prince Consort in 1861 prompted further great development of Framlingham, for a school, the Albert Middle-Class College in Suffolk (now known as Framlingham College) was built with surplus money from the Prince Albert Memorial in Hyde Park, and from local and public subscription, and with monies from the Sir Robert Hitcham fund. The school was the brain-child of Lady Kerrison and her husband, Sir Edward Clarence Kerrison, who reflected that the number of small schools, along with the Sir Robert Hitcham's schools, were no longer adequate for this developing community. Also it was pointed out that 'there was a definite place in the county for a school that would fit boys for their life's occupation, and would replace the small private schools and academies, few of which were of any great practical value, or were really satisfactory'. Sir Edward Kerrison had been trying 'to see fuller and better use made of the Framlingham estate, bequeathed to Pembroke Hall by Sir Robert Hitcham in 1636' and the opportunity to put these ideas into practice came in 1861 with the death of Prince Albert, who had suggested in 1851 on a visit to Suffolk, that 'Middle Schools or Colleges might be formed and conducted upon the plan of the German Schools, subject to periodical inspection'. The Kerrison proposal 'to erect a memorial to the late Prince Consort in the shape of a College, for affording a Scientific Education to the Middle Class at a moderate cost, was supported by a large and influential portion of the Gentlemen residing in Suffolk'. By 27th May 1863, 15 acres of Sir Robert Hitcham's manorial lands were allotted, a competition for the buildings had been arranged, and the design submitted by Frederick Peck accepted.

A Charter was granted by Queen Victoria on 30th July 1864 under the style and title of 'The *Albert Middle Class College in Suffolk*'. The building of this large college for 250 boys, 'where each boy had a separate bed', stands on the south hill facing the castle and Church. In time this led to the general development of this area of 'greater Framlingham'. It is likely that the bricks for this and nearby buildings were made from the clay hill, now known as 'the dip', puddled in the mere, and fired in the kiln built in Kiln Field, probably on the site of the present Territorial Army H.Q. The school opened in April 1865, with the Rev. Albert Cooke Daymond, M.A. as Headmaster, about 10 resident and 4 visiting masters, and 145 boys. A week later a further 123 boys arrived, making a total of 268, filling the whole of the available accommodation.

Section 4.1

FRAMLINGHAM from 1863 - 1901

Great changes occurred during this period, initially brought about by the convergence of three factors within the four years 1859 - 1863, namely the coming of the East Suffolk Railway in 1859, the sale of Frederick Corrance's extensive property in Framlingham by his Executors, and the building of the Albert Memorial College. These factors were further stimulated by the enterprise of several of the older families in Framlingham and the advent of several entrepreneurs to Framlingham from elsewhere.

Jasper Peirson was instrumental in encouraging the East Suffolk Railway to build the five mile, five furlong railroad from Campsey Ash to Framlingham (at a cost of £40,000). This facility was enhanced by the sale in lots of Corrance land, part of which lay between the Kettleburgh Road and the rail track, while another lot lay adjacent to the land selected for the building of Framlingham College, north of Red Rose Lane which became the residential area known as Pembroke Road. Further lots of his land included the Regency House and 9 Double Street, used by Robert Lambert as his house, his shop and his printing works, which he bought, and the Tudor houses on the south side of the Market Hill, which in 1872 was sold to Hatsell Garrard and used as his grocery and drapery shop. Additionally, Corrance property beyond the south end of Fore Street, commonly known as the Freehold, was bought by Abraham Thompson and developed in 1864 as Albert Road and Albert Place. This area at the end of the Kettleburgh Road (to be renamed Station Road) marked the western end of the growing residential, commercial and industrial area that was established as far as the railway terminal and beyond along the old Kettleburgh Road.

Industrial Buildings

The coming of the railway was the signal for a chain of developments; the Kettleburgh Road became the main artery for traffic from Woodbridge and Wickham Market to Framlingham, supplanting the old route via Fairfield Road and using the recently brick-built bridge that links these two roads. A building impetus followed with the building of the railway station and engine houses, then the Station Hotel 'with good stabling' and from 1863 the establishment, by T. Twidell Buckmaster of nearby brickworks, and the building of the railway terrace, followed by a further building programme. Entrepreneurs who would benefit from the movement of bulk commodities bought land between the Kettleburgh Road and the railway track, some of which had become available from the sale of part of the Corrance property.

Notable among the Framlingham families at this time were the Fruers, the Bridges, the Barkers, the Thompsons, the Edwards, the Roes, the Lamberts, and the Mauldens, while Messrs. Buckmaster, Smith, Clarke, Potter, Manby, Walne and Baldry were drawn to Framlingham from neighbouring villages; Buckmaster, a Bedford man, had bought the Mill at Letheringham, Smith was a brickmaker from Badingham, Clarke came from Worlingworth, Potter from Wickham Market, Manby from Dennington, Walne from Kettleburgh and Baldry from Hacheston. The Fruers, Abraham

Thompson and Frank Baldry were builders, George Edwards owned a tannery, as well as a grocers shop, with the local savings bank; the Bridges were blacksmiths, the Barkers watchmakers and ironmongers, and a son, Joseph Barker, developed gas for Framlingham. A. Roe and his son (as well as inventing small cooking appliances) founded the manure works at Broadwater, which later was changed to a bacon factory. James Maulden ran and developed the Maulden Maltings which gradually became one of the largest employers in the town.

In 1872 Sir Henry Thompson, the distinguished surgeon and son of Henry Thompson, a successful local grocer, draper and Deacon of the Congregational Chapel, presented a clock to the town in memory of his father. This clock was established on the south wall of the Church tower and accepted as the parliamentary timepiece for the town, and was the responsibility of the R.D.C., who paid a local watchmaker £8 per annum to wind and care for it.

Robert Lambert, a printer, founded and produced the *Lambert Annual Almanack*, which sold for one penny from 1857 to 1896 before it was taken over first by Messrs. Maulden & Sons, then from 1903, by Arthur Fairweather of Woodbridge. In the 1874 edition of the *Almanac*, a short description of several of the important buildings and of the widely varying activities and interests of the townspeople was included and **is reproduced here** (in spite of the risk of some duplication).

A selection of *Almanac* advertisements over a period of about 40 years is included, (in Printing).

Church Clock

"During '73 very few remarkable events have transpired to break into the even tenor of the way of the inhabitants. Early in the year the Ipswich and Suffolk Freehold Land Society allotted by ballot 'college Hill Estate' into 23 building plots; but not one of the allottees have speculated in bricks and mortar. The rural dress of Mulberry-lane has thus been thrown aside, the ditch filled up, and the road is now almost as much used for vehicle traffic as Mount Pleasant.

"Death has taken away during the short period of twelve months three respected tradesmen of the town, viz, Messrs. Richard Green, Jonathan Hart, and Thomas Dale. The first of the three was well known as taking delight in matters of Antiquarian research. He was the author and publisher of an excellent HISTORY OF FRAMLINGHAM & SAXTEAD; and THE STRANGER'S GUIDE TO FRAMLINGHAM, both of which have commanded considerable attention. As an old inhabitant he was highly esteemed for his strict integrity and uprightness in conduct and principle; and he was carried to his grave amidst tokens of respect in the good old age of 85 years. Mr. Hart, for many years the principal of the firm of Jonathan Hart & Co., Grocers and Drapers, and of late years manager of Messrs. Gurneys Banking business, was extensively known and respected for his good business habits and tact, and for his kind, gentlemanly and courteous conduct to all with whom he came in contact. Mr. T. Dale, for many years Secretary to the 2nd Suffolk Volunteer Rifle Corps, and more or less a member of the Framlingham Band from his youth up, and an employer of several artisans, was undermined in his health by a painful malady, and died at the age of 49 years. He won the respect of a large circle of friends, and was interred with military honours in the Cemetery.

The Albert Memorial College

"The ALBERT MEMORIAL COLLEGE has had a very successful career during 1873. In the Cambridge Examinations it has taken the fourth position in all England; and under the management of its present head master the numbers of pupils have increased by 30, and it is more than probable the College will be filled to its utmost extent of accommodation in 1874. The public distribution of prizes in October was a grand success, Lord Henniker, Earl Stradbroke, and several other of the nobility being present and taking part in the events of the day. The concert by the College Choir in the evening was crowded with visitors; and the head master was congratulated on the proud position he had raised the College to occupy. We understand the Governors have determined to admit a limited number of day scholars into the College. This will prove a boon to Framlingham; and it is hoped that it may induce persons of limited means to take up their residence in the town and give an impetus to building. The College Cricket Club was generally successful in the several matches of the season; and the Football Club is in an efficient state.

"CONGREGATIONAL CHURCH. The celebration of the jubilee of this place of worship - known by older inhabitants as the 'New Meeting' - took place on the 24th September. The first brick of this Chapel was laid April 6, 1823, and opened for religious services August 6th following. The first members composing this Church were Samuel Dale, John Fruer Snr., S. Dale Jnr., Henry Thompson (father of Sir Henry Thompson) John Fruer, Francis Runnacles, Frances Bush and Mary Taylor. The present pastor is the Rev. C.E. Gordon-Smith.

"THE OLD WESLEYAN CHAPEL was held by the late William Edwards, Esq., solicitor, the mortgagee, and was sold some time after his death to Mr. A. Clements, landlord of the Railway Inn, who, pulled the chapel down in 1868, and the site thereof thrown open for the purposes of an inn-yard. A bowling-alley is on the site of the Vestry, and there are graves of those who once were worshippers in the Chapel which can be found in the yard of this inn. To what strange purposes are sacred spots sometimes devoted! The Chapel, which was built in 1808, was preached in for the last time by the Rev. J. Renshaw, of Ipswich, on Sunday March 15, 1868. The congregation adjourned to a building called "THE PEOPLE'S HALL". This hall was converted from a steam flour mill, erected by J. Peirson, Esq., in 1853, and adapted to its present uses by a Limited Liability

Company, composed principally of the worshippers at the Old Wesleyan chapel. The independent Wesleyans worship there on Sundays and have the use of the Hall certain other days in the week; and the Hall is lettable for any moral, literary, scientific, social or political purpose. Mr. R. Lambert is Secretary to the Company.

"THE OLD MEETING HOUSE being the oldest of the Dissenting places of worship, was erected in 1717. There is a minister's house adjoining the Chapel; and in addition thereto there are several other gifts, viz., an annuity, freehold tenements in Castle-Street, and a money donation. The two former are received under the Wills of William Mayhew (Thomas Mills' servant) and Mrs. Martha Smith. Mr. Mayhew charged his Estate at Dennington with £4 per annum to be paid to the 'Dissenting Minister of Framlingham as long as there should be one' and the tenements in Castle-Street were left by Mrs. Smith 'in support of the preaching of the gospel at the Meeting House, in Framlingham, whereof the Rev. Mr. Richard Chorley was then minister'. The money donation is £180 invested, and the interest is applied in aid of the Meeting. During the pastorate of the Rev. Samuel Say Toms the congregation, which originally had been Baptists and Presbyterians, espoused Unitarian principles, and as such the worshippers meet there to this day. During the year 1873, the Rev. T. Cooper, after 20 years pastorate, resigned his charge, and only remains with the congregation until the appointment of another minister.

"FRAMLINGHAM CHURCH is dedicated to St. Michael the Archangel and is supposed to have been erected prior to 1353. Others contend it was not erected until about 1400. The steeple is 96 ft. high, and in it there is a peal of eight bells. The first, second, and eighth were made in 1718, and the third in 1720. There were only five bells until 1718, when the peal was made up to eight, The rector finds the ropes for the bells out of the income of 'Bell-rope meadow' containing 3 acres, 20 poles, situated on the Kettleburgh-road. The length of the Church in 125 ft. and height of nave 44 ft. The gallery and organ were erected about 1708, the former being presented to the parish by the Master and Fellows of Pembroke College, the patrons of the living. In 'Green's HISTORY OF FRAMLINGHAM the Rectors who have held the living are given from the year 1311. The present Rector is the Rev. George Attwood, M.A., and his Curate the Rev. J.S. Cattlow, M.A. The rule with the Masters and Fellows of Pembroke College is to present the living to their Senior Fellow, and the present rector was instituted on the 19th May, 1837. The income ranges from £1,500 upwards. The tombs in the Church are very handsome and astonish many visitors as regards their number and beauty.

"Prayers are read in the Church every morning at the tolling of the bell, according to the Will of Sir Robert Hitcham, for which £45 a year is paid the Reader - the Rev. T.J. Brereton - and £7.10s. the Sexton - Mr. A.G. Barker. The Reader has also a house in Castle-street wherein to dwell rent free, to which there is a capital garden attached.

"FRAMLINGHAM CASTLE is one of the many fine ruins to be found in our sea-girt isle. It occupies a site of 1 acre, 1 rod, 11 poles, and is generally believed to have been erected between 521 and 614. It has fourteen towers, and its walls are six feet in thickness. It is surrounded by an inner and an outer moat, being bounded by the Mere on the west and the town on the south. History says the Danes, under the command of their captains Hingwar and Hubba, in 866, entered the land at the mouth of the Humber, and pursued their warlike enterprises through the entire province of Mercia. They next proceeded into the East Anglian territories, and having, after a sanguinary battle, made themselves masters of Edmund's capital at Thetford, he retreated before them with the remains of his army into his Castle at Framlingham, wherein he was beseiged, and being hard pressed and without hope of succour he again fled, but was closely pursued towards Hoxne (originally called Heglisdune), where he was defeated and made captive under the following circumstances. Having in his flight reached that village, he concealed himself from his enemies under a bridge which to this day is known by the name of the Gold Bridge, in which situation he was discovered by the glittering of his golden spurs, by a newly married couple on their way home by moonlight, and who betrayed him to his ferocious pursuers; they sought him at the bridge, but having left that spot and secreted himself in an oak tree upon the Abbey Farm, in Hoxne, the Danes traced him by his footsteps thither, upon which, in the warmth of resentment, he pronounced a curse upon all who might pass over the bridge to be married or buried.

"Martyrdom was the immediate consequence of his captivity, which, upon the authority of Francis Palgrave, Esq., in his *History of the Anglo-Saxon Period*, is thus narrated: 'A particular account of Edmund's death (he says) was given by his Sword-bearer, who, having attained a very advanced age, was wont to repeat the sad story at the court of Athelstane. Edmund was fettered and manacled, and treated with every species of cruelty and indignity. The heathen Danes bound their captive to a tree, beat and scourged him, and shot their arrows at him as a mark - taunting him and urging him to deny his faith; but he continued steadfast amidst his sufferings, until Hingwar, wearied by his constancy, commanded that he should be beheaded. Upon this, follows a legend, that the monarch's head was thrown into a thicket nearby, where, after a long search, it was found by some of his faithful subjects in the possession of a wolf, who, holding the head up between his fore feet, very civilly delivered up his charge, which being immediately joined to his body, the whole was interred at Hoxne, but not without the attendance of the wolf, who afterwards withdrew to his native woods. The notice of this legend is called forth from its intimate connection with Bury St. Edmunds, where even the arms of the town have long been formed to commemorate the savage protector of the royal monarch's head, as did also the capitular seal of the once sumptuous monastery of that place, which represented St. Edmund sitting on a throne, with a bishop standing on each side; on the reverse, he was bound to a tree and transfixed with arrows; below is another compartment, the body of St. Edmund, headless, and near it a wolf, bringing back the royal head to restore it to the body.

"Roger Bigod, eldest son and heir of Hugh Bigod, in 1183 came into Possession of the Castle; and he was one of the 25 barons appointed to enforce the observance of *Magna Carta* by King John on the plain of Runnymede in 1215. In the same year King John took Framlingham Castle with other possessions in Suffolk and Norfolk.

"Queen Mary, in July, 1553, after the decease of Edward VI, took up her abode at Framlingham Castle and continued there from the 10th to the 31st. Upon her arrival, the first gentleman who took up arms and levied men in her defence was Sir John Sulyard, who, as a reward for his fidelity, was appointed to guard her person during her residence in it. Though her stay at the Castle was short, yet she issued her commands from hence to the lords lieutenants and sheriffs to march with the power of their counties to her aid. The gentry resident within the county who came forward as her adherents were Sir John Sulyard, of Wetherden Hall, near Stowmarket; Sir Thomas Cornwallis, of Brome, then high sheriff of Norfolk and Suffolk; Sir William Drury, of Hawstead Place, M.P. for the county; Sir Henry Bedingfield, of Redlingfield, who brought with him 140 men completely armed, and was appointed by Mary knight-marshal of her army; Sir Henry Jerningham, with many others, whose vassal troops followed their standard, by means of which she was at the head of 40,000 men, to whom she declared that she would disturb nothing established in religion, but reserved to herself the right of following her own creed, which was that of the Catholic Church; a pledge which it is almost needless to add was no sooner given than it was forgotten.

"The following lines are the closing portion of a CHRONICLE OF CASTEL FRAMLINGHAM by Miss Charlesworth:

> 'The bloody flag of Popery was reared upon thy walls;
> The Protestants' lone chronicler was sheltered in thy halls;
> Royal and noble have they been, thy dwellers in the past;
> The poor man and the homeless now tenant thy gates at last:
> The bridge which hath seen leaders pass, to conquer or to die,
> Is trodden by the quiet foot of way-worn poverty.
> So fadeth the memorial of that which hath been high!
> So worketh round the viewless wheel of human destiny!
> Oh ! beautiful in ruin ! - most lovely in decline !
> Be ours an age as ruffleless, as full of calm as thine !
> And thou who should'st have clos'd for me my long unfinished song,
> Heaven watch above thy happy home, and grant it stand as long,
> Sweet quiet, with its shadowing wings, guard over its roof keeping,
> As have the solemn isles, where thine ancestors are sleeping."

"The Castle is now held by the Masters and Fellows of Pembroke College, who came into possession thereof under the will of Sir Robert Hitcham, Knight, the last possessor. They are also Lords of the Manor of Framlingham and Saxtead. Mr. G. Goodwyn acting as steward.

"The lands surrounding the Castle, comprising 671 acres, were left in trust by Sir Robert Hitcham to the poor of Framlingham, Coggeshall, and Debenham (see Sir R. Hitcham's Will, published by R. Lambert, Double-street, Framlingham).

'JEMMY' CHAMBERS, the poet. This eccentric man was born at Soham in Cambridgeshire; and when he came to man's estate indulged in wandering throughout Suffolk, sleeping in any outhouse he could crawl into. He prowled round about Framlingham, Woodbridge, and the neighbourhood for several years. He was beastly dirty in his habits; and stunk from filth as he walked. He generally had five or six dogs with him. A Mr. Cordy of Worlingworth, befriended and also secured him assistance; and a house was placed at his disposal to live in; but he soon took to his old life of outhouses and wandering. Help was also afforded him by Woodbridge ladies and gentlemen, but the poet's eccentricity was unmanageable. The poet Bernard Barton, of Woodbridge, wrote thus of him: 'Ladies are somewhat fond of pet oddities. An old, tattered, weather-beaten object like old Chambers, is the very thing to take their fancies. Why, when the poor wretch was living, and had located himself hereabouts, his best friends were the ladies. When they stopped to speak to the old man, to be sure they would get to windward of him as a matter of taste, for he was a walking dunghill, poor fellow, most of his wardrobe looking as if it had been picked off some such repositories; and his hands and face bearing evident marks of his antipathy to soap and water. Yet, though he was the very opposite of a lady's lap dog, curled, combed, washed and perfumed, he had his interest - and it was pretty effective too - with the sex. His wretched appearance was sure to appeal to their compassion; the solitary, wandering life he led, his reputed minstrel talent, some little smattering of book learning, which he would now and then display - in short, I might write a regular treatise, giving very philosophical reasons why Chambers was quite a lady's man.'

"MR. GEORGE WRIGHT. George Wright (a Baptist Minister) was born at Framlingham May 19, 1789, and preached the gospel at the Baptist Church at Beccles from April 21, 1822 to April 24, 1870. He was at one time connected with and preached for the Wesleyans; but was afterwards led from conviction to adopt Baptist principles. After preaching for 48 years at Beccles, during which period he was made the means of saving over 300 souls, he was compelled through failing health and old age to resign his charge. He died October 7th, 1873 in his 85th year.

"THE FIRST GAS-LIGHT AND GAS WORKS USED IN FRAMLINGHAM. The first oxy-hydrogen light apparatus used in Framlingham was made and exhibited by Mr. Joseph Barker, sen., about the year 1845, on the premises now used by Mr. Lambert as a printing office in Double-street. It was also used in the Castle-hall by the Rev. C.C. Nutter, Unitarian minister, to illustrate a lecture given by him on 'The Seven Ages of Man' by a pair of magic lanterns, to dissolve the views on the canvas. On the same premises in Double-street the first complete gas-works were erected by Mr. Joseph Barker, and used for lighting his shop and that of Mr. W.D. Freeman during the winter.

"THE FIRST PAPER FRONT(?)
Paper cuffs, collars, and fronts, are common enough in our days, and even paper coats, trousers, and window blinds are manufactured extensively in America. But 60 or 70 years ago these things were not even dreamt of as articles of attire. It is believed, however, that the first front manufactured from PAPER was made at Framlingham; if not, the following fact is not without a little interest. There lived, about 1820, in the town an auctioneer named John Ludbrook, who was a clever old man in his way. He had been a farmer at Earl Soham, but became reduced in his circumstances. He removed to Framlingham and commenced business as an auctioneer. Having lost his wife he had a housekeeper he called 'Ria (Maria Copping). One morning there was a rap at his door, which his housekeeper (rather of an oddity) answered. She received a letter from the postman, which she handed over to her master. Ludbrook said 'A letter! bless me, where's that from?' He opened it, and exclaimed 'God luv my heart, 'Ria, it is from the great Mr. Blumfield, of Billingford. I ha' got to go and meet him for a waleration'. 'Ria replied, 'A waleration indeed; you ha' got nothing to go with'. 'Ah ya, 'Ria, there'll be a way made out' replied her master. 'But' continued 'Ria, 'You ha' got no shirt to go in'. 'We shall manage', said her master; whereupon he goes out and purchases a sheet or two of paper at one of the shops in the town, and on his return he and 'Ria contrive to make a paper frilled front. The morning arrived for meeting Mr. Blumfield who was a great auctioneer in his day, and a wretchedly saddled horse was led to Ludbrook's door. Out comes John with his paper frilled front ready for a mount; but on viewing the animal he insists upon a better bridle and saddle for his journey, which the man succeeds in obtaining. John mounted, off he goes, with his paper front, feeling his own and the importance of the business of the day. Reaching Earl Soham Falcon Inn, John, who was a thirsty soul, went in for his 'six punna'. James Kent, the landlord, knowing John well, supplied him with his grog, and, twigging John's paper front, he, with a view to teaze and on mischief bent, made a snatch at it and tore it from John's bosom. John with great warmth, cries out 'James, you are a fule; 'Ria and I ha' been trying hard to make this here front: I hav' to meet the great Mr. Blumfield of Billingfor' on a waleration today; and now I don't know what to du'. After teazing John a little while and holding up his front to the gaze of all in the house, the landlord says to his wife, 'Hannah, run upstairs and find John one of my frilled shirts'. John, after donning the landlord's shirt, pursued his journey all the more comfortable if not the smarter for the change.

"John Ludbrook was the first to introduce printing into the town of Framlingham, and many of his catalogues were quite curiosities in their way; for instance, it was not amiss for him to place the swill tub in the pantry, nor arithmetically a difficulty to sell three bird cages in four lots, nor anything uncommon to sell an eight-day corner cupboard."

Great Britain was riding high in the 1850s and 1860s; Australia and New Zealand received constitutions for representative governments, transportation ended and a gold rush to Victoria accounted for a sizeable emigration from the United Kingdom. In 1867 the confederation of the North American Colonies became the Dominion of Canada and numbers of farm labourers made their way there. England was looking outwards, changes were afoot, people were more mobile and were more affected by mass movements and combinations of like-minded workers.

Innovations in machinery were suspect and resented in this agrarian agricultural area. By the 1870s Framlingham was no longer an independent self-governing unit, but was influenced by

national and local movements. The development of agricultural machinery had caused much antagonism, and rendered unnecessary some large numbers of agricultural labourers. Furthermore, poor harvests had reduced farming incomes. In 1874 a large open air meeting of labourers was held. This was followed in 1875 by the formation of the Labourers' Union, and by a walk-out of agricultural workers in the Wilford Hundred when their demand for higher wages and shorter working hours was refused by their employers. This provoked a situation of extreme antagonism between employers and employed, unknown before in East Anglia. Weekly processions of Union men were formed at Framlingham and elsewhere. Flags and banners were flown and blue ribbons and rosettes were worn by Union members. In June, at the height of the dispute, 2,400 men, locked out by the farmers of East and West Suffolk, were reduced to receiving only 9s per week from Union funds. Time-honoured relations between masters and men were severed for ever; some leading landowners were in opposition to the demands while others took up the cause of the workers. Sir Edward Kerrison, who refused to lock out the men on his estate, acted as mediator. During the harvest 'Union' delegates advised the men to return to their employers and ask for work, but numbers of them were encouraged by emigration agents to leave with their families for Canada, while others migrated to the towns. The numbers of agricultural workers were reduced, some were never to return to the local farms. The eighteen-week lock-out with responsibility for strike pay, emigration and migration, cost the National Agricultural Labourers Union about £25,000. Times were hard, and harvests were poor for several years together. An increasing number of farmers joined the Framlingham Farmers' Club, one of the oldest in the country, and some regularisation of labourers' wages was agreed. The workers who remained were better off than before; the public houses were selling more beer to these workers, who were criticised for joining neither the benefit societies nor the savings banks. The Mutual Improvement Society founded in 1844 by Sir Henry Thompson, with James Larner as its Vice-President, was wound up in 1876 for lack of support.

In order to ameliorate the situation, the chapels became very active and in 1877 the new Benevolent Society of the Framlingham Court of Foresters was established in a brick building in Albert Road. The Brook Lane library was bought by the James Larner Lodge of Good Templars; a Young Men's Christian Association, which met in rooms in Crown & Anchor Lane, was formed, with a good library given by Mrs. Barker. Times remained hard, and three suicides were recorded in Framlingham, but a sense of responsibility by those who were prospering was being shown to those in need: a drama performance was given in the Castle Hall to raise funds for the reading-room, a spelling bee was organised to raise funds for the Suffolk Volunteer Reserve Corps, a cricket club was formed, and the Whit Tuesday gala was well attended; a ploughing match was organised by the Framlingham Farmers' Club, and the Duke of Hamilton distributed game in Framlingham from his shoots.

By 1878 outings were arranged for chapel Sunday Schools. Lectures were arranged by the Temperance Society, for it was noticed that the labourers were drinking rather than paying their bills.

At the height of the success of its energetic Headmaster, the Rev. W.W. Bird, an epidemic of scarlatina hit the College. This was most unfortunate for since 1874, when day boys were introduced to the school, the numbers had steadily risen and had reached 350. The epidemic caused the withdrawal of 150 boys and for many years the numbers in the College remained below 300.

The Foster Education Act of 1870 made provision for School Boards to be elected by the local ratepayers with authority to build and maintain 'Board Schools' at the expense of the ratepayers. Since it was felt that the Charity Commissioners were failing the poor children of Framlingham, Board Schools were established and the Hitcham and Thomas Mills Free Schools were closed, but following the Royal Sanction given to the Hitcham Charity Scheme, steps were taken to build a new school in College Road for the poor boys and girls of the town. This was opened with very moderate fixed fees in March 1879 amidst cries from the ratepayers of Framlingham that the donors had bequeathed money for FREE education.

The Thomas Mills Schoolroom was used as a library aud reading-room for the town, and in 1886 enlarged, following gifts amounting to £60, and was then used as a club as well as a reading-room for the young men of the town. Plans were launched for the building of a fee-paying grammar school for middle-class girls, which should be realised when the Mills estate could reach £2,000. This scheme, initiated in an era of agricultural depression when rents were reduced by 30% - 50% and the incomes from both the Hitcham and Mills charities were much reduced, had to be deferred until 1902. While anxiety was felt in 1880 by the farming and trading classes in Framlingham, in the country at large there was further concentration on a religious resolution to the difficult times. This was reflected in Framlingham by the formation of a Bible Society and a Religious Tract Society, and, to a lesser degree, by the first outing to Aldeburgh of the Church Sunday School. In an attempt to improve conditions, the Agricultural Benevolent institute was established in Framlingham and affiliated to the London H.Q. Money was collected locally to be distributed to farmers or their widows in need. Attempts to involve members of the community included a shooting competition between the R.V.C. and the Framlingham Volunteers, and the formation of a quoits club in Framlingham to challenge similar clubs in nearby villages. The Framlingham Amateur Dramatic Society was formed, performances being given in the Castle Hall.

Religious Caravan

The 18th January 1831 was marked by the great gale from the N.N.E. which uprooted trees and brought bitterly cold conditions with snowdrifts so severe that rail and vehicular traffic was delayed and deaths were caused. Another gale, this time from the W.S.W., assailed the town on 14th October of the same year, when fruit was stripped from the trees, trees fell, and the four sails of T.T. Buckmaster's Victoria Tower mill were blown off. Harvesters reported the wettest-ever harvest, which stretched over seven weeks. Farming losses were so great that many farms were offered for sale, and the census of 3rd April showed a decrease of 51 to the 2,518 persons recorded in 1871, with 31 empty houses; but at the same time the census had illustrated the growing prosperity of some in Framlingham, for of the 83 trades listed (see Trades), three provided for leisure activities, and included one photographer, one piano tuner, one gun-maker; three for the elegance of ladies' fashion, including three milliners, two glovers and three hairdressers; the three harness-makers, three coach-builders, three watchmakers and two stone-masons provided services for the well-to-do, while the 62 persons listed as servants demonstrated the relative affluence of some of the 2,518 persons registered in Framlingham. Demand had encouraged four bakers/confectioners and two chimneysweeps to practise their trades, which were hitherto undertaken by the householders, and nine men were employed on the railway. By 1871, 13 schoolmasters/mistresses were employed both for the fee-paying students and for the children provided for by the newly-established elementary school.

The world was changing as a result of the Franco-Prussian War of 1870, the Ashantee Wars and the Russo-Turkish War of 1877/78. These wars did not immediately affect Framlingham apart from the development of the Suffolk Volunteer Rifle Corps and the competitive shooting-matches, which produced Dan Scase, who became the national champion shot for many years, and the 'march-outs' of the volunteers which produced a nucleus of trained young men led by local officers.

Harvest Time

In spite of two disastrous floods in 1882 a better harvest gave heart to the people of Framlingham. New Societies were formed, such as the new Teachers' Association, the Unitarians, and the old Framlingham Farmers' Club with a new Committee. Concerts by the Harmonic Society, lectures, competitive shooting and quoits matches were arranged.

A number of changes occasioned by deaths and retirement took place in Framlingham in 1884. The 89 year-old Rector, the Rev. George Attwood, after 44 years in office with some years of failing health, died and was succeeded by the Rev. Edward Bickersteth, a Fellow of Pembroke College, Cambridge, who, with the P.C.C. perceiving the precarious state of the Church fabric, appointed Mr. Prior, a London architect, to assess its condition.

St.Michael's Church

It was decided that major repairs should be undertaken at once, first to the nave and then to the chancel. Edward Bickersteth, having launched an appeal and invited subscriptions towards the estimated cost of £8,000, was then appointed the first Anglican Bishop in Japan. After just 14 months in Framlingham he resigned the living, to be succeeded by the Rev. James Holme Pilkington, also a Fellow of Pembroke College.

The Rev. J.S. Cattlow, the well-established and highly regarded Reader and Curate, also retiring in 1884 after 14 years service, was presented with a gift of more than £100. The Rev. W. Fielding resigned from the Unitarian Chapel as did the Free Methodist Minister, the Rev. W. Hammond, who was replaced by the Rev. W.R. Mullett, while the Particular Baptists opened a mission-room for Sunday-night services. A notable local figure, Mr. G. Goodwyn, who had changed his name from Peirson, died. He had succeeded several generations of Peirsons who had been leading figures in the town, owning much property; at his death all these estates and effects were sold by his executors. The Clodd & Larner firm that had been established almost 75 years past ceased trading and was bought by John Self. Other changes included new and improved management for the Bowling Green Club and an extra reading room for the young men of the town, which was opened daily from 6-10 p.m. in Double Street.

The Free Methodists, who had been in Framlingham for 17 years sold their chapel in Station Road and bought for £670 the Peoples' Hall as a United Methodist Free Church. *The Railway Inn* was built on the site of the old chapel.

It was recorded at the 1885 General Meeting of the local gas company that 8% was being paid to shareholders and that the price of gas was to be reduced to 5s.7½d. per thousand therms.

The political parties were active. In 1886 after the third Great Parliamentary Reform Act of 1884 which redistributed seats, Framlingham became the centre of the new division called the North Eastern or Eye Division. A tide of Liberalism swept the country, and again F.S. Stevenson was elected. Gladstone's Home Rule Bill for Ireland was a central feature of policy, aud local lectures were given including an important one in Framlingham Castle; the local consensus was in favour of Home Rule.

In 1886, Framlingham lost an influential friend by the death of Sir Edward Kerrison who, it will be remembered, had been instrumental in the setting up of Framlingham College and in mediating between the farmers and workers during the lockout of 1874.

On 21st June 1887, while Queen Victoria, accompanied by her family and a number of European monarchs and Indian potentates, attended a thanksgiving service in Westminster Abbey, Framlingham celebrated her 50 years' reign and the growing importance of Great Britain in the world, with a public holiday. The Church bells rang out; an ecumenical service of thanksgiving was held in St. Michael's Church, followed by a public dinner in the Castle for the poor of the town and by a sports afternoon, with tea, for the children. It was hoped that a public playground could be established in honour of the occasion, but Pembroke College turned down the proposal.

Concentration on local affairs included the Allotments Act of 1887, allowing the compulsory purchase of land for allotments. In Framlingham in 1894 the Rev. James Holme Pilkington gave glebe land for this purpose and in 1889 an Horticultural Society was formed with the Rector as President and the Headmaster of the Board School, E.G. Warren, as Secretary. Framlingham was reassessed by the county and found to be responsible for 27½ miles of road - the seven approach-roads to the town costing approximately £20 per mile, or about £500 per annum to maintain.

Favourable comments had followed the metalling of the roads with granite and the cementing of some of the principal paths in the town. In spite of these costs, which were greater than those of neighbouring towns, the rateable value was reduced from £10,666.15s.0d to £9,975.12s.6d.

Changes were occurring in Framlingham year by year, in 1888 James Maulden, establishing a new steam rolling mill in his maltings at the lower end of Bridge Street was able to produce flour, bran, pollards and meals 'at the lowest market prices', and in 1899 the old local savings bank, operated by Mr. Edwards for so many years, closed, and most of this business was transferred to the relatively new Post Office.

The nave of St. Michael's Church was reopened on 17th October 1889 with the High Altar placed in front of the temporary wall across the chancel steps, and the Thamar organ between the first two pillars on the south side of the nave, which was furnished with 500 chairs for the congregation (See Church). Repairs for the chancel were held up for lack of funds, since the estimate given by Mr. Prior was found to be grossly inadequate. The PCC dispensed with his services and the Rector increased the fund-raising efforts. However, the Church bells were rehung by Messrs. Day & Sons on 1st June 1892 at a cost of £200 which had been raised by subscription.

Maulden Chimney

Developments in that year also included the setting up by Mr. Preston of the stock-yard on the corner of Bridge Street and New Road, where regular popular and profitable sales of animals took place. In 1892, J. Maulden installed in his maltings one of Wickham Market's new Whitmore & Binyon steam rolling mills, which enabled him to increase his flow and output of 'Best roller flour' to 20 sacks of flour per day. (See Mills/Maltings). Perhaps on account of these developments the railway platforms were extended, although we read of the low state of farming in the district, with tenants being given notice to quit. However, this did not deter the 15 members of the town band under the control of S. A. Wright emerging in new regimental suits of dark blue with yellow facings, said to have a 'taking appearance'. Possibly this description may also have been given to the attire of the newly-formed bicycle club! (See photograph).

The important Parish Councils Bill became law in 1894. It was designed to pass to local councils matters which had hitherto been handled by Parliament. They included the Burial Acts, Public Improvement Acts, matters concerning parish property and the raising of certain rates and the management of land for allotments. This act necessitated the election of Parish Council officers and the end of the offices of Overseers and Guardians of the Town.

Accordingly on 4th December 1894 at 6 p.m. in the Castle Hall the first Parish Meeting under the Local Government Act was convened by the Overseers to elect a Chairman of the meeting and to elect 15 Parish Councillors. The meeting was well attended; T. W. Read of Albert Place was elected

Chairman of the Meeting. He asked that nominations for Parish Councillors be handed to him, and within 15 minutes, Francis Read, Fellmonger, of Fore Street, seconded by Robert Lambert, Printer had presented the following nominations:

>John Bridges (Tailor)
>Samuel Green Carley (Grocer)
>John Howard (Tailor)
>John Martin (Clerk to Justices)
>Rev. James Holme Pilkington (Rector)
>Savill Joseph Savill (Farmer)
>John Robert Watson (Farmer)
>Samuel Wright (Music Seller)
>Thomas Twidell Buckmaster (Farmer)
>Charles Harper (Labourer)
>George E. Jeaffreson J.P. (Surgeon, JP)
>Benjamin Norman (Gunsmith)
>William Pipe (Farmer)
>Calvin Denny Smith (Farmer)
>Reuben Whitehead (Merchant)

These nominations were accepted, and the 15 were considered to be duly elected.

The first meeting of this Council was held on the 14th December 1894 in the Boy's School, Framlingham, when all the 15 signed the Declaration of Acceptance of Office. Dr. G.E. Jeaffreson J.P. was elected Chairman and John Martin Vice-Chairman. F.G. Ling and H. J. Damant were proposed to act as Clerk to the Council. A vote was taken and Mr. Ling was elected Clerk and asked to continue his duties as clerk to the Burial Board. By 1895 John Martin was Clerk to the Council, and Messrs W. Rodwell, J. Savill and J. Watson became District Councillors.

One of the first undertakings of the new Parish Council was to resolve the ever-recurring question of disposing of the sewage of Framlingham. Mr. Hill of Maidenhead completed the comprehensive sewage works designed by Mr. T. Miller of Ipswich, near to the Castle Bridge on the Kettleburgh Road, at a cost of £3,000. This money was borrowed by the authority of the Plomesgate Union, to be repaid by the Town in 30 years. It was hoped that the scheme would be successful. (See Services). The Council bowed to the plea of 1895 that the town pond should be cleaned and repaired. However, criticism of mismanagement of the Hitcham Trust was levelled at the Councillors, and at the 1897 annual parish meeting a poll was demanded, and Messrs. F. Read, J. Self, R. Lambert, J. Fuller, W. Rodwell, E. Gardner, A. Amey, G. Dorling, W. Pipe replaced all but the Rev. H. Pilkington (Chairman) and Messrs. J. Martin, T. Buckmaster, J. Savill, J. Bridges and B. Norman. It was agreed that the weekly allowance of 4s., reduced from 7s., was to be paid as before to the twelve inmates of the Hitcham's Almshouses.

Framlingham was alive with clubs and societies ranging from quoits, bowls, bicycling, golf, cricket, and the rifle corps, to farming, freemasonry, and a choral society. Skating, chess and competitive sports were also added in 1897, with continuation classes in mathematics and woodcarving and ambulance classes run by the Police. The War in South Africa, 1899/1900, led to a new emphasis on training for the volunteers, lectures in First Aid and fund raising for benefits for the soldiers. Seven of the Framlingham force volunteered to go to South Africa and five were chosen. Others were called to the colours. Private Dan Scase was not chosen to go to South Africa, but gained a certain distinction by winning the shooting cup and £5 in prizes at Bisley, where he was representing G Company for Framlingham, and in 1901 he became a Gold Medallist.

The year 1897 was memorable. It included an advance in technology with the connecting of Framlingham with Earl Soham by telecommunication, set up in a specially designed new building in Fore Street. The 70 ft. boring for water at the Haynings crossroads having been found to produce unwholesome water, a further boring to a depth of 250 ft. was undertaken, with the insertion of iron pipes to reach an artesian well with an inexhaustible supply of good water that could easily be pumped up to supply the nearby houses. This pump was covered by a shelter, and the whole given to the town in 1898 by the Jeaffreson family, who had served the community with three generations of doctors since about 1825.

Jeaffreson Pump

The various flourishing clubs and societies were joined by a branch of the Young Men's Friendly Society for 'the moral, social and intellectual improvement of the mind ... of all young men, in the Town'. In this year, Framlingham also joined in the national celebrations to mark the sixtieth anniversary of the Queen's accession to the throne by decorating the town with flags and bunting, by firing a royal salute at break of day and by having a holiday marked by the ringing of the Church bells, the playing of the volunteer band on the Market Hill and by the volunteers firing a *feu-de-joie* followed by three cheers. After this a Thanksgiving Service was held in St. Michael's Church before the local children formed a procession, sang and then marched to the Castle Meadow for sports and games before a sumptuous tea in the Castle Yard. The Committee had raised over £100 for the day's events and gave the balance of this fund for a cot or cots at a local hospital.

Framlingham Ladies Cycle Club

By the Lent Term of 1901 Framlingham College formed an Officers' Training Corps of 73 as a Cadet Volunteer Rifle Corps., and one Company was attached to the first Volunteer Battalion Suffolk Regiment, led by a retired Royal Marine Artillery Quartermaster-Sergeant. The College also played its part in the town with concentration both on successful examination results and on swimming; 41 medallions and 42 certificates of competency were awarded by the Life-Saving Society, and 229 of the 300 boys in the College were able to swim 60 yards. Quite a good record at the turn of the century.

In spite of the low death rate in Framlingham there had been 1,586 interments since 1856 when provision was made for 1,615 grave spaces, so in August the Parish purchased land adjacent to the cemetery for £400. The last burial took place in the churchyard in March 1901, that of Mrs. Stephen Blomfield, a Free Methodist in her 90th year who was buried in her husband's 1851 vault.

Section 5.0

FRAMLINGHAM 1901 - 1930

20th Century

Queen Victoria died aged 82 on 22nd January 1901 at Osborne House on the Isle of Wight, and on 24th January 1901 King Edward VII was proclaimed King. The body of the late Queen was ceremoniously brought to Westminster Hall London, where it lay in state before being taken to Windsor on 3rd February 1901, and buried at Frogmore on 4th February. On 14th February, King Edward VII read the speech from the throne at the State Opening of Parliament, and on 27th February joined his brother-in-law in Germany, Emperor Kaiser Wilhelm, who had been gazetted a Field Marshal of the British Army on 27th January 1901.

The return of the volunteers from South Africa early in May 1901 was celebrated by the local G Company of volunteers, 2 troopers of the Suffolk Yeomanry, the band and C Company Cadet Corps. meeting them at the railway station. Then, amidst much enthusiasm, the town, led by the Rev. J. Holme Pilkington, welcomed them on the Market Hill. At the official reception in the Castle Yard, each of the 5 men was presented by Mrs. Holme Pilkington with a £5 note and an illuminated address. This was followed by tea for about 150 guests.

Framlingham people had made great and loyal plans for celebrating King Edward's coronation on 26th June and although they joined in the nation's concern for the King's health and safety when it was learned that he had appendicitis, they decided to keep to their arrangements, and on 26th June, a fine day, they fulfilled their programme but in a 'gloomy manner'. (King Edward was one of the first sufferers to experience a successful appendisectomy - he was pronounced well enough for his coronation on 9th August 1902).

One citizen, C.P. Dowsing, a tailor, was prepared to celebrate the coronation by giving one suit free of cost in every ten ordered before Christmas. He had prepared tickets printed 1-10 K, 1-10 I, 1-10 N, 1-10 G, to complete the words 'King Edward' and a blind-folded man had inserted these tickets into the envelopes of receipted bills.

The Balfour Education Act of 1902 for the first time made provision for elementary and secondary education to be brought under public control as a duty of the state. (This led to the doubling of numbers of secondary schools in the country in 5 years). The Boards set up in 1870 were abolished and elementary and secondary education was placed in the hands of statutory committees of the boroughs and county councils. In practice in Framlingham one parish councillor and one county councillor were to replace the three elected parish councillors who had been on the board. The cry went up 'This is Mr. Balfour's method of **increasing** representation and control by those who find the money'. Many opposed the Act, and six inhabitants of Framlingham, known as 'passive resisters', were summoned before the magistrates on 29th August 1903, when distraints were made. Their goods were sold on 25th September 1903. Immediately there was a protest meeting on the Market Hill followed by another meeting in the evening in the Free Methodist Church. The passive resisters continued to maintain their stand against the 1902 Education Act by attending the half-yearly Magistrates' summonses in the distinguished County Court House built in 1876 behind the Police Station in Bridge Street. (The local J. P.s were Dr. G. E. Jeaffreson, Francis Read, Robert Lambert and John Self).

It was clear that Framlingham resented any loss of control over its affairs and their spending powers. This resistance was put to the test in 1905 when a resolution was passed in the Parish Council by a small majority of 34 with 230 abstainers for Framlingham to apply to the County Council for urban powers, a condition that all but Framlingham and Saxmundham enjoyed among the neighbouring towns. The influential men of Framlingham, misunderstanding the implications and rallying supporters to reject the decision, sent a signed petition to the County Council. This was accepted, much to the dismay of a number of inhabitants, who saw that by the acceptance half the salaries of officials was lost and Framlingham was contributing to civic affairs in other towns in the Plomesgate Rural District while losing much of the grant for the roads for which they were responsible. Framlingham did not apply again for urban powers until 1927.

It was inevitable that trading changes should reach Framlingham, for the National Tariff Reform League was campaigning for protection for prices of corn, flour, meat, dairy produce and certain manufactures. The day of the small individual supplier was threatened. In 1901 the nationwide 'International Stores' opened in Bridge Street, and in August 1904 the Framlingham & District Agricultural Co-operative Society bought, for £800, premises near the railway station, so that they could buy in bulk. They set out to extend their number of shareholders (146 holding 1, 890 shares) in order to increase their capital to £1, 250. In the same year J. T. Page disposed of the *Castle Brewery* to Messrs. Truman, Hanbury, Buxton & Co. Ltd. a large firm with its headquarters away from Framlingham, which became responsible for the hitherto locally owned brewery. It may also be noted from the annual advertisements that A. G. Potter had become an agent for SWIFT cycles and for the locally known cheaper WULFRUNA cycles, and that his business was moving from the locally made skips, sieves 'and fancy baskets' to that of an agent for mass-produced articles. Other shop owners by 1903 were combining the sale of goods supplied to them from factories with the production and sale of goods made on the premises, as had been the practice in the past.

Fire at Framlingham

On 26th August 1905 a serious fire broke out in Fore Street, which could not be controlled by the Fire Brigade as there was insufficient pressure of water. Five houses with their contents were burnt to the ground, leaving 27 townspeople homeless and destitute. They were helped by local people who raised a fund of £123 for them. Three houses built by Frank Baldry in 1908, and Hillside House built for Miss Lambert replaced the five burnt down cottages.

The Campbell Bannerman Liberal Government, which ran from 1905-1914, bringing in some sweeping changes, including a change in the Education Act to appease the non-conformists, introducing measures aimed at social amelioration. The Old Age Pension law of 1909 was among these.

How To Obtain the Old Age Pension.

ON January 1st, 1909, the Old Age Pensions Act comes into force, and on that day all who have satisfied the Pension Authorities of their claim may draw their first week's pension of 5s. or less. Both men and women are entitled to pensions. In the case of married persons, both husband and wife may draw a pension, provided they fulfil the conditions of the Act.

Who is Entitled to the Pension?

Any man or woman who has attained the age of 70, who has satisfied the Pension Authorities that for at least 20 years he or she has been a British subject and has resided in the United Kingdom.

The yearly income of a person applying must not exceed £31 : 10 : 0.

The age of the applicant can best be proved by the production of a birth certificate. If this cannot be produced, the following may be put in as evidence:—
(1) Certificate of baptism
(2) Certificate of service with any forces of the Crown.
(3) Certificate of membership of any Friendly or Provident Society or Trade Union.
(4) Certificate of marriage.
(5) Any other evidence which appears to the Pension Authority to be sufficient for the purpose.

[In this last may be included entries in Family Bibles, old books with the applicant's name and age inserted, samplers, or even the evidence of friends that to their belief the applicant is 70 years of age or over.]

Residence in the British Dominions during the preceding 20 years may be accepted as proof that the applicant is a British subject. If it appears that the applicant was not born in the British Dominions, he may prove that he is a British subject, either by producing a naturalisation Certificate, or by showing that his father was a British subject. To prove residence, the evidence of two witnesses should be produced, if possible, who have had personal knowledge of the applicant and his business for 20 years.

Temporary absence from the United Kingdom will not disqualify for receiving a pension if—
(a) before his absence the claimant was living in the United Kingdom, and throughout his absence was employed in the service of the Crown, or was employed by a servant of the Crown, provided he was paid out of money provided by Parliament;
(b) before the absence he lived in the United Kingdom, and during the absence was serving on a vessel registered in the United Kingdom;
(c) throughout his absence his home was in the United Kingdom, provided that the sum of such absences does not exceed 8 years in the prescribed 20 years.

When once a person has become a pensioner he must not be absent from the United Kingdom for more than three months at a time.

The Amount of Income.

The amount of the claimant's private income (see table) is calculated on the amount of any money likely to be received during the year, in the form of wages, income from property, or any other benefits.

Means of Claimant from all sources except pension.	Rate of Pension per week.
	s. d.
When the means of the claimant do not exceed £21 a year (about 8s. 1d. a week)	5 0
Exceeding £21, but not exceeding £23 12s. 6d. (about 9s. 1d. a week)	4 0
Exceeding £23 12s. 6d., but not exceeding £26 5s. 0d. (about 10s. 1d. a week)	3 0
Exceeding £26 5s. 0d., but not exceeding £28 17s. 6d. (about 11s. 1d. a week)	2 0
Exceeding £28 17s. 6d., but not exceeding £31 10s. 0d. (about 12s. 1d. a week)	1 0

The income of one of a married couple living in a house is reckoned as at least half the total income. That is to say, if the husband has £30 a year, his wife is considered to have £15, even though she may not have a penny of her own. Claimants are not allowed to part with any of their income or property for the purpose of qualifying for a pension. Children's earnings do not count as disqualifying for a pension.

Who May Not Claim?

The following classes of people are not entitled to pensions:—
Men and women under 70.
Aliens.
Persons whose income is over £31 10s. a year.
Persons who have been absent (except temporarily) from the United Kingdom during the last 20 years. (See above.)
Persons in receipt of Poor Relief, except medical or surgical assistance, or expenses in aid of maintaining a dependent in hospital, asylum, or infirmary, etc.
Lunatics.
Criminals who suffered imprisonment without the option of a fine, for 10 years after release.
Habitual drunkards.
Persons who have habitually failed to work.

How to Claim.

Apply at the local post-office for an Old Age Pension form, and send it to the Local Pension Officer. Application should be made three months before reaching the age of 70. If for any reason a claim is refused, application should be made within seven days to the Clerk of the Committee for a form of appeal to the Local Government Board, which must be promptly filled up and forwarded. The decision of the Local Government Board is final.

NORTH EAST SUFFOLK ELECTION.

VOTE FOR PEARSON

Land for the People.   Free Trade & Prosperity.

Printed and Published by Hudson & Son, Edmund St, and Livery St, Birmingham.

The divisive radical budget of 1909, known as the 'Peoples' Budget, caused the critical general election of 1910, which was fought to sanction the budget, consider the veto powers of the Lords and to support Home Rule for Ireland. The aim of the Liberals in the Lloyd George budget was to shift the tax burden from producers to persons of wealth through income and inheritance taxes, levies on unearned income and increments on land. These measures were reflected locally. The Plomesgate No. 2 Old age Sub-Committee of nine had three Framlingham members: Messrs. R. Lambert and F. Read with F. G. Ling as Clerk, and the Small-holdings Sub-Committee for Plomesgate was set up to extend ownership of land to a wider public, but this was not found to be a popular pursuit. More open government was also an aim, and from 1908 the press was authorized to attend meetings.

Daisy Rose Bricks

In 1909 'daisy-rose' bricks from Peter Smith's brickworks in the Kettleburgh road were used in the building of the Rowan Cottages at the bridge end of Station Road (See Brickmaking).

The death of King Edward VII on 6th May 1910, and his funeral on 20th May, followed by the coronation of King George V on 3rd May 1911, came at a time which may be seen as a constitutional and revolutionary marker in the annals of the nation. The former because of the reduced powers of the Lords, and the latter because of the National Insurance Act of 1911. The National Insurance Act for the first time made provision for payments of employers and the whole working population to take out insurance against loss of health and for the prevention and cure of sickness, and secondly made provision for the unemployed wage earners between the ages of 16 and 65 with less than £26 per annum income from property, who worked in trades that were especially liable to fluctuations. They would be eligible for 15 weeks' benefit when out of work. This caused much interest in Framlingham, and a wordy political duel between John Cobbing of the *Crown Hotel* and J. K. Badshah of Ipswich was well attended and enthusastically followed.

In spite of these important national developments the even tenor of life in Framlingham continued as usual, with the varied functions of the local clubs, the schools and the changes of ministers in Church and Chapels. However, two important decisions were made for the Town; the first by a joint committee of the District and Parish Councils. Since the town's sewage was still giving offence, it was decided to spend a further £520 to improve the disposal of sewage, but to hold over a proposed scheme for piped water to the Town. The second was taken by Pembroke College following a fall of masonry in February from one of the western towers of the castle into the armoury at the rear end of the Castle Hall. They arranged for the Hall temporarily to be closed while repairs were made. These were put in hand using flints from the fallen tower to the north of the main entry. The Hall was reopened in September of the same year.

Another untoward occurrence for the town was the great flood of December 1910 when Albert Place, the sale ground and other low-lying areas of the town were under water and the Maulden Maltings kiln fire was put out by the flood. This calamity was followed by a plague of rats, so bad that in January 1911 a rat committee was set up and payment was made for every rat caught. The boys and young men cooperated in this search and were rewarded when they produced the rats' tails for the Committee. But by March of that year, Plomesgate Rural District Council refused to give further money for the extermination of the rats, and it was not until October 1929 that the government introduced a National Rat Week, to end on 9th November 1929, that rats were again a matter of general concern.

The Great Flood of 1910

Framlingham was again in tune with the nation and the Empire in its rejoicings and preparations for the coronation of King George V. To mark the occasion it was decided to inaugurate a fund for the establishment of a Parish Nurse. This was fulfilled in January 1911 when a much-needed and appreciated Nursing Association was set up in connection with the Cottage Benefit Nursing Association, with Miss Jeaffreson as Hon. Secretary, with two full-time nurses; it was run by a committee of ladies, and supported by voluntary contributions.

Arrangements for coronation day were to include a tea for all children, a meat tea for all people of 65 years and upwards and sports and amusements for all. The day started with a peal of Church bells at 7 a.m. followed by an hour's music provided by the Territorial Band on the Market Hill before they were joined by the Territorial Company and the College Training Corps who marched to St. Michael's Church for a special service conducted by the Rector. A procession then formed of the Band, Territorials, O.T.C., veteran townspeople, public officials, members of Friendly Societies and school children, who marched through the decorated streets to the Railway Station, where an oak tree was planted in an enclosure by F. Read J.P. In addition to the sports and games on the Castle Meadow, motor car rides were arranged for the old people. The day finished with a bonfire on the Castle Meadow.

Motor Car Rides.

The Rail and Miners' Strikes of 1911/12 do not appear to have impinged on Framlingham, beyond limiting the lighting of the streets, in spite of their serious effects in the country and in Parliament.

The River Ore flooded on 26th August 1912, cutting off all approaches on foot to the railway station, including the new iron bridge from Fairfield Road leading to the fens. Many occupiers of the houses in Albert Place and Station Road were compelled to take to the upper floors. The farms suffered, too, and the farmers and farm-labourers were badly affected. The flood accentuated the poor condition of the roads, and in 1912 the Parish Council arranged for some roads to be steam-rolled and covered with a coating of tar with the expectation that all the main roads in the town would be similarly treated by 1913. On account of a dispute over payment between the Rural District Council and the County Council further tarring did not take place until 1914.

There was further regularisation from 1st January 1912 when the Shops Act came into force, and Wednesday was declared an early closing day from 1 p.m. throughout the country.

The two outstanding events for Framlingham of 1913 were the handing over of the castle by Pembroke College, Cambridge, to H. M. Commissioners of Works and Public Buildings, who set about putting the building into a proper state of repair. The ivy was stripped from the walls, and scaffolding was erected round part of the exterior; earth was removed from the foundations in readiness for cement to be poured in to steady the walls. Of the three wells which were believed to exist, two were found, one of these being 7½ feet wide at the top, more than 60 feet deep, and said to be in excellent condition. The other great change was the retirement of the Rev. Dr. O. D. Inskip after 26 successful years as Headmaster of Framlingham College. He was succeeded by F. W. Stocks.

The local elections of 1913 to the Rural District Council engendered considerable interest with a 76% poll of electors. John Self continued his 15 years as a County Councillor and was joined by George Mann and A. T. Wicks. At the Parish Council Meeting fifteen Councillors were elected, six for the first time, Messrs. W. T. Brunger, H. Coleman, J. Fuller, H. C. Howlett, H. F. Ling, H. B. Maulden, C. C. Nesling, J. T. Page, Rev. J. H. Pilkington, A. G. Potter, J. Robinson, A. E. Runnacles, J. Self, A. T. Wicks and W. Woodgate. These Councillors continued their services through the War and on account of the 1914 Disqualification Relief Act those of them on active service remained Councillors although they were not available to attend meetings.

The Volunteers, now known as the Territorials, continued their usual routine of drills, scouting competitions and mock combats using 'Broomsticks'. All were apparently unaware of the preparations being made by the Germans to extend their western boundary and overrun part of France and Austria. Although the Schlieffen Plan had been worked out, no one expected war, even in July 1914. Sarajevo changed everything. The Territorials, as was their custom, went to camp at Great Yarmouth. They were there when war was declared between England and Germany, but speedily returned to base and in two days were mobilised. Amidst much enthusiasm, they left for Felixstowe by train. They were seen off by a great procession of townsfolk headed by a large Union Jack and with the Territorial Band playing martial music.

Framlingham Town Band Circa 1910.

They were addressed by Alfred Pretty, a senior citizen, who urged the men to be prayerful, vigilant and to acquit themselves like men who were going forth to defend their country and their homes. Framlingham not only sent their Territorials but also 14 men who served in the Royal Navy. Later in the year a large and enthusiastic meeting was held for recruits for Kitchener's Army. Among the speakers were Major General Sir Ronald Lane and Mr. Stevenson, the M.P. for Eye Division from 1885-1906 who, it was said, 'created a great impression'. On a further occasion Lord Kitchener, whose home was at Aspall near Debenham, came himself to search for recruits; young men answered the call to the colours, and, in order to be accepted at the front, several lads made out that they were older than they were, often to the apprehension of their parents.

On 1st July the new Assembly Hall, built as the Working Men's Club behind the Framlingham Conservative Club, was opened by the Marchioness of Graham, and in the evening the fairy operetta, 'Beauty and the Beast', was enjoyed by an enthusiastic audience. All too soon the hall was used to billet soldiers. Riding horses for officers and Suffolk horses for gun carriages were supplied by the local farming community and were accommodated in stables erected on the north side of the Saxmundham Road.

Horses and Mounted Soldiers

Pageant Field, then known as Gun Park, was commandeered by the Army, and a military camp with accommodation for the soldiers in charge of the horses was built. Additionally the 2nd/3rd London Brigade R. F. A. Territorial force was in training in Framlingham. The water for this area was supplied from the Jeaffreson pump newly equipped with a portable steam engine which greatly speeded up the supply. The military authorities required the four hour chimes of the Church clock to be silent after 4 p.m. These were stopped until 1916. After the War the carillon was found to be worn out and was left silent.

The threat of invasion must have been very real, for an extant map of 26th July 1915, issued to 'Lawyer' Read of Framlingham, (see colour plates by Church section), shows parishes coloured within the Eye Parliamentary Division and certain roads outlined in red to be reserved for "Military movements". This map was accompanied with instructions for evacuation in the event of invasion, and for him to be the last to leave Framlingham. He, with his wife and Mrs. S. Greene Carley (his assistants), were provided with the necessary poison' to be taken, should the invasion take place, to prevent them from being captured and forcibly disclosing the evacuation information'.

Yet as 1915 slid into 1916, Framlingham, in common with many other small towns mourning the loss of well-known young men who had fallen in France and at sea, received back the wounded, some of whom were cared for at Easton Hall, which was turned into Lady Hamilton's hospital. House-to-house collections were made to raise money for comforts for the troops and for the Suffolk P.O.W.s. A branch of the War Hospital Supplies was formed and a concert was arranged to raise money for the newly formed Volunteer Training Corps, but always there were the secret plans for evacuating the area should the need arise.

Several annual functions were cancelled, including the Whit Tuesday Gala and the Farmers' Club Show. The gas lights were shaded for fear of air raids, and were not employed for the four days of the full moon, since increased coal prices threatened the gas prices. The Y.M.C.A. opened the school-room of the United Methodist Church in Albert Place, which was much appreciated by the 'Boys', the room being crowded every evening.

In March 1916 guns were located on the Market Hill and street lighting was stopped; a new War Time Association was formed with T.W. Read as Hon. Secretary. Summer time was introduced. Allotment-holders were encouraged to grow food and low price Scottish seed potatoes were made available.

The War Savings Committee under the County Committee for National Service acted as canvassers for volunteers. Already Framlingham and district had sacrificed 250 - 260 men, and Lieut. Col. Richard Brettell suggested there should be a war memorial on the Market Hill. Subsequently it was agreed it should stand in the churchyard and be paid for by voluntary subscriptions after the war had ended. Framlingham through its War Savings Committee raised £4, 735 in 12 weeks ending 19th March 1918 and passed £1,984 through the War Savings Association but did not take part in the War Bonds Scheme that was established. One of the first flag days was held to raise money for wounded horses.

The veteran Rector the Rev. Holme Pilkington died suddenly on 28th December 1916, following his exertions in controlling youths who had invaded the belfry. His successor at St. Michael's was the Rev. H.C.O. Lanchester of Pembroke College. The Rev. Holme Pilkington had played a full part in the town having been a Parish Councillor from 1894 and Chairman from 1907 until his death. The Vice-Chairman, J. T. Page, of the *Castle Brewery*, became Chairman of the Council, with the Veterinary Surgeon, C.C. Nesling, Vice-Chairman. The Council was approached by Lady Rendlesham who asked that a Village Food Production Committee be appointed, but the Council declined to co-operate, feeling that the War Savings Committee was enough. But food shortage was a real national problem and the Board of Agriculture and Fisheries required Committees to promote pig production and appealed for help. A local committee was established. In order to save fuel, from October 1918 shops were required to shut at 5pm on Monday, Tuesday, Thursday and Friday, 1 pm on Wednesday and 7 pm on Saturday.

The armistice, which signalled the end of hostilities, was arranged by the high command for 11 a.m. on the 11th day of the 11th month of 1918. The four terrible years of carnage, the gas attacks, the trench warfare, the lost convoys and naval battles, the separations, were over. There were still shortages of food and a great dislocation of industry for so much had been focused on armaments and the needs of the fighting services. The situation was further aggravated by the spread of a virulent influenza germ which proved fatal in many instances. Framlingham made preparations for the return of 36 wounded and discharged soldiers who had been prisoners of war, and on 18th January 1919 a welcome back tea party was arranged for them in the Assembly Hall.

War homecomings at the railway station

By 25th January 1919 a representative committee was set up, with Canon Lanchester as chairman and A. T. Wicks the secretary, to welcome home and to entertain the war disabled. The cry of 'Honour to whom honour is due' reflected the attitude of the inhabitants. Names and addresses were to be supplied to A. T. Wicks so that personal invitations might be sent to each service-man to the 'Welcome Home' evening on Thursday 27th February, where arrangements were made for a meal provided by F. Pullan of the *Crown*, to be followed by entertainments by professional entertainers and an orchestral band. Further preparations were to be made for the later return of the 4th Suffolks.

There was a real desire for a return to normality, the gala was to be held again and peace celebrations were to be arranged for 17th June. Following the official signing of peace on 5th July a short joyous ring of the church bells signalled the display of flags throughout the borough. A National Peace Sunday was held with special services and thanksgiving followed by a concert given by blind musicians. Very special preparations were in hand for the peace celebrations to be held on 19th July 1919. The day was to follow and out-do the pattern of the Jubilee days, with a short peal of bells, a *feu de joie*, a march to the Church, sports for children, followed by tea at 4. 30; then dancing, a great military tattoo, fireworks and a bonfire. The procession included transport for wounded soldiers and Red Cross personnel and three cars for elderly inhabitants and the marching 'Comrades of the Great War' the College O.T.C., school children with flags and Miss Kiddle on a specially decorated bicycle representing Peace, and Miss Semmence representing Britannia. The resettling of the war service-men was not an easy task. It was established that twenty houses were required in the area, jobs were scarce, and wages low.

Comrades of the Great War

Much concern was felt for the increasing number of blind men returning from the front and in March 1919 the National Institute for the Blind was established, and a local committee formed which organised a concert to raise money for St. Dunstan's with a further two concerts in April. Support for different schemes were developed as war memorials via the Lord Kitchener War Memorial Home at Lowestoft, and included cottage holdings for ex-Service men. The County Land Agent asked for plans which were discussed at a public meeting.

Marching Comrades: Victory Parade 1918.

The four years of war had upset the old social order. Women had played a responsible part in nursing the wounded, raising money and releasing men for the front. The 'khaki' election of December 1918, with an increased electorate to include all men of 21 years and over, whatever their financial status, and all women over 30, reflected these changes. The coalition government won a huge majority on a platform promising punishment of the German war criminals and full payment of the costs of the war by the defeated powers. The privations, losses and lasting difficulties were thought to be mitigated by the display of a captured German machine-gun which arrived in June 1919 followed by a German field-gun which some wished to display on the Market Hill and others in the Castle and some in Gun Park. This matter was not resolved and in 1927 Mr. Scoggins again suggested that these guns should go from his care to the castle but the Ministry of Works would not accept them.

By 1922 the need for entertainment and a more 'normal' way of life engendered the re-establishment of some of the old societies. The Framlingham Amateur Dramatic Society was one of these. It was re-formed in April 1922 following letters printed in March in the Framlingham Weekly News from F. J. Shirley, an assistant master at Framlingham College, suggesting the formation of a choral or operatic society, endorsed by Mr. Hulme-Welsh in his reply. Twenty people attended a meeting in the *Crown* on 21st April 1922, and the F. A. D. S. were re-formed and since then have presented annually (apart from 1931, the year of the pageant) productions of one sort or another, as had been the case from 1903 to 1912, by earlier F.A.D.S., the Society that had been wound up in 1916. (See 'Drama in a Suffolk Town' by Sidney Gray).

During the War and for nearly thirty following years the three most pressing problems for Framlingham's Parish Council were sewage disposal, the provision of good drinking water and the lighting of the ever-enlarging town on account of the various building programmes. Also of importance to the residents were the care of footpaths with their bridges and the maintenance of the roads, along with the matter of collecting and disposing of household waste.

Between the years 1898 and 1936 the fire brigade developed from a private concern with its own committee and its four fire-engines to being part of a nationally run establishment with uniforms and a modern fire engine (See Fire Brigade).

The years immediately following the Great War were years of adjustment and resettling for the market town of Framlingham, where the previously well-adjusted and self-sufficient population of about 2,500, where everyone was known to each other, was the victim of the gradual regularisation of local affairs from Whitehall. Intrusion came, for example, from the Board of Education's letter requiring the management of the independently and locally founded Mills Girls Grammar School to be administered by the East Suffolk County Council. In 1921 the Ministry of Health's circulars sought to arrange for the registration of electors and some reorganisation through the transfer of powers, and in 1923 the same Ministry introduced the 'Payment into the Bank Order' for all local Government business.

The Government made assessments for housing needs throughout the country. For Framlingham it was calculated that 20 dwellings were required, but only 12 were sanctioned. Frank Baldry built the five double houses along the Saxtead Road, then known as the Government houses. Also in 1923 the Workmen's Compensation Act became law following negotiations on wages and hours of work which attempted to settle the volatile and disgruntled workers - men who had fought for their country and who found no sure means of livelihood in the difficult years of the 1920s.

Horses 'on the farm'.

Furthermore, mechanised transport was being introduced into farming. Cars and lorries were replacing horse-drawn vehicles. Work was scarce, farming profits were reduced and by 1931 the population of Framlingham had fallen to just over 2,000. The 1920s were years which included strikes of coalminers, the general strike of 1926, and the first Labour Governments, interspersed with coalition governments, which attempted to resettle the redundant military and to regenerate industries in the country with 'Buy British' slogans and attempts to capture international markets. Money was short; even the caretaker of the Cemetery, Pageant Field and Churchyard was required to take a cut of £10 p.a. in his salary to £80 p.a.

The basic County Rate was reduced by £70 on account of reduction in railway assessments; the Special Expenses rate was changed. But no-one, that is, not Pembroke College nor the R.D.C. nor Framlingham Parish Council was prepared to spend money on repairing the dangerous steps to the Castle pond. Eventually repairs were paid for by private subscription.

Locally, the people of Framlingham were complaining of the condition of their footpaths with dangerous footbridges, and of the local roads that connected farms with the town. These local roads were the responsibility of the Parish Council while the through roads had become the responsibility of the County Council. In 1927 the County Surveyor identified whale bones in use as a fence to hold back the bank at Button's Corner, opposite Button's Mill on Mount Pleasant, but had them removed in spite of the request from the Parish Council that they should be kept in the town and perhaps housed in the Castle. There was a general feeling of frustration as the old local responsibilities for the welfare of the people of Framlingham were gradually removed from them by instructions and injunctions.

The Courthouse.

Among these was the order to remove the Judge's Courts from the purposely built 1876 Court House in Bridge Street to Saxmundham. Representations were made by Councillor John Self at County level and by Lord Huntingfield to the Lord Chancellor. Yet in spite of the strong local feeling Judges Courts were removed from Framlingham by order from the Lord Chancellor's Office in July, 1924. Magistrates' Courts were to continue on a fortnightly and then monthly basis until 1978.

The question of the ownership and powers and regulations for the Market Hill, raised in March 1925, was settled in September 1926 when Pembroke College conveyed the area to Plomesgate R.D.C., who in turn delegated these powers to Framlingham Parish Council. But there were complaints of dirt and rubbish left behind by stall-holders, and the Parish Council was concerned that the stalls were too near to the roadway for safety. Controversy continued and came to a head in 1973 when the Parish Council became the Town Council. Researches were made to find the charter relating to the rights for stalls on the Market Hill. This was not forthcoming in spite of the 3 market days in the week claimed to have been granted to Roger Bigod in 1285 for Tuesday, Friday and Sunday markets. The matter was eventually resolved in 1977 with the Market Traders' Byelaw, which allowed stalls to occupy only the sites at the top end of the Hill, for £2 per stall (£1 for charity stalls) to be paid to the Town Council.

Market Stalls.

There was no public collection and disposal of rubbish until the matter was discussed in September 1925 when it was proposed that a horse-drawn cart should operate on one day in the week. In July 1927, Plomesgate undertook to provide an incinerator (for £145) but it was not until 1935 that a plan for 'scavenging', similar to that in operation in Halesworth, was presented by Blyth R.D.C. (the successor to Plomesgate) and arrangements were made for a limited service.

Framlingham Parish Council, in 1926 was sent appeals for more allotments from the Ministry of Agriculture & Fisheries; in answer to these requests T. T. Buckmaster laid out a number of 15 rod plots in Victoria Road with provision for further plots, and 18 plots were made available in College Road, with others in New Street, Vyces Road, Mount Pleasant and Fore Street.

The War Memorial.

The War was not forgotten. The War Graves commission made provision for graves for three soldiers 'killed in action'. The War Memorial, to the 70 men who had fallen was subscribed for and sited in the Churchyard and was handed over to the care of the Parish Council. By 1929 it was noted that the cemetery was likely to be full and plans were therefore made for the provision of an additional piece of land.

Section 5.1

FRAMLINGHAM 1930 - 1950

The 1930s became years of growing anxiety, with a severe economic depression, when land was worth only £4. 10s. 0d, per acre, when prices were slashed and competition was keen, unemployment was high and privations were real.

In spite of this, however, the spirits of the people of Framlingham remained undampened and with people from surrounding villages they staged six performances of an historical pageant in eight episodes, in Framlingham Castle, from 8th to 11th July, 1931. This was a huge undertaking involving hundreds of people - sponsors, committee members, officials, besides the two authors, the producer, performers, musicians and those who designed and made the clothes and scenery, those responsible for the horses, heraldic garments and the Flodden helmet (facsimile now in the museum).

Pageant in Castle.

The organisation even included a Welfare Committee. The pageant was pronounced a great success. Gun Park was bought with the proceeds and presented to the Parish Council as 'Pageant Field', to be an amenity for the people of Framlingham, including the growing number of children. Pageant Field became an added cost and responsibility for the Council - the grass was kept down in some years by grazing sheep, and in others by arrangement with Framlingham College or the Football Club, until a suitable grass cutting machine was bought for the purpose. A detachment of the Royal Engineers encamped in Gun Park in 1930 and as before, used water from the Jeaffreson pump which had on 13th May 1930 been officially opened by the Rev. Canon H. C. O. Lanchester.

Arrangements were made for a Band to play, (at £2. 0s. 0d. per evening) on some evenings between June and August. Equipment was bought and presented for a play area for the younger children, trees were planted around the perimeter, and the ancient road, from Castle Street to the Saxmundham Road, which had become a footpath, was diverted.

The Plomesgate Rural District Council was to be superceded by Blyth Rural District Council, and

1931 also witnessed other changes, for A. T. Wicks, a parish councillor, died. His death was followed by the sale and break up of his property, the draper's shop in the dominating Guildhall building, which stood on the terrace on the Market Hill behind a glass awning supported by iron pillars. In the same year the grocers and drapers department store on the other side of the Market Place, established in 1872 by Hatsell Garrard and more recently owned and run by the Wareing brothers, was bought in 1930 by A. G. Potter, the authorised Ford car dealer. When he bought this important site (see plans) the right of way through from Market Hill to Riverside was bordered with flower beds, greenhouses and mulberry trees, with a short crinkle-crankle wall. Alas, most of this was replaced by a steel framed large workshop, of indifferent design, supplied at a low cost by Messrs. Cocksedge of Ipswich, and erected by Potter employees.

From August 1934 preparations were in hand to celebrate (in May 1935) the Silver Jubilee of King George V. A public collection reached £128. 13s. 9d., to be spent on the various entertainments and prizes for the childrens' sports: 1s. 6d. for winners, 1s. 0d. for second, and 6d. for third prizes. A programme was printed and sold, and raised a further 9s. 6d.

Fancy Dress.

The day included 7 a.m. bell-ringing, 10.00 to 10.30 the Band on the Market Hill, 11.00 to 11.45 a Service in St. Michael's Church, and at 1.30 a muster and procession from the Market Hill to the Pageant Field behind the Band, and the planting of an oak tree. Luncheon was provided for 72 Old Age Pensioners at 12.15, tea for 320 children at 4.15, and at 5.00 p.m. a meat tea for 275 adult workers and wives. The streets were lit for the evening free of charge by the local gas company. It was an enjoyable and successful day and ended with a profit of £12. 4s. 3d. from which £5 was sent to the King's Jubilee Fund, and £2. 10s. 0d. each was spent on Jubilee seats, one for the Pageant Field and one for Station Road.

The new Council Area School was built on the north side of Saxtead road and opened in the Autumn term of 1935, with John Self and Canon H. C. O. Lanchester as the local Council representatives on its board of Governors. The Eastern Electricity Board brought light to private houses from underground cables within Framlingham, but as yet could not undertake to light the streets, which were lit from the local gas works in College Road at an annual cost of £175. Building was going on with seven privately sponsored bungalows along the north side of Saxmundham Road and twenty-four Rural District Council houses in King's Avenue, on two acres of land between the Saxtead and Dennington roads. In spite of the increased population and of limited means of travel, Framlingham was losing some of its facilities. Magistrates' Courts were held on Wednesdays only in each week, and the office of the Registrar for births and deaths closed and henceforth the Registrar made only four one-hour visits in each month, despite recommendations for at least eight from the Parish Council. Litter bins were ordered from the Rural District Council.

On 20th January 1936 King George V died and King Edward VIII was proclaimed King, but due to his attachment and intended marriage to Mrs. Simpson, an American divorcee, he abdicated the throne on 30th December 1936 without ever being crowned. His brother King George VI was proclaimed King and was crowned in 1937. This 'unsteady' year followed Germany's announcement in 1935 that she was re-arming, which gave rise to international disquiet as the world witnessed the fanatical German Chancellor, Hitler, capturing the support of many of the German people by disregarding the Locarno Pact and in 1936, by re-militarising the Rhineland and forming the Rome-Berlin pact. In 1937 persecutions of Roman Catholic and Protestant clergy were followed in 1938 with the annexation of Austria and the Munich Pact, signed by Hitler, Mussolini, Chamberlain and Deladier, which enabled Germany to absorb the German speaking Sudeten land of Czechoslovakia. The plans laid out in *Mein Kampf* were being fulfilled. Slowly the people of Great Britain began to react to this threat. The Anglo- French Conference in London was the signal for Great Britain to put its defence of the realm in order by ending the Anglo-German naval agreement, among other things, and by instigating Air Raid Precautions throughout the country. Framlingham had its preliminary Air Raid Precautions meeting in September 1936. The Home Office sent out A. R. P. instructions. Streets were to be named and numbered, the Fire Brigade was to be regularised and given uniforms. Following the 1938 Fire Brigades Act, the Rural District Council became responsible for Framlingham's Fire Brigade, with certain powers delegated to the Parish Council. Soldiers were billeted in the town following Great Britain's declaration of war on Germany on the 3rd September 1939.

Shortages of food were anticipated and potatoes were offered to assist in the food supply. Ration books were issued for food and clothing. Suggestions were broadcast that air raid shelters should be built. Children were evacuated from London and other vulnerable towns to inland and country areas, including Framlingham and district. Air raid sirens were fixed to Police Stations and public buildings. Black-out restrictions were in force. While the rural area of Framlingham was concerned with producing food in ever-increasing amounts, in bringing the fire service up to strength and in observing the black-out, others were concerned to counter the German plans for invasion; this war involved everyone.

On 11th May 1940 Winston Churchill became Prime Minister of the National coalition government. The Germans invaded France on 24th, and on 27th May the Belgians capitulated to them. The situation was desperate. Between 27th May and 4th June 335,490 officers and men were evacuated from the continent; our shores were vulnerable to invasion and our army was in disarray, plans for a German assault were known. Winston Churchill proposed that a secret 'stay behind' force should be mobilised at once under the command of Col. Colin Gubbins, R.A. This secret force of locally recruited independent men should be under the immediate command of one of eight young hand-picked officers, to cover the coastline from Gravesend to Devon and Cornwall and later to the east and north of Scotland. Captain Andrew Croft, responsible for Essex and Suffolk, was to enrol his network of secret 'stay behind' patrols, members of which included Herman Kindred of Parham and Joseph Woodrow, two local independent farmers who were to find four others to be in their platoon. Although only five or six came from any one area, and were known to each other, about 35,000 men were secretly recruited and trained within weeks in the arts of sabotage, using explosives known as 'time pencils', 'machine carbines' and 'sticky bombs'. The force had a cover name, the 'Auxiliary Units' and it was linked to the Local Defence Volunteers, later called the Home Guard. The men were vetted by MI5 and sworn to secrecy. They were shown how to construct hide-outs where they stored ammunition and food rations for four weeks, for their work was to sabotage the enemy on a given command. Members of the Framlingham platoon attended secret meetings at Little Glemham or special training sessions at Coleshill House in North Wiltshire, where they were taught to greet each other with 'the Germans are coming' and learnt how to decapitate a motor cyclist on the move by using high tension steel wire. Although trained to commando standard of guerilla warfare they masqueraded as 'ordinary' members of the local Home Guard, leaving notes for each other in pre-arranged hiding places and usually working at night. They were considered the last ditch troops who knew that speed in action was all- important, and that the first fourteen days of invasion were crucial. So well was the secret of this force kept that it only became public knowledge in the late 1960s and only in 1990 was the first reunion held of these unknown gallant men.

During the first year of this war Framlingham's tenor of life was much as before, but on 5th December 1940 a stick of incendiaries destroyed the elementary school staff house in College Road, killing the headmistress. Another fell on Percy Stannard's house in Albert Place killing his wife and a child. The year 1941 not only marked the setting up of the Framlingham Parish Invasion Committee but also the integration into the National Fire Service of the Framlingham Auxiliary Fire Service, with a brigade of 30 members and a new 4-6 ton Ford truck added to the equipment. The sum of £52 was raised for war charities and a salvage scheme was inaugurated for paper, bones, rags, tins, glass and scrap iron, including many decorative fences. Blyth Rural District Council advocated scrounging for wood because of the uncertainty of getting coal. A National Air Raid distress fund was started and gifts of money for War Weapons Week, and later food, were sent to Framlingham from Massachusetts, U.S.A. The U.S.A., not yet in the war, passed the Lend-Lease Act in March 1941. Invasion was still a serious threat, and in July 1941 an Invasion Committee was set up in Framlingham to coordinate services under the heads of the Civil Defences, and in September this Committee was addressed by Major Marriott of the Home Guard and by Colonel Panton, R.A.M.C.

Following the June 1941 invasion of Russia by Germany, Great Britain in July signed a mutual aid treaty with Russia. This was followed in August by the Atlantic Charter signed by President Roosevelt and Winston Churchill. It was a declaration of peace aims by the two countries and endorsed by a further 15 countries in September. Bit by bit the whole world was becoming involved in this destructive war.

In December 1941 Japan bombed Pearl Harbour in Hawaii, and the U.S.A. declared war on Japan; this was followed three days later by Germany and Italy declaring war on the U.S.A., which from then on was Britain's active ally. Framlingham received the 95th Bomber Group, soon to be replaced in 1943 with the 3,000 strong **390th Bomber Group,** which operated from a newly-prepared airfield at Parham. Many of the men bought bicycles and used Framlingham as one of their entertainment bases, and men from Massachusetts, especially, were offered hospitality. A building in New Road became the Anglo-U. S. Forces Club, with a canteen. The Americans believed in daylight precision bombing, persisting with it until heavy losses forced them to make nightly sorties to bomb their targets. These became of concern to the local people, who were aware of the dangers and losses of these airmen.

Dennis Fire Engine.

Once the U.S.A. had joined beleaguered Great Britain plans were afoot to invade the continent, but always the threat of air attacks was paramount. Framlingham's Dennis fire engine went to assist in fighting the blitz on London and never returned. Framlingham built an air-raid shelter on the Market Hill, which was kept locked with the key nearby. Static water tanks in brick and steel were erected. The state of readiness of the various services was apparent. Dennis fire pumps, attached to lorries, were available to fight local fires and reciprocal arrangements for help in case of disaster were made with Ipswich and other nearby towns. The Blyth Rural District Council surveyor visited Framlingham and agreed sites for water reservoirs in case of fires; two sandbags were issued to each householder and stirrup pumps were distributed throughout the town. Brick air raid shelters and Morrison table shelters were to be provided, and a more efficient siren was to be based on the Police Station in Bridge Street. Various flag day appeals were held for Warship Week, hospitals, and distress funds.

Local concern was aroused when Dr. Allen received his call-up papers. He was one of only two doctors in Framlingham and was responsible for 6,600 patients, including the pupils of Framlingham College. The local Council made representations for his exemption but in September 1942 he joined the R.A.M.C. Not only were there fears of air raids and consequent fires, but also of a gas attack and the Ministry of Health built a gas cleansing station in the Badingham Road. Gas masks and anti-gas clothing were issued to fire-fighters, police and other officials, while each member of the public had a gas mask. There were calls for more A.R.P. fire-guards, and regular duties were assigned to the Home Guard. A further call for iron railings for fighting equipment was made.

Police House & Station.

The 390th Bomber Force at Parham played its part in the D-Day landings on 6th June 1944, the great day of the invasion of France from the southern shores of Britain, under the command of

S.H.A.E.F. (Supreme Headquarters of the Allied Expeditionary Force) supported by the Mulberry Harbours which were towed across the channel and sunk to facilitate the landings. This whole operation had been kept a close secret and marked the turning point in the prosecution of the war.

Following Hitler's suicide on 1st May 1945, Churchill and President Truman on 8th May 1945 proclaimed the end of the war in Europe. A welcome home fund was started in Framlingham and orders were given by the County Council for the removal of the tank traps and protective pillboxes that flanked the entries to the town, especially those in College Road and Well Close Square. Elections for the Parish Council were fixed for 15th April 1946; and the Church chimes were to be restored. Plans for the V.E. Day celebrations were put in hand, including a Service in the Castle.

The war in the Pacific seemed to be far away but all were affected by the dropping of an atomic bomb on Hiroshima on 6th August 1945. This was followed by the surrender of Japan on 14th August, V.J. Day being declared on 2nd September 1945 when the formal terms of surrender were signed. This was acknowledged in Framlingham by the V.J. Day celebrations that included children's sports. The costly war was over.

On account of the many losses of local men, there was little enthusiasm for the V.J. victory celebrations, apart from the entertainment for the children, but parcels of food which included 100 lbs. of dried fruit, beans and tinned fruit were received from South Africa, and distributed to the needy of the parish in 1 lb. bags. To the many people in Framlingham and district with husbands and sons in the Suffolk Regiment, made prisoners of war by the Japanese at the fall of Singapore, and forced to work on the notorious railways on starvation rations, the celebrations had great poignancy, since no news of them had ever been received from the Far East.

The Parish Council could again concentrate on facilities for Framlingham. Piped water came to the town and consent was given by the Ministry of Health, Ministry of Labour and Home Office for the street lighting to be supplied by electricity. Life was resuming a sense of normality. M.C.O. Todd, the Parish Clerk was demobilised from the R.A.F. and returned to his duties at £30. 10s. 0d. per annum; and the Council advertised for a groundsman to replace Mr. Borritt who had carried on until after V.E. day, his 87th birthday, at a wage recently increased to 45s. 0d. per week. New applicants were to be over 50 or certificate-A discharged and wages were to be £3 per week, to rise to £4. 10s. 0d. per week in 1947.

Following the 1944 Education Act, the Local Education Authority proposed closing the Mills Girls Grammar School and building an area school in Saxmundham. This brought an outcry from the people of Framlingham, for as they rightly pointed out this school had been built with the local Mills Charity money. A petition was signed by householders and Mr. Granville the local M.P. took up the matter.

Two wartime buildings were available for re-use: a building on Badingham Road used by the Americans in connection with Parham Air Field, which the St. John Ambulance Brigade asked to have, but from 1964 to 1971 was used by the Framlingham Fire Brigade before becoming the H.Q. for the Scouts and Guides; and the Anglo-U.S. Forces Club, which, it was suggested, might become a sports centre, but which first became the bias binding factory and then in 1968 the headquarters of the Framlingham Farmers Co-Operative.

DAN SCASE'S CYCLES

have been before the Public for Ten Years and still have a large Sale. This has been achieved without the publication of testimonials. The convincing fact is that

SCASE'S CYCLES RECOMMEND THEMSELVES.

Gent's Machines with Clincher Tyres £8 10s.

Ladies' Machines with Dunlop Tyres £10.

SEWING MACHINES OF BEST MAKE.

ATHLETIC OUTFITTER, ETC.

Footballs, Cricket, Lawn Tennis, and Golf Requisites.
GUNS, RIFLES, AIR GUNS, REVOLVERS & CARTRIDGES.
In fact everything in Stock for Sportsmen.

CHEAPEST HOUSE IN SUFFOLK FOR ALL KINDS OF
FURNITURE, PAPER-HANGINGS, PICTURE FRAMES, ETC.

DAN SCASE,
Market Hill, Framlingham, Suffolk.

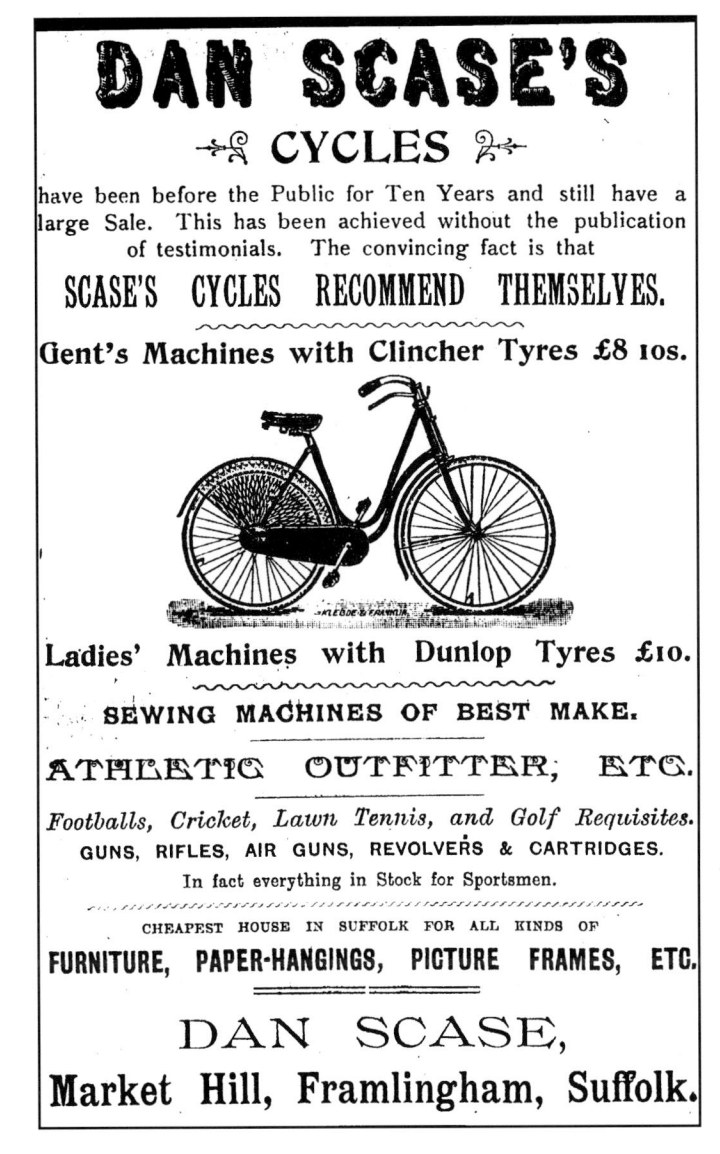

The war had brought great changes to Framlingham: the number of small shops had been much reduced, the drift from selling home-produced goods to being outlet agents for mass produced goods had intensified. Craftsmen were considerably fewer and the number of trades plied had been reduced from 83 in the 1890s to about 20. The horses and gigs which had still had their place in the 1920s and early 1930s had gone; bicycles had become all important, with no fewer than four suppliers in Framlingham. The motor car was beginning to be in general use with attendant parking problems. The Parish Council, while husbanding its money carefully was keen to improve standards and amenities within the borough. It decided to remove the pens and coops from the old saleyard, to plant new shrubs and trees in the cemetery, to improve street lighting to repair and floodlight the Church clock. A 'Public Convenience' was supplied in Crown & Anchor Lane by the Rural District Council, who also removed the smaller air raid shelter from the Market Hill. The Council examined the field paths and recommended repairs to bridges, arranged for refuse to be collected on Mondays and Tuesdays, and limited the stalls on the Market Hill to Saturdays only. At last in 1947 the static water tank was removed from the Market Hill, and the housing shortage was alleviated by the Rural District Council building 24, not 8, houses to be let to tenants in Victoria Mill Road (and to be called Victoria Place). Food parcels were still arriving from the U.S.A. in April 1948. A District Nurse was employed from 1st September 1949.

The Duke & Duchess of Athlone were invited by the Council in 1949 to drive through Framlingham en route to the College. They were greeted by the ringing of the Church bells and the applause of school children in a flag-bedecked town. Framingham, U.S.A., were planning celebrations for the 250 years since the foundation of their town, and invited representatives from Framlingham to join them. Miss Brunger and her brother sailed in the Queen Mary with a gift of a painting of Framlingham by Leonard Squirrell to mark the occasion. She addressed a meeting in Framlingham on her return, and Framlingham invited Mr. Merriam from the U.S.A. on a reciprocal visit, when a party was held in the Corn Hall at the *Crown*, and a gavel was presented to the Parish Council made from wood from Framingham, U.S.A.

Arrangements in 1950 were made for the people of Framlingham to use the Framlingham College pool through the summer months as a Sports Club amenity, at a cost of £50 for two months. The Parish Council to pay £25 and the Sports Club to be responsible for £25 and for the proper conduct of the users.

Section 5.2

FRAMLINGHAM 1950 - 1977

By 1950 the immediate effects of the second World War were giving place to the Cold War, with two main rivals and protagonists on the world stage, the U.S.A., and the U.S.S.R. Nations were searching for partners to strengthen their trading and defence programmes, and technology and experimental sciences were concentrating on space travel and the race to be the first to land a man on the moon. Framlingham was experiencing change, competition and uncertainty coupled with a wish to maintain the security of the past. These sensations were expressed with an understanding of the possible dangers of a nuclear threat in the future which were still to be considered. In December 1950 an Air Raid Precautions officer spoke to a public meeting in Framlingham on the requirements of the town in the case of an emergency, which included an H.Q. report centre manned by 18 people, 9 of whom should be voluntary, an ambulance section of 10, 15 men for a reserve team and 11 women welfare volunteers as well as the Police and wardens. A course starting on 25th January 1950 would instruct the wardens. This was followed in May 1951 with the County Civil Defence Organiser appealing through the press for volunteers, and again in March 1952 when Framlingham was appointed a subcentre with 30 dependent parishes and was required to provide four rest centres with sleeping for 100 and cooking for 800, under the Blyth Rural District Council Civil Defence Committee. There was another call for volunteers for rescue squads, and that in the year that West Germany was admitted to the Council of Europe.

September 1951 marked the end of the passage through the *Crown Hotel* as a right of way for traffic from the Market Hill to Fore Street. By 1954 lighting costs had risen from about £187 per annum to £385 per annum, and from 3rd November 1952 the branch L.N.E.R. line from Wickham Market was to be closed to passengers, and goods trains to be reduced to one per day (see Railway).

While world decisions were being made of the possible uses of atomic development, radioactive carbon-dating was establishing the ages of fossils and 'finds'. Framlingham in 1951 was considering the performance of a second pageant to mark the Festival of Britain. This was produced and arranged by the Girl Guides and performed in the grounds of Helmingham Hall. Princess Margaret attended the gala performance. 'Vikings' in 'long boats' crossed the 'North Sea' represented by the lake, invading East Anglia where the Saxons were peacefully ploughing with oxen; a white Alsatian dog ably guarded the head of Saint Edmund, and Mary Tudor's courtiers formed a colourful procession.

There was both national and local concentration on the future of education in the country. In 1950 the Hitcham's Church of England Junior School was granted voluntary aided status and in 1954 the direction for the future trends in education was heralded when London opened its first comprehensive school, to be followed in the 1960s with a boom in higher education which included the foundation of the University of East Anglia.

Domestic problems centred round the Castle pond (which in earlier times had been used for drowning witches, see illustration next page), with many projects for its improvement. It was established that Pembroke College owned it and before they handed it over to the Parish Council they repaired the wall that borders Castle Street. The Church gates were pronounced dangerous and in 1949 they were removed at a cost of 17s. 6d. and sold on behalf of the Town Council by A.G. Potter for £7. 4s. 6d. The new Telephone Exchange was built in Fore Street in 1958 and in

1959 the College Road pump was removed. The Playhouse Cinema of Saxmundham planned to re-open the Regal Cinema in New Road in 1957, but were discouraged by the Parish Council which forbade Sunday opening. This proviso was over-ruled and the Cinema opened in 1961.

Castle Pond.

The European Economic Community was set up in 1957 followed by Great Britain joining the European Free Trade Association in 1958. The farming community, especially, was to watch developments as this country became more closely involved with regulations and limitations evolved on the Continent. Great Britain did not join the E.E.C. until 1973, and this move was confirmed by a national referendum in 1975. The later 1950s found the Rural District Council concentrating on housing the elderly and in 1959 an outline plan was drawn up. It showed that the population in Framlingham grew from 1801 to 1901 then dropped until 1951, and it increased again to about 2,500 by 1961 within the 36 square mile catchment area. The only means of employment included the schools, the bias-binding factory and small building firms, banks, shops and professional practices, with industrial developments in Station Road and Badingham Road; 566 men and 22 women were employed in agriculture and mining; 87 men and 30 women in manufacturing, and 452 men and 304 women in the service industries; so different from conditions in the nineteenth century (see classified trades) when 83 trades and means of work were current.

It was found in 1971 that Framlingham had 74 buildings of architectural and historical interest and the centre of Framlingham was declared a conservation area. As a result of the outline planning a comprehensive building programme was inaugurated, with the Council developing ten plots in the Saxmundham Road and 28 in Fairfield Road, with 4 plots in Pembroke Road, 5 in Brook Lane, 2 in Station Road, 3 in Victoria Mill Road and 2 in Badingham Road being privately developed. Stage 2 was for ten plots on each side of Pembroke Road, 1 in College Road, 3 in Albert Road, 6 in Station Road and 3 in Badingham Road to be followed by 26 houses in Mount Pleasant, 40 in Brook Lane and 24 in Fairfield Road, making a total in the three stages of 54, 33 and 90 houses. Additional accommodation for classrooms and games fields was also planned for the Area Modern School and the Hitcham's Junior School.

The Parish Council agreed to rent the Castle Meadow from Pembroke College from Michaelmas 1963 on a seven year renewable lease at £50 per annum, since which time it has been let to caravan clubs, for fairs, and to other organisations and annually the Gala is held there in Whitsun Week, and as before to the Framlingham Livestock Association for the Annual Suffolk Horse Colt Show.

Glass Canopy.

In 1967 the glass canopy on the terrace in front of the Guildhall, where A.T. Wicks had held his 'stalls' was said to be in a dangerous condition and was removed; this changed the look of the Market Hill as the new building work which extended the area of Framlingham beyond its earlier boundaries markedly changed Framlingham from its earlier compact form. However, the names given to the newly developed areas linked them to the past of the town; they included Norfolk Crescent, the Mowbrays, Danforth Drive and Victoria Mill Road, with further reminders of the occupants of the castle in the closes off Brook Lane.

Mr. and Mrs. P. Heffer at home.

The Church clock, the responsibility of the R.D.C., had been manually wound three times a week and when necessary, adjusted. From 1969 it was worked by electricity with constant expert attention for the first few months until the electrical mechanism was mastered.

Framlingham had its share of the country's ageing population and the R.D.C. in 1960 was concerned to provide accommodation and help for them. Meals on wheels were provided for twenty people in 1968. The Elms was developed with flats, and formally opened in 1970 and in 1972 a community care scheme was started.

1973 saw another reorganisation of local government with the objects of devolving more power to the local Parish Councils. In spite of this, plans to help the young to have 'affordable' housing even in the form of a controlled caravan site were turned down by Suffolk Coastal District Council. The new authority, involving 120 parishes, was set up in 1974 with the new Regional Water Authority becoming responsible for the supply of water and the disposal of sewage.

From 1973 Framlingham was twinned with Coucy le Château, a town with similarities, for example, the Seigneur de Coucy of 1130 held a comparable status with the Earl of Norfolk. Each ruling family lived in its own Castle, and in each case the castle had been besieged. The castle at Coucy is an extensive ruin, while that of Framlingham has only its curtain wall standing, with its seventeenth century building inside.

Framlingham's Parish Council became the Town Council in 1974 working no longer with the old East Suffolk County Council but with the Suffolk Coastal District Council, which reassessed the roads programme for the district, and was prepared to include a £41,000 sports hall, for the use of the community, within their plans for the new Framlingham High School to be built by 1978 and called the Thomas Mills High School. A new National Health scheme became operative and Framlingham Town Council was asked to furnish Suffolk Coastal District Council with the activities and clubs that were operative in the town; they included:

Bowls Club	Over 70s Club
Conservative Club	Rotary
Cricket Club	Round Table
Cruse	Royal British Legion
Football Club	St. John Ambulance
Foresters	Scouts
Flower Club	Sports Club
Framlingham Assn.	Suffolk Territorial Assn.
Free Church	Territorial Army
Guides	Twinning Assn.
Knoll dwellers Assn.	Workers Educational Assn.
Labour Party	Women's Institute
Liberal Party	Young Farmers Club
Over 60s	Youth Club

In 1975 the fens, which also included the Fairfield, was offered to the town by A.K. Cooper, to be maintained as an open space and to be run by a Trust. Plans for the Queen's 25th Jubilee celebrations included a 'wet wellie race', a medieval market, a fancy dress competition, with parties for the 3 to 5 year-olds and for the pensioners, and a treasure hunt, a disco and dancing on the Market Hill, followed by a torchlight procession and community singing.

Framlingham has in many ways changed and developed through the centuries. The Town is now an integral part of a wider horizon and subject to national and world-wide influences. The shops in the main are outlets for pre-packaged goods. Motor transport has enabled its residents to journey far afield; but perhaps a recognizable rose found in 1976 in the fabric of Romsey Abbey said to date from 1160 is an indication of the permanence and persistence of national qualities and characteristics, strongly reflected by the inhabitants of Framlingham!

Subjects

BANKING

The earliest record of a banking transaction in Framlingham is that of a letter written on 30th March 1761 by Samuel Lodge to Mr. Henry Alexander - (possibly the son of Waldegrave Alexander, and attorney of Cransford, the husband of Amy of Wingfield) asking that:
'At sight hereof please to pay to Thomas Mendham or order Ten shillings value received and place the same to the Account of Sd. Tr. Numb. Sert. Sam + Lodge'.

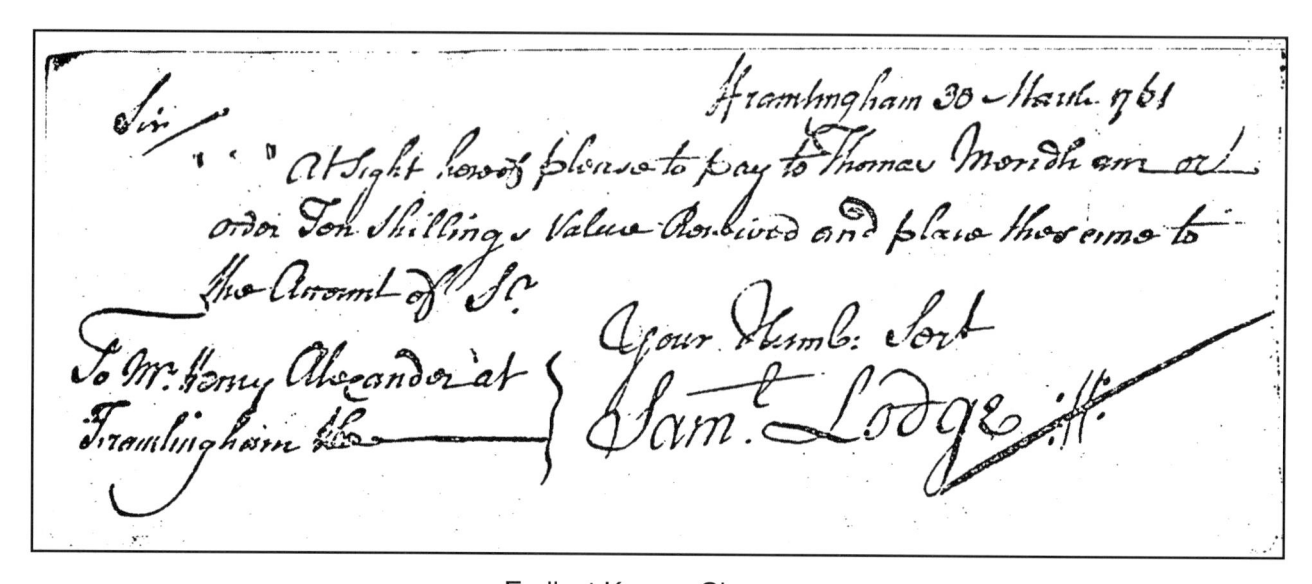

Earliest Known Cheque.

It is recorded by Barclays Bank that this is the earliest country cheque known to them, but that there is no record of a Bank in the name of Alexander in Framlingham. There was 'Alexander & Co. Ipswich Bank' from 1744 which merged with the Gurney Group under the title of Gurneys Alexander & Co. in 1878, and later became Barclay & Co. Ltd. in 1896.

Before 1855 when the first purpose-built Bank was established in Framlingham, on the site of the present Barclays Bank, by Robert John Harvey Harvey Esq. of Norwich, banking transactions were carried on from about the 1820s by Mr. Manning Keer, an agent for the Norfolk & Norwich Joint Stock Banking Co.. He operated in a back room of the old *Black Horse Inn*, approached from Church Lane and incorporated into Mr. G.B. Keer's house, known as Stair or Step House. This arrangement ended in 1832, when Mr. G.B. Keer was declared a bankrupt. 'The agent had diddled the Bank out of £10,000'. In Church Street, Harvey & Hudson, with agent Mr. Bloom, were issuing drafts on Hankey & Co.. By 1858 the Harvey & Hudson Bank was operating in its new premises on the Market Hill site.

It would seem that Gurney & Co. had an agency in Framlingham, 'after 1815 and before 1826' which became Gurneys Turner & Co. in 1823. Their agents were George and Charles Edwards, who operated from the best counter in their shop, which stood on the north side of the Crown Hotel, where Carley & Webb now stands. The Norfolk & Norwich Joint Stock Banking Company was absorbed into the East of England Bank in 1836, but failed in 1864. (In White's Directory of 1855, Framlingham is listed with Gurney & Co. on the Market Hill North, and Jonathan Hart, Grocer, as agent.

Sold for £270 in 1850.

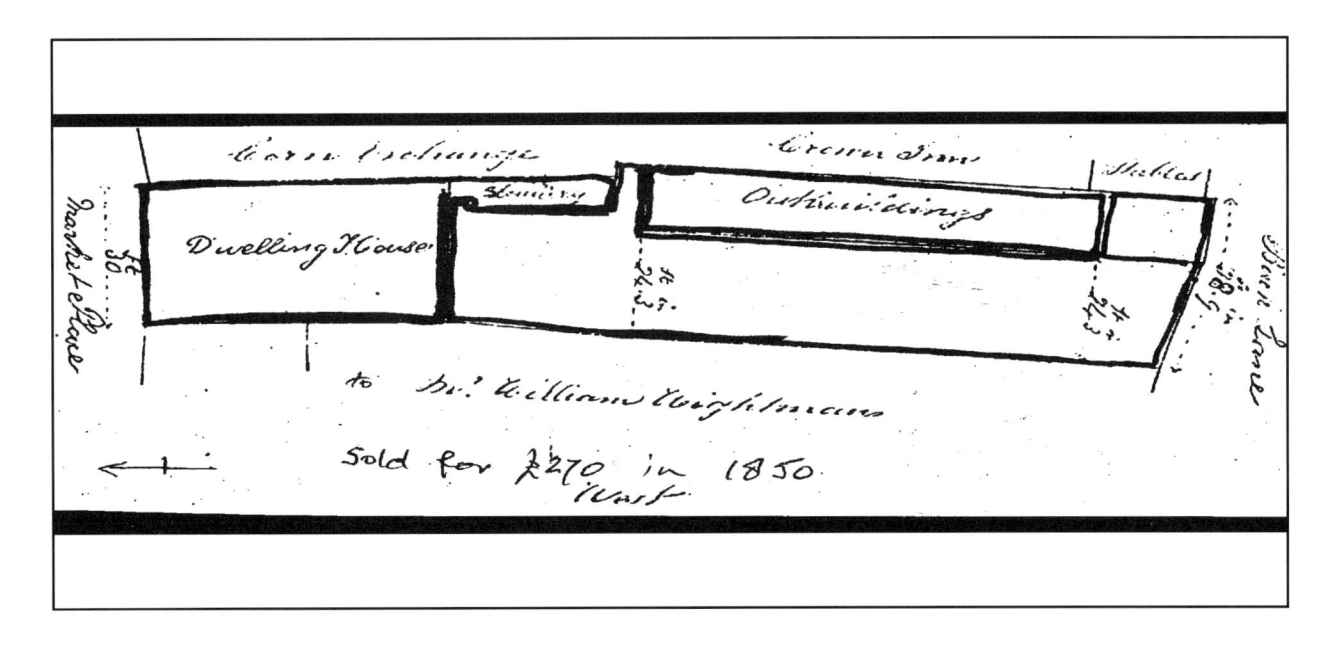

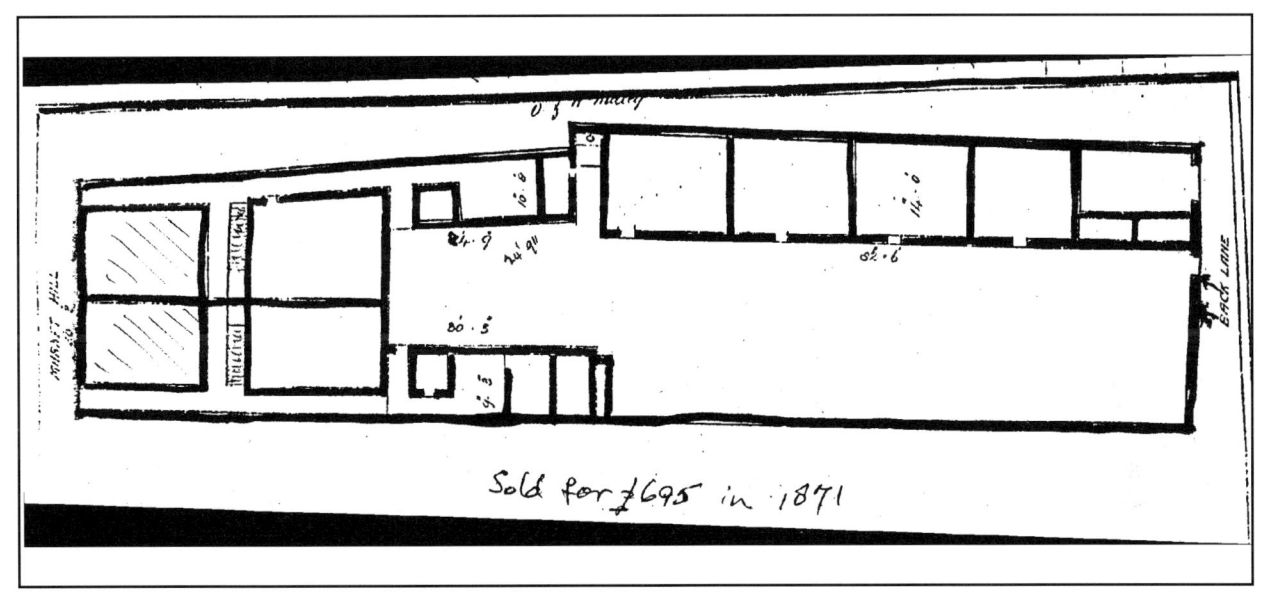

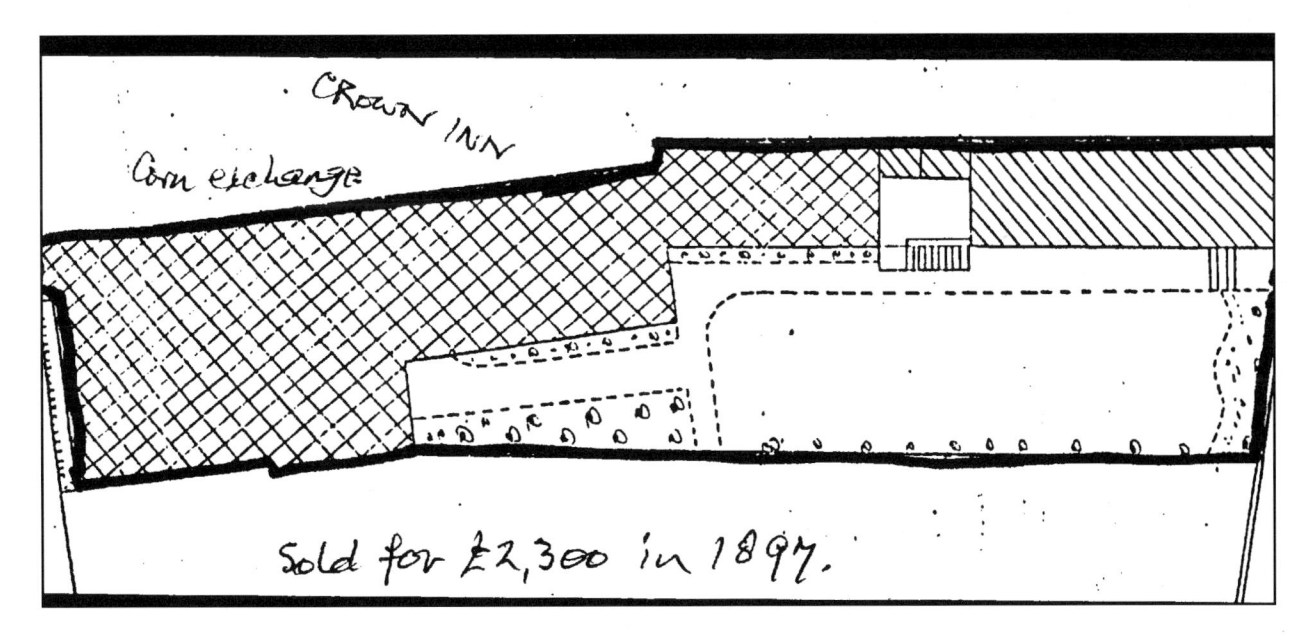

Sold for £695 in 1871.

Sold for £2,300 in 1897.

In 1855 Robert J.H. Harvey, the Senior Partner of Harvey Hudson & Co., Norwich Crown Bank, bought the present Barclays Bank site and the adjacent buildings for £410 from Mrs. Catherine Sparkes and James Brighten Grant. The bank pulled down the existing dwelling house, and erected two sizeable buildings on the site (see plans) - a bank, and within the property, a dwelling house with supporting stables and out houses that reached to Back Lane/Fore Street. They continued the agency for the Alliance Fire & Life Assurance Company run by George & Charles Edwards. From 1873 the manager was clerk to the Burial Board.

The Franco-Prussian War of 1870 caused prices to fall, and Sir Robert J.H. Harvey (as he had become) having speculated with the bank's funds, committed suicide. The bank failed, his partners were declared bankrupt, and the remaining goodwill of the bank was bought by Messrs. Gurney & Co. of Norwich. The Framlingham site, without adjacent buildings, was bought for £695 from the Harvey Hudson Trustees by William Birkbeck and John Gurney, representatives of Messrs. Gurney. Further alterations were made to the buildings, which were extended and restructured.

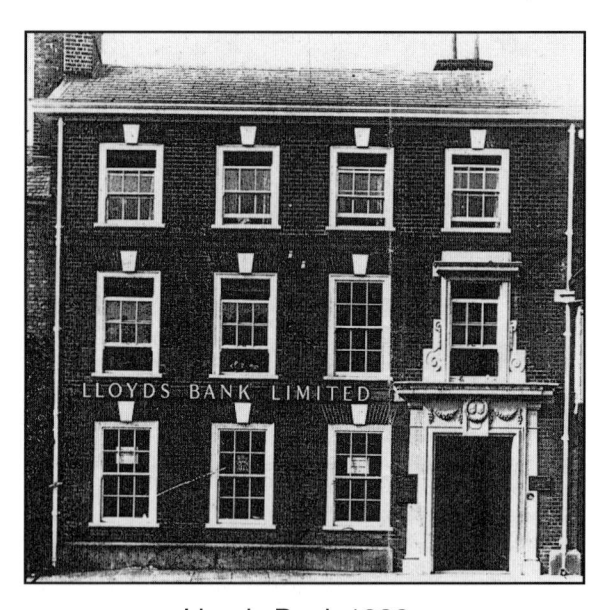

Barclays Bank

Lloyds Bank 1932

An amalgamation of the Gurney Banks with Barclays Bank & Co. Ltd. was effected in 1896, and in 1897 William Birkbeck, Trustee for Gurney's Bank, sold the property for £2,300 to Barclays Bank & Co. Ltd. The interior of the building was redesigned and the imposing brick and stone front was added. It has elaborate mouldings over the upper windows, and carved heads of the Muses grace the tops of the lower windows, while Neptune's head is over the doorway. A carved stone cornucopia divides the bank's chimney from the roof of the neighbouring *Crown Hotel*. These are all signs of the affluence of this late Victorian period.

In 1919 Lloyds Bank bought the red brick No. 12 Market Hill from Mr. George J. Summers, the Postmaster, and gave it an imposing doorway with the black horse carved over the door. This building ceased to be used as a bank in 1941, when an agreement was made between Lloyds and Barclays in respect of their banks in Suffolk. Lloyds retained its bank in Long Melford in return for closing its Framlingham branch.

The Midland Bank in 1966 bought from the Misses Carley part of George Brooke Keer's old property known as the Manor House. This is a Grade II listed building of Georgian design. The façade of the building remains, but extensive internal reorganisation was carried out by Messrs. Thomas F. Trower & Son of Norwich before the Bank was opened to the public on Monday 11th March 1968 as part of their scheme to extend their business in East Anglia.

The photograph here shows the new branch of the Midland Bank.

BRICKMAKING

There must have been brickmaking in Framlingham from at least the sixteenth century, for the Tudor chimneys of the castleand bricks, later to be used in the building of Sir Robert Hitcham's Almshouses, are of this date. There were probably at least 7 or 8 brickmaking sites. One is referred to in the Surveyor's report of 1817 under 'Gall, Jno. (old brick kiln)' sited in College Road. A site near to Station Road is marked on the 1888 map of Framlingham, the Kettleburgh Road Brickworks is known of (see following details), and there is strong evidence that bricks for the building of Framlingham College were made 'at the bottom of the hill'. Local people talk of the 'dip' by the allotments in New Road, from which the clay was probably dug and then puddled in part of the Mere. Until recently, a shed where bricks were dried before being fired was extant, and one nearby field is called Kiln Field. Brick Lane leaves the Framlingham to Parham Road by Gate Cottage Nursery, to the N.E. - and has a disused sandpit to the S., and a branch of the River Ore to the W., suitable adjuncts for brickmaking. This land in 1835 belonged to Frederick Corrance Esq., marked 503 on the apportionment map 4, labelled 'Brick Kiln'; he also owned No. 90, Kiln Field. Nathaniel Bennington on the apportionment map is listed as the owner of 139, Brick Kiln Ground at Hacheston.

THE KETTLEBURGH ROAD BRICKWORKS

In company with several other men of acumen and endeavour, Peter Smith came to Framlingham from a neighbouring village about 1845. He already owned and worked his brickworks in Badingham, and, after prospecting part of the Duke of Hamilton's land around Rookery Wood, where there was a deep pond, he rented 22 acres, 1 rod, 36 poles of this land at an annual rent of £26. 10s. payable at Michaelmas, recognising that building material was required for the burgeoning borough of Framlingham, as it was developing its industrial area.

This ingenious man had spotted a second pond lower down the hill, and he planned to make use of these two natural ponds in the considerable hill of clay that had been laid down in the Ice Age. He cut a channel from the upper to the lower pond, and further channels to three man-made lagoons, near to the River Ore. He could control the supply of water to these lagoons, and the hill would provide the clay for bricks. It was to be cut from the hill and puddled in the lagoons, to free it from stones, and then transported to sheds that were built at the foot of the hill. The next stage was the moulding of the clay in wooden moulds for bricks, and shaping the clay round wooden supports for drainage pipes of varying circumference. Once the clay was dry, the bricks or pipes were loaded into one of the two large kilns that stood nearby. Each kiln could hold approximately 30,000 bricks, and the kilns were fired three or four times a year. Coal was brought to the site to fire the kilns, and local builders such as Messrs. Baldry of Framlingham or Mr. Elliott of Bedfield came to the site for their bricks. Some of the bricks were made in the daisy-rose decorative moulds, and can be seen on houses in Station Road.

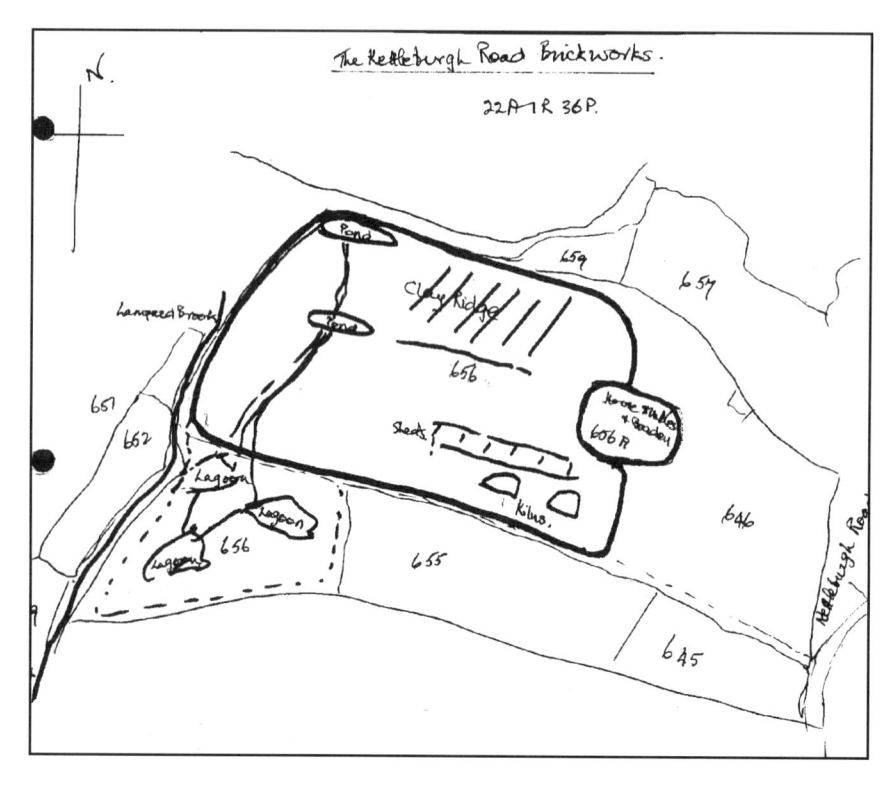

Peter Smith built himself a house with stables on half an acre of land, and incorporated 3 acres, 2 rods and 6 poles for the garden, near to the sheds and kilns, for which he paid a ground rent of £1 per annum. His son William took over the business and the house and ran the works until 1934/5.

The 1930s were a time of unemployment and slump, and the annual rent for the house and orchard was reduced to £11.10s. Building work stopped; there was no demand for pipes for improving agricultural land and therefore no demand for bricks and pipes.

In 1935 this whole industry came to an end; the land was reclaimed as farming land, the lagoons were filled in and the kilns and huts were demolished. The Smith's house was on a 50 year lease from 11th October 1917. It still stands and is now surrounded by arable land that is ploughed and sown at the lower level, with a vertically cut hill to the south, now grassed over, and Rookery Wood and the deep pond on its summit mark the area of so much activity for nearly 100 years. All this may be viewed from the bridle path which leads from the Kettleburgh Road through to Broadwater.

BUILDINGS

THE ANCIENT HOUSE

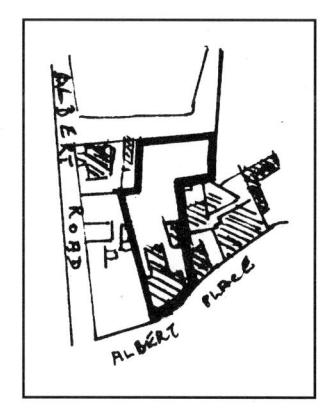

Ancient House Site

Deeds for the Ancient House which fronts on to Albert Place only go back to 1862 but the original timber framed building is is much older. The distinguished façade that we see is probably late seventeenth or early eighteenth century with plastering and pargetting between the windows on the front of this important two storey building. It is decorated with a laurel leaf pattern with swags at the top and roundels at the bottom. In the nineteenth century the house was divided into two properties known as 6 and 7 Albert Place and partly occupied by the Fairweather family who had a bicycle and motor car workshop at the present 'Wheelwrights'. The house was restored to a single residence in 1957 when Lieut. Cmdr. Sitwell, an historian of Framlingham bought the property.

The Corn Hall or Corn Exchange

Framlingham, the market centre of the area, built a corn hall in 1847 within the *Crown Inn* courtyard. This was a sizeable building and at first was used each Saturday as a corn market, and as a Law Court on alternate weeks on Fridays until 1872.

In the 1930s general sales were held fortnightly on Fridays.

The Corn Hall was also used for dances and entertainment, and in 1950 it was to serve for the reception of Mr. Merriam of Framlingham, Massachussetts, the representative of the 'Danforth Community' in the U.S.A.
It was used from 1948 to 1951/2 by the local Roman Catholics for their weekly Sunday Mass. From 1952, Trust House Forte have redesigned the interior for use as bedrooms and offices for the *Crown Hotel*. It is no longer recognisable as a Corn Hall.

The Crown Inn

Commercial Hotel
Market Hill

The *Crown Inn*, now known as the *Crown Hotel*, and earlier *'The Crown'* stands in the centre of the eastern side of the market Hill. Until 1951 there was access for vehicles to use the old main road from Framlingham to Parham by driving through its yard. When in 1952 alterations were carried out by the new owners, Trust House Forte, early sixteenth century beams were revealed, with some walls of painted daub and wattle. The best of these may be seen in the entrance hall and lounges. These renovations also established that the front elevation, which faces the Market Place, is an eighteenth century refacing of the original Tudor inn, possibly first built about 1553, when Mary Tudor occupied the castle. She was collecting support from the important local gentlemen, such as Sir Thomas Cornwallis of Broome, and High Sheriff of Norfolk and Suffolk, Sir William Drury of Hawstead Place, M.P. for the county, and Sir Henry Bedingfield of Redlingfield, who was to become her Knight Marshal. It may be supposed that the *Crown*, recently built, accommodated part of Queen Mary's retinue for whom there was not room in the castle when she came with Philip of Spain to support the Earl of Surrey's son Thomas, a minor, when as the fourth Duke of Norfolk, he held his first court at the castle in 1557.

The *Crown* has always been a focal point in the town and has played host to many disparate concerns, for example in 1749 it was to be the meeting place for two 'boxers' Mark Pettet of Earl Soham, and Robert Colthorp of Bedingfield, before their fight, for two guineas, in the castle. In 1774 James Smyth attended on Saturdays to receive deficient gold coinage, and it was used as an excise and inland revenue office. In 1803 the Yeoman Cavalry used it as an enrolment centre, and in 1804 the shoemakers of Framlingham and neighbourhood met, in view of the recent increases in the price of leather, to agree on prices for boots and shoes.

In 1823 a dinner 'to be served punctually at 2 p.m.' was held to mark 50 years of service in Framlingham by Samuel Say Toms, the Unitarian Minister, and in 1830 signatures were collected against the tithing system on a petition deposited at the Crown.

From 1830 to 1847 the *Crown* was used as a court, which from 1847 to 1872 was held in the newly built corn hall in the yard of the *Crown*.

The Court House

In 1830 Framlingham was chosen as the legal centre for the jurisdiction area of thirty-three surrounding parishes. Initially Petty Sessions were held at the Crown Hotel Framlingham, and at Wickham Market, but from 1847 they were held in the new Corn Hall in the Crown Hotel yard until the Court House was built in 1872.

The Court House, a distinguished square shaped building with a glass cupola in the centre of its roof was built behind the Police House in Bridge Street, a private dwelling that had had cells erected at its back in 1847. Judges Courts were held in the Court House from 1872 to 1924 when they were removed to Saxmundham. Magistrates Courts were held on a weekly, fortnightly, then monthly basis until 1978 when they were altogether removed to Saxmundham.

Parish Council Meetings were held in the Court House from 1894 until 1981. From 1979 to 1984 Mr. Lanman's collection of artefacts which were the foundation of Framlingham's Museum were housed on its upper floors.

The Court House now has the Arms of Framlingham and of Coucy le Chateau, its 'twinned town' in France, on its south wall and is currently used to house the public library.

The Griffin Inn

In the early seventeenth century, the Griffin Inn was in two parts, and owned by Robert Bradshaw, who left it in his will of 1647 to James and Alice Stopher. They first rented it to Richard Porter who in 1686 bought the whole property from them as his residence. In 1695 Richard Porter sold the north part of the property, known as the Yard House, to Edward Keere, grocer, and a wooden 'pale' was constructed from the Market Hill to Back Lane to divide the properties, with two gateways for access.

1747   Plans of Griffin Inn   1845

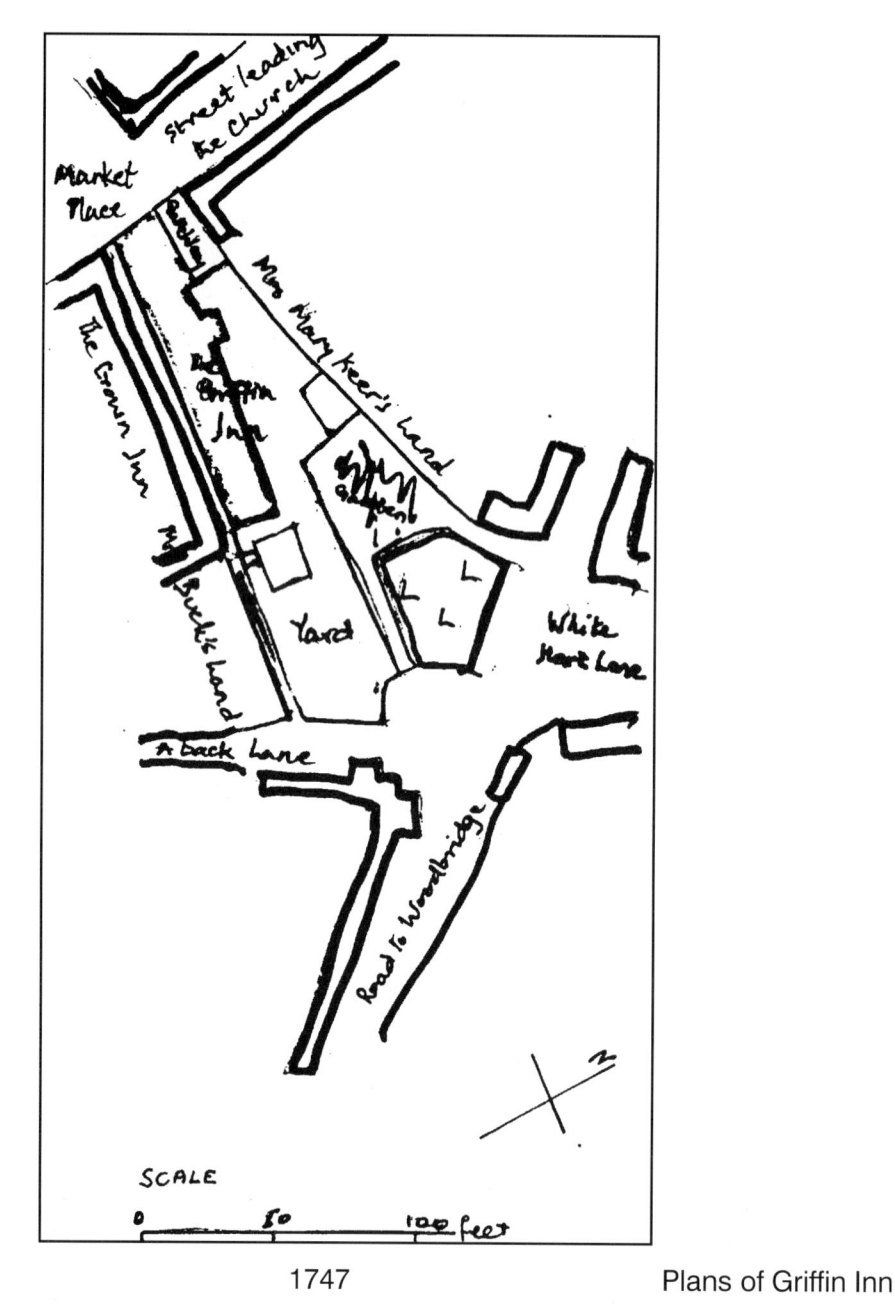

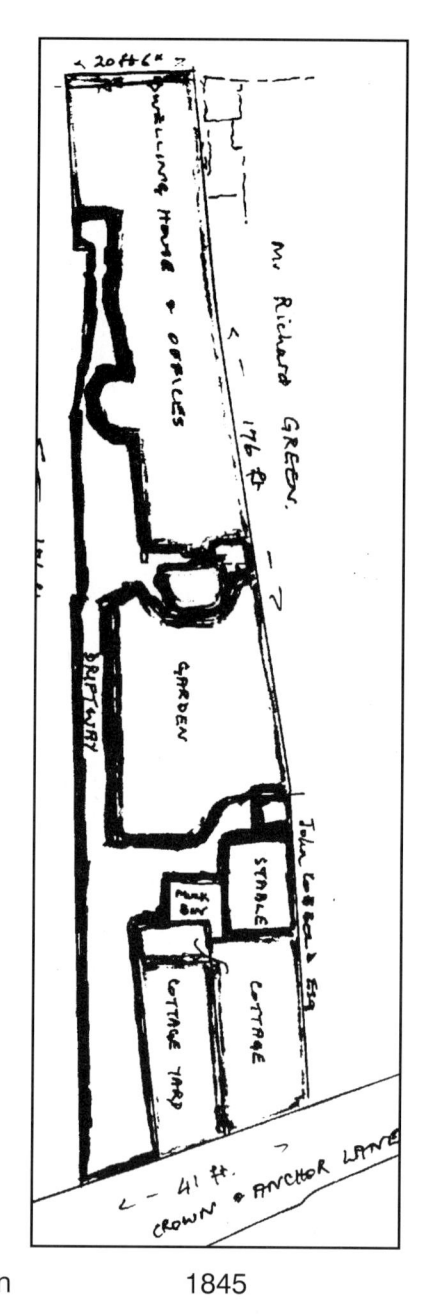

In 1797 when George Edwards sen. and Thomas Barker were the respective owners of the Griffin and Yard House a brick wall replaced the wooden fence and the gateways were bricked up.

The properties were next owned by the sons George and Charles Edwards, and Samuel Barker, and then respectively by S.G. Carley and Hatsell Garrard for his son Charles. Charles Garrard's was bought in 1965 by A.G. Bridges and in about 1948 Mr. Wood's small cottage on the corner of Crown & Anchor Lane and Back/Fore Street was removed to make room for more storage; and in 1950 the R.D.C. installed public lavatories on a part of this land.

S.G. Carley was joined in 1929 by P.J. Webb who took charge of the wine department and the Lankester/Cocks sale room in Crown & Anchor Lane was in 1950 replaced by a wine shop with cellarage built in the yard, now freed from stabling and cartsheds. This in turn was pulled down in 1970 and the wine department was set up in the front of the shop, using the 'Best Counter' which earlier had served as the banking counter for Gurney's Bank, run first by George and Charles Edwards in 1844, and then by Jonathan Hart in 1851 (see Banking). Jonathan Hart was joined by

S.G. Carley as his partner, and S.G. Carley became the owner of the shop with P.J. Webb. (It is likely that the Edwards brothers installed the crane in the yard, near to a stone carved with the date 1796; the crane raised the stores that were delivered in bulk; it swivels on its post and has a large wheel that was turned by hand to operate the chains).

Further alterations were made to the layout and service of this shop in 1977 in order to accommodate themselves to the sale of prepackaged goods from their suppliers. The fine mahogany counters, drawers, and shelving with their large green and gold cannisters for the special lines in tea, gave place to prefabricated central shelving. The distinguished coffee bean roasting machine left its dominant position, with its delicious aroma, to make room for the self service store in the front shop, and a delicatessen was established towards the back, and the wine shop moved again, this time to the old store room premises.

The Guildhall

The building popularly known as the Guildhall was built in part in 1564 by Simon Pulham, a woollen draper, on the site of the Guild Hall of St. Mary, known to have existed since 1363.

It is a two-storey building with attics, faced with mathematical tiles (tiles hung on batons to give the effect of a brick wall) and stands on a terrace in a most prominent position on the north side of the Market Place. On the ground floor three large nineteenth century shop windows project from the face of two-thirds of the building, while a door leads into the western one-third of the existing building. Within this section, in a rear wing on the first floor, is a finely panelled room fitted with a remarkable revolving cupboard and with shutters to the windows that have two secret drawers at their base. This part of the building may have been built by Simon Pulham to include a council chamber where official meetings could be held. (Commander Sitwell suggests that the old guild may have had some lingering responsibilities in the town and required that provision be made for them).

The gateway in the brick wall that divides this house from the Churchyard leads to the south porch of the Church through an eight feet wide avenue between gravestones, suitable for a procession of guildsmen.

This building when owned and occupied by the Kilderbee family who followed Simon Pulham, had a further section to the west, which was burnt down in 1958 and replaced by the incompatible modern Eastern Electricity showrooms and offices.

Regency House or 7 Church Street

The Regency House stands opposite the gates of the Church. It was earlier known as Tudor House or Church House since in the sixteenth and seventeenth centuries it was the building customarily used by the clergy of St. Michael's Church. In about 1810 a Captain Thomas Poole from London bought the property, and in about 1813 had the present false front, including the central curved and balustraded verandah, made up in London and fixed to the front of the house. From 1870 Robert Lambert, the author of the Lambert Almanacks and printer of the Framlingham Weekly News, owned this house and used it for his booksellers and stationers business. He was able to reach his printing works at No. 9 Double Street from the back of this property (see diagram). Recently, Regency House has been in the possession of T. Fleming and used as a showroom for antique furniture. (See picture in Subjects: Roads).

THE CASTLE

Since there is a guidebook to the Castle produced by English Heritage, no description, apart from these three extracts and a drawing of 1658 is included in this work.

The Dining Hall - Circa. 1658.

Castle Hall

Chimney

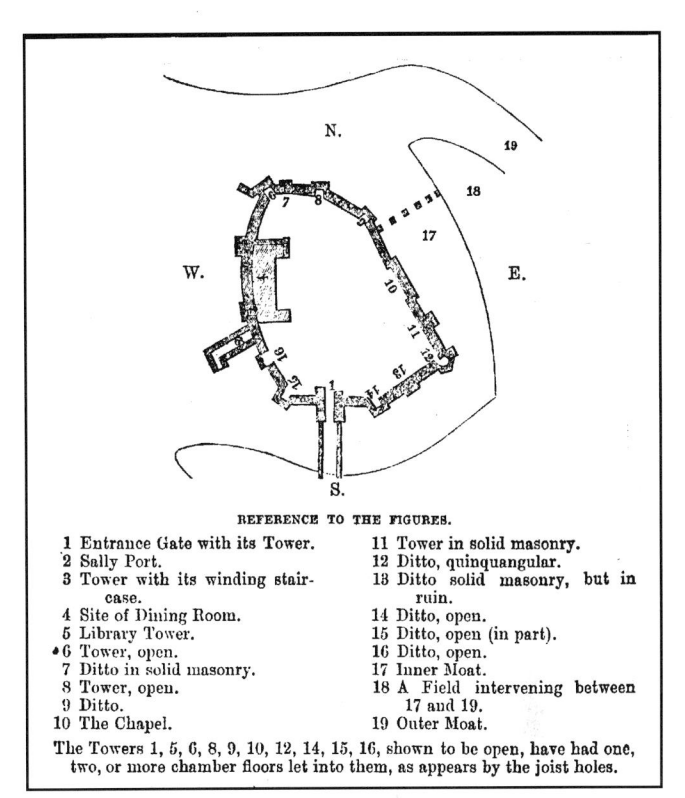

Site Plan

REFERENCE TO THE FIGURES.

1 Entrance Gate with its Tower.
2 Sally Port.
3 Tower with its winding staircase.
4 Site of Dining Room.
5 Library Tower.
6 Tower, open.
7 Ditto in solid masonry.
8 Tower, open.
9 Ditto.
10 The Chapel.
11 Tower in solid masonry.
12 Ditto, quinquangular.
13 Ditto solid masonry, but in ruin.
14 Ditto, open.
15 Ditto, open (in part).
16 Ditto, open.
17 Inner Moat.
18 A Field intervening between 17 and 19.
19 Outer Moat.

The Towers 1, 5, 6, 8, 9, 10, 12, 14, 15, 16, shown to be open, have had one, two, or more chamber floors let into them, as appears by the joist holes.

Castle and the Mere in winter.

THE HISTORY OF FRAMLINGHAM CASTLE

In the County of Suffolk,

[Written by Dr. Sampson of Pembroke Hall Cambridge, in the Year 1663.]

Framlingham Castle is a very ancient Structure, and said to have been built in the Time of the Saxons. It was One of the principall Seats of St. Edmund the King and Martyr. When he fled from Dunwich, being pursued by the Pagan Danes, hee took refuge in this Castle, but being hard besieged, and having no Hope of Rescue, he fledd from thence, and being overtaken by his Enemies was beheaded at Hoxon, from whence long after, his Corps was removed and re interred at Bury, called since St. Edmund's Bury. Mathew Paris informs us, that William Rufus gave this Castle to his favorite Roger Bigod; and learned Mr. Camden says, that this Castle, if not rebuilt, yett was repaired by his Son Hugh Bigod, who was created Earl of Norfolk by King Stephen, becaufe he testified upon Oath before the Archbishop of Canterbury and others, that King Henry willed upon his Death-bed, that Stephen, his Nephew, and not Maud, his Daughter, should succeed him in the Kingdom of England.

This Hugh was the Sonne and Heire of the before-mentioned Roger, who was Sewer to King Henry the First, by Adeliza the Daughter and Heire of Sir Hugh Grantesmenill, High Steward of England. He married Juliana the Daughter of Almerick de Vere, the King's Chamberlain, and had Issue Roger Bigod Earl of Norfolk, and William a second Son, who dyed in the 24th Year of Henry the Second, and was buried in the Priory of St. Bennet in Thetford. Afterwards this Castle was given by King Edward the First to his Second Son Thomas of Brotherton Earl of Norffolk, and Marshall

Marshall of England, who repaired it as appeareth by his Armes in diverse Places thereof. This Thomas married Katharine the Daughter of Sir Roger Hayles of Harwich, Knight, and had Issue Edward, and Margarett. Edward succeeded his Father as Earl of Norfolk, and Marshall of England, but dyed, the King's Ward, in the same Yeare with his Father, leaving his said Sister Margaret his Heir. She was first married to John Lord Segrave, who built the Church of St. Michael in Framlingham, and the Church of our Lady in Woodbridge.

This Castle was very faire and beautifull, fortified with a double Ditch, high Banks, and Rampiers. The Walls, which are of great Height and Thickneffe, are strengthened by Thirteene Towers square built, all which are yett to be seene, as are likewise the Remains of Twoe Watch Towers or Barbicans on the West Side. These Barbicans are now corruptly called by the common People, The Burganys.

This Castle was inwardly furnished with Buildings very commodious and necessary, able to receive and entertaine many. In the First Court was a very deepe Well of excellent Workmanship, compassed with carved Pillars, which supported a leaden Roofe, and though out of Repayer, was in being Anno 1651.

In the same Court also was a neat Chappell now wholly demolished, Anno 1657, and transported into the Highwayes.

There were in the Building diverse Armes, some in Stone, some in Wood, to be seene Anno 1651. As of Bigot, Brotherton, Segrave, and Mowbray; and under a Windowe, largely carved and painted, were quarterly the Arms of St. Edward King and Confeffor, and thofe of Brotherton, under a Chapeau turned up Ermin, supported by Two white Lyons, for the bearing whereof Thomas Earle of Surrey, the Son of Thomas Second Duke of Norfolk of that Name, lost his Head in the 38th Year of Hen. the 8. Also on the Hall Gate fayerly cutt in Stone were the Armes of Brotherton impaling Bourchier, quartered with Lovayne, supported with a Lyon and an Eagle. There was likewise on an old Dore a great Iron Ring garnished with Ms. with Ducal Coronets thereon.

On the West Side of this Castle spreadeth a great Lake, which is reported to have been once navigable, and to have filled the double Ditch about the Castle. But it is now much less than formerly it was, being every Day filled upp with Earth and Sand washed into it by the heavy Raines: People now call it the Meare. It is said that from thence cometh

cometh the River Ore, which emptieth itself (having taken in diverse other Waters) into the Sea at Orford.

This Castle had a Drawe-bridge and a Portcullis over the Gate, which was the strongest Tower: and beyond the Bridge, without, was a half Moone of Stone, about a Man's Height, standing Anno 1657. There was on the East Side a Posterne, with an Iron Gate, leading over a private Bridge into the Parke wherein the Castle standeth, which was, not long since, thick beset with Trees, as the stumps yet shew.

In the Year 1173, when King Henry the younger rebelled against his Father King Henry the Second, Robert Earle of Leicester, with his Flemings, infested the Countrey, farr and neere, from this Castle. This Robert, together with his Amazonian Countesse Parnell, were taken Prisoners at Farneham St. Genevesa, not far from St. Edmund's Bury, by Richard Lucy Lord Chiefe Justice of England, and Protector of the Kingdom (in the Absence of King Henry the Second) in a pitcht Field, wherein were put to the Sword about Tenn thousand Flemings, which the said Earle Robert had levied and sent forth from this Castle to rob and Spoile the Countrey, all or most of which Number were buried in and about the Village of Farnham, in the Year 1173 aforesaid, the twentieth of K. Henry the Second.

Since the Conquest the Possessors of Framlingham Castle were, viz.

1. Roger Bigot and his Posterity.
2. Thomas de Brotherton Earle of Norffolk, Second Son to King Edward the First.
3. John Lord Segrave whoe was the First Husband of Margaret the Daughter and sole Heir of Thomas of Brotherton, and to hir Brother Edward that dyed *sine prole*. She was afterwards married to Sir Walter Manny, Knt.
4. Thomas Lord Mowbray, Son of John Lord Mowbray and Elizabeth his Wife, Daughter and Heire of Margaret Dutchesse of Norffolk, and John Lord Segrave her Husband. It continued in their Family divers Generations.
5. Sir John Howard, Knt. Son of Sir Robert Howard, Knt. and of Margaret his Wife, Daughter and Coheire of Thomas Mowbray Duke of Norfolk.
6. Thomas Lord Howard, the First Son of Thomas Howard Duke of Norffolk, by Margaret his Second Wife, Daughter and only Heire of Thomas Lord Audley of Walden, Lord Chancellor of England, which said Thomas was summoned to Parliament as Baron Howard of Walden, and afterwards

afterwards created Earl of Suffolk, whose Heirs afterwards sold it to

7. Sir Robert Hitcham, Knt. Serjeant at Lawe, who by his Will dated in August 1636, devised the Castle, Manor, and Lordship of Framlingham, and the Manor of Saxted, being of the yearly Value of One thousand Pounds, to the Master and Fellows of Pembroke Hall in Cambridge, and their Successors, Part thereof, of about One hundred Pounds *per Annum*, to be employed for the Good of the College only, and the Rest for erecting of a Work-house in Framlingham for imploying the Poor of that Town, and of the Poor of Debenham and Coggeshall in Essex, and for providing a Stock to sett them on Work, and for Building of Alms-houses in Framlingham for Twelve poor People, who should be allowed Two Shillings a Piece weekly for their Maintenance, and Forty Shillings a Piece yearly for a Gown and Firing; and for building a School-house at Framlingham for the poor Children of that and the said other Towns, and for Ten Pounds a Piece to bind them Apprentices, and for the yearly Stipend of Forty Pounds for the Schoolmaster, Twenty Pounds for One to read Prayers there Twice a Day, and for Five Pounds *per Annum* for the Sexton. By the said Will he likewise directed, that if the Masters and Fellows of Pembroke Hall should willfully refuse to perform the Directions thereof, then that the Devise as to them should be void, and that the Premises should go to Emanuel College in Cambridge in the same Manner and to the same Uses.

This is all I knowe, or can gather from Antiquitie concerning this Castle. What it was when it flourished you have heard in Part, but now through Age and Ill-handling, it is ready to give up the Ghost.

FRAMLINGHAM CASTLE, SUFFOLK.

THIS view shews the inside of the castle, the ruins of several of the dwelling-houses, with others lately erected on their foundations. The large house nearest the left hand of the spectator, in all likelihood was in being when the castle was entire; as, both by the bricks and stile of building, it appears to have been constructed about the time of Henry the Eighth, or Queen Elizabeth.

THE chimneys, many of which are still standing in the towers, are worthy of observation, being curiously wrought into various figures with ground or rubbed bricks: indeed the artificers of those days gave many extraordinary instances how perfectly these materials might be worked into the different mouldings and ornaments of architecture.

IN the year 1173, Queen Elinor, out of revenge (as it is supposed) for the matrimonial infidelities of her husband, Henry the Second, incited his son Henry, an ambitious and ungrateful youth, to raise a rebellion against his father in Normandy. He was assisted by the kings of France and Scotland, and joined by many of the barons, amongst whom was Robert earl of Leicester, who crossing the sea, with a body of French, and three (some say ten) thousand Flemmings,

FRAMLINGHAM CASTLE, SUFFOLK.

landed at Walton, in this county, and was received by Hugh Bigod, earl of Norfolk, into his caftle of Framlingham. From hence they made frequent excurfions, to the great annoyance of the neighbourhood, which they repeatedly laid under heavy contributions, robbing and defpoiling all paffengers, burning villages and caftles, and committing diverfe other enormities; infomuch that Hugh Lucy, the chief-juftice of England, affifted by Humphry de Bohun, attacked and defeated them in a pitched battle, fought at a place called St. Martin's, at Farnham, near Bury St. Edmond's. In this engagement the earl of Leicefter and his wife, a lady of a mafculine fpirit and deportment, were taken prifoners, together with many of the French; but the Flemmings were, to a man, all either flain or drowned. Their bodies were afterwards buried in and about that village.

HENRY having reduced his fon to obedience, foon after returned to England; when he befieged, took and difmantled this caftle. Its owner, Hugh Bigod, obtained his pardon, on paying to the king four thoufand marks; but the earl of Leicefter did not efcape fo eafily, for he was conveyed prifoner to Roan in Normandy, where he was clofely confined; his caftle at Leicefter was demolifhed, the town burned, its walls razed, and the inhabitants difperfed into other places.

HITHER likewife, in the year 1553, Queen Mary retired, on notice being fent her, by the earl of Arundel, of the death of her brother, Edward the Sixth, and of the patent for the fucceffion of the lady Jane. She chofe this place, not only as being near the fea, whereby fhe might eafily efcape to Flanders; but alfo becaufe the great flaughter of Ket's followers, by the duke of Northumberland, in the late reign, made him, and confequently his party, extremely odious in the neighbourhood. The event juftified her choice; for fhe was joined by almoft all the inhabitants of this and the adjacent counties, who encamped near the caftle, to the number of thirteen thoufand men. From hence fhe foon after fet out for London, to take poffeffion of the crown, relinquifhed by her unfortunate competitor. She was met on her way by the lady Elizabeth, at the head of a thoufand horfe, which that princefs had raifed for her fervice.

IN the year 1653, an act of parliament paffed, fettling and confirming the manors of Framlingham and Saxtead, in the county of Suffolk, with the lands, tenements and hereditaments thereunto belonging, devifed by Sir Robert Hitcham, knight, late ferjeant at law, to certain charitable ufes.

This drawing was made in the year 1769.

FRAMLINGHAM CASTLE, SUFFOLK.

THIS Caftle ftands in the hundred of Loes, and is fituate on a clay hill, north of the town, having on the weft fide a mere or marfh, formerly a lake. It is a very ancient ftructure, and is faid to have been erected in the time of the Saxons; but Hiftory does not record the name of the builder. Kirby, in his Suffolk Traveller, conjectures it to have been conftructed by Redwald, the moft powerful King of the Eaft Angles, who kept his court at Rendlefham, in this hundred.

IT was one of the feats of St. Edmunde, the King and Martyr, who fled hither from Dunwich, when purfued by the Danes. Hither, likewife, they followed him, and laid fiege to the Caftle; when he, being hard preffed and having no hopes of fuccour, endeavoured to efcape; but being overtaken in his flight, was beheaded at Hoxton: from whence, long after, his corpfe was removed, and interred at Bury; therefore called St. Edmund's Bury; the Caftle being taken, remained, as it is faid, fifty years in the poffeffion of the Danes.

WILLIAM THE CONQUEROR, his fon Rufus, or, according to others, Henry the Firft, gave this Caftle to Roger Bigod; by whofe fon Hugh it was either rebuilt or much repaired, having been difmantled in the year 1176, by order of King Henry the Second. This Hugh Bigod was created Earl of Norfolk by King Stephen, as a reward for having teftified upon oath, before the archbifhop of Canterbury and others, That Henry the Firft had, on his death-bed, nominated Stephen for his fucceffor to the Crown of England, in preference to his daughter Maud.

IN the poffeffion of the Bigods it continued till the twenty-fifth of Edward the Firft; when that family being extinct, it reverted to the Crown, and was by that King given to his fecond fon, Thomas de Brotherton, Earl of Norfolk and Marfhal of England, who repaired it, as appeared by his arms fet up in diverfe parts of the building. On his deceafe it came to his two daughters, Margaret and Alice; the latter married Edward de Montacute, who, upon the divifion of the eftate, had, in his part, this caftle and the demefnes thereof. He left it to his daughter

FRAMLINGHAM CASTLE, SUFFOLK.

Joan, who marrying William de Ufford, Earl of Suffolk, carried it into that family; from whence it came to the Mowbrays, dukes of Norfolk, who fome time refided here. From the Mowbrays it defcended to the Howards, earls and afterwards dukes of Norfolk. After them it was granted to the De Veres, earls of Oxford; from whence it returned to the Howards; and was, by Theophilus, earl of Suffolk, fold, together with the manor and demefnes, to Sir Robert Hitcham, Knight, Attorney general, in the reign of King Charles the Firft; who, by his will, dated in Auguft, 1636, devifed the caftle, manor and lordfhip of Framlingham, together with the manor of Saxted, being then of the yearly value of one thoufand pounds, to the mafters and fellows of Pembroke Hall in Cambridge; one hundred pounds per annum to be expended for the benefit of the college, and the remainder to be appropriated to charitable ufes, for the emolument of the poor of the parifhes of Framlingham and Debenham, in this county, and thofe of Coggefhall in Effex.

The account of the various poffeffors is differently ftated by Dr. Samfon, of Pembroke Hall, Cambridge; who, in the year 1663, wrote the hiftory of this Caftle, printed in the laft edition of Leland's Collectanea. He gives as follows:

I. Roger de Bigod, and his pofterity.

II. Thomas de Brotherton, earl of Norfolk, fecond fon to King Edward the Firft.

III. John, lord Segrave, who was the firft hufband of Margaret, the daughter and fole heirefs of Thomas de Brotherton, and to her brother Edward, who died fine prole; fhe was afterwards married to Sir William Manny Kt.

IV. Thomas, lord Mowbray, fon of John, lord Mowbray, and Elizabeth his wife, daughter and heir to Margaret, duchefs of Norfolk, and John, lord Segrave, her hufband. It continued in their family diverfe generations.

V. Sir John Howard, Knight, fon of Sir Robert Howard, Knight, and of Margaret, his wife, daughter and co-heir of Thomas Mowbray, duke of Norfolk.

VI. Thomas, lord Howard, the firft fon of Thomas Howard, duke of Norfolk, by Margaret his fecond wife, daughter and only heir of Thomas, lord Audley, of Walden, and afterwards created earl of Suffolk, whofe heirs afterwards fold it to Sir Robert Hitcham.

This Caftle was a large, ftrong and handfome building, fortified with a double ditch; its walls, which are forty-four feet in height, and eight in thicknefs, inclofe within their circuit an area of one acre, one rood, and eleven perches; and are flanked by thirteen fquare towers, which rife above them fourteen feet: two of thefe were watch towers, and are called by Doctor Samfon, Barbicans; who fays they were, by the common people, corruptly called Burganys.

This author, defcribing the Caftle, fays, "It was inwardly furnifhed with buildings very commodious and "neceffary, able to receive and entertain many; in the firft court was a deep well of excellent workmanfhip, "compofed with carved pillars, which fupported a leaden roof, and, though out of repair, was in being anno "1651. In the fame court alfo was a neat chappel, now wholly demolifhed, anno 1657, and tranfported into "the highways.

"There were in the building diverfe arms, fome in ftone, fome in wood, to be feen anno 1651; as of Bigod, "Brotherton, Segrave and Mowbray; and under a window, largely carved and painted, were, quarterly, the "arms of St. Edward, King and Confeffor; and thofe of Brotherton, under a chapeau turned up ermine, fupported "by two white lions; for the bearing whereof, Thomas, earl of Surry, the fon of Thomas, fecond duke of Norfolk "of that name, loft his head in the thirty-eighth year of Henry the Eighth. Alfo on the hall-gate, fairly cut in "ftone, were the arms of Brotherton impaling Bourchier, quartered with Lovayne, fupported by a lion and an "eagle. There were likewife an old door, a great iron ring garnifhed with Ms. with ducal coronets thereon.

"On the weft fide of this caftle fpreadeth a large lake, which is reported to have been once navigable, and to "have filled the double ditch of the caftle: but it is now much lefs than it formerly was; being every day filled up "with earth and fand, wafhed into it by heavy rains. People now call it the Mere. It is faid that from hence "cometh the river Ore, which emptieth itfelf (having taken in diverfe other waters) into the fea, at Orford.

"This Caftle had a draw-bridge, and a portcullis over the gate, which was the ftrongeft tower; and beyond "the bridge without, was a half moon of ftone, about a man's height, ftanding in 1657. There was on the eaft "fide a poftern, with an iron-gate, leading over a private bridge into the park, wherein the Caftle ftandeth, "which was not long fince thick befet with trees, as the ftumps yet fhew."

This drawing, which reprefents the outfide of the Caftle, was made in the year 1760.

CHARITABLE BENEFACTION

In the seventeenth and eighteenth centuries, Framlingham had its charitable benefactors for the poor of the town. Notable among them are Sir Robert Hitcham, a lawyer, John Pulham, a woollen draper, John Smith, a yeoman, Thomas Mills, a wheelwright and William Mayhew his assistant, and c. 1890 William Warne, a farmer; and in about 1965 Mrs. Pryke left money to relieve the poor of the parish.

Sir Robert Hitcham gave to Pembroke Hall all the demesne lands and the manors of Framlingham and Saxtead, apart from the castle and the meres, for the relief and education of the poor, including the almshouses that were built in 1678 for twelve persons in New Road. Income from the rents earned for the trustees an annual sum of about £418. Hawes & Loder lists John Pulham, and his imaginative gift of £20 on 21st September 1639, to be lent to six poor tradesmen or young beginners, at 'five marks apiece'. John Smith, a yeoman, left £50 in his will of 1673 for a similar purpose for £5 to be allotted to poor tradesmen, interest free, as three year loans. Neither of these two bequests was well administered, and in 1780 only £5 could be traced, then in the hands of William Roe.

Richard Porter left in his will of 1701 provision for 18 twopenny loaves to be given to the poor weekly. Thomas Mills in 1703 left money to build and maintain six almshouses in Framlingham, and some £9 per annum to supply bread for the poor, as well as money for a school for the education of poor children, which was built off Brook Lane. His assistant William Mayhew left money to build two additional almshouses.

Robert Hawes comments, 'This Town is not rich but pay as much collection as Neighbouring Parishes do, from whence the Poor flock to Framlingham as eagles to a carkas. And those who save most by these gifts are tradesmen and Innkeepers, occasioned by the circulation of money through the hands of the Poor Persons relieved thereby.' (*Hawes & Loder*, p. 398 ff.)

In 1967 Brigadier Blaker suggested at a public meeting that there should be some regularisation and amalgamation of the charities, but it was not until May 1981 that the three bread charities of 1701, 1703 and about 1890, with the Townland Trust of 1862 were incorporated into the Framlingham United Town Charity. The Pryke Charity of 1965 was administered independently from 1973 until 1990 when all the charities were combined and registered under the name of the Pryke Charity.

CHURCH

ST. MICHAEL'S CHURCH.

The Church of St. Michael, Framlingham, stands with its records as a reflection of the hopes, aspirations and everchanging fashions of the inhabitants of its parish through the ages. It is assumed that the Bigods, the new overlords of Framlingham in the twelfth century, built not only their walled castle, but also a church on the site of the present church in 'New Framlingham'. This was to replace a Saxon church, recorded in Little Domesday, which very probably stood within the walls of the Saxon castle, on the site of the present castle car park, surrounded by the Saxon burial ground for which there is evidence. There is a record of Rectors from 22nd March 1311, but the first known bequest to the church comes from John de Harleston (Rector 1374-1387) who specified in his Will that 'the work on my chancel [is] to be wholly perfect', so reflecting his care and his attitude to that part of the church for which he was responsible. There is a carved top of a putative priest's tomb against the South wall of the present chancel. This first chancel had three altars: the high altar, a Lady Chapel, and an altar to St. Nicholas.

The church was enriched, c. 1350, with at least one wall painting, that of the Trinity, on the south side of the north arched wall of the nave. This church has a fine East Anglian octagonal font, c. 1380, which earlier dominated the West end of the nave. It was carved with emblems of the four evangelists, and between them four angels holding shields carved with (1) three cups with wafers, (2) emblems of the Trinity, (3) emblems of the crucifixion, and (4) defaced, but thought to have depicted three crowns. It stands on a step on which were carved in Latin the words 'Pray for the souls of John Plomer and Margerie his wife who caused this font to be made'. The font has four lions sejant and four green men known as woodwoses, each holding a club, at the foot of its stem. Its cover, also thought to be c. 1380, is conical in shape, with its eight ribs decorated with carved crockets upon which may still be seen the remains of red and gold paint. At the apex of the cone is a religious symbol: an acorn about to split in order to bring forth new life, symbolizing the emergence of the new spiritual life of the baptised. Unfortunately, the base of the font cover is missing. It was probably about 2'3" high, and is likely to have had doors similar to those at Bedfield so that the priest could administer the sacrament of baptism and the god-parents could view the ceremony.

In order to facilitate the management of popular processions, north and south aisles were built on to the thirteenth century nave in about 1350. At the west end of this north aisle is an area, possibly once furnished for the guild of the Blessed Virgin Mary. (The guildhall stood on the Market Hill, and, though separated from the church by a wall, enjoyed access by a pathway to the south door). On the north wall of this area is a beautiful canopied niche, now empty, bearing the monogram of the Blessed Virgin Mary and 'IHC help'. Three carvings support the niche: to the west a head with a triple crown, in the middle a winged figure of the Blessed Virgin with an MR on her shield, and to the east, possibly a representation of Margaret of Antioch. From a kneeling position in front this niche the full beauty and impact may be appreciated.

The fifteenth century church chest which stands against the south wall near the steps to the chancel was carved out of solid wood and bound with iron bands; it has, as usual, three locks, one for the Rector and one each for the two churchwardens.

It is supposed that the present church was built by one of the Mowbrays - their coat of arms is twice emblazoned on the tower which was built between 1483 and 1534. All was not left to the lords of the castle; many benefactors left money 'to the High Altar of the Church', as was the practice in the fifteenth and early sixteenth centuries, in order to atone for shortcomings during their lives, and to expedite their passage through purgatory. Also, in 1447, Margaret Crane gave 'a chalice with a vestment and two towels' (may they have been sold in 1557, as part of the £80 raised by the churchwardens to pay for necessary repairs to the Church ?) During the fifteenth century, the addition of towers to churches became popular. Some Wills made after 1497 reveal that a number of parishioners were making bequests for the new 'stepyll' so that the tower to St. Michael's Church Framlingham might rival others in the neighbourhood. it was built against the west wall of the church, with two string courses, supported by four six-step buttresses with flint and flush designs, and with four four-light windows above the string courses and two two-light between the string courses to give light to the ringing chamber, the whole being 96' high, with a battlemented top, and four heraldic lions with shields, one on each of the four top corners. The fine west door was set in an arch with St. Michael (now missing) and the dragon depicted in its spandrels.

The roof of the church was twice raised to give more light to the nave through the clerestory windows. - Money was left in 1464 by John Pulham for 'the clerestory of Framlingham Church', and in 1520, when much building work was in hand for the church, Joan Maggs left money 'to the new clerestories of the Church'. Pillars on the nave walls bear evidence to the earlier height of the nave roof. Three legacies in 1500, 1501 and 1504 were for lead for the church roof. In 1558 wood for the Rood was brought from Saxtead's New Haugh Wood.

The interior roof of the nave is one of the great beauties of the church. A single oak hammer beam construction is covered by unusual wooden fan vaulting, similar to that of St. Peter Mancroft in Norwich. The corbels with carved faces in the aisles possibly once supported figures, now missing, which further beautified the church and gave support to the aisle roofs. Monies were being left for the beautifying of the interior of the church and for items for the greater comfort of the congregation: five bequests were made for stooling, (pews) between 1512 and 1520, when carved oak pews were made for the church, as was the fashion of the time.

By 1553 the church had five bells and a sanctus bell. The foundry of Richard Brasyer I or II made a bell between 1423 and 1513, William Bread cast a bell for the church in 1583, and John Bread another in 1622, with inscriptions '*Omnis sonus laudet domino anno domini*' 1583 RG and '*Anno domini*' 1622 W I B.

St. Michael's underwent a great change c. 1543 when the third Duke of Norfolk caused the chancel to be razed to the ground to make way for an area large enough to accommodate both tombs from Thetford Priory, disbanded in 1540, and for further memorials to the Howards. This Duke was imprisoned in the Tower during Edward VI's reign, and on this account the rebuilding of the chancel was completed on the orders of the King. The 68' wide chancel was built on to the 50' wide nave in 1553. The chancel built by the Dukes of Norfolk was felt to be their property.

The chancel arch has four twelfth century pillars, two of which are free standing. They are the oldest existing pieces of masonry in the church. Did they mark the original chancel arch, or did they come from Thetford priory when the Norfolk sarcophagi were transported, and the present wide chancel was built, around 1550 (The pillars on the south side were cut to accommodate a three-decker pulpit, about 1700). Tombs were brought from Thetford Priory and placed to the south and north of the High Altar. That of Thomas Howard, third Duke of Norfolk, with his effigy and that of his wife, Elizabeth, stands to the south of the Altar, while that of his poet eldest son, Henry Earl of Surrey, is the coloured alabaster tomb on the north wall.

Tomb of the 4th Duke of Norfolk and his two wives.

The fourth Duke of Norfolk may be seen kneeling at his feet. His own tomb lies east of his father's tomb, with effigies of his two wives upon it. Between this tomb and the High Altar stands the tomb of Henry Fitzroy, Duke of Richmond, a natural son of Henry VIII, with his wife Lady Mary Howard. Finally a small tomb on the north wall, lying between that of the Earl of Surrey and the fourth Duke is the tomb of Elizabeth, the infant daughter of the fourth Duke and of Lady Margaret. The niche below the ogee arch is empty, and the two shields are unemblazoned.

The fine Norfolk and Richmond tombs in the specially built chancel of St. Michael's Church Framlingham bear a remarkable resemblance to the French Royal tombs of Francois I and Louis XII in the Cathedral at St. Denis, which date from c. 1500 - 1530. Francois I and Henry VIII were friends, and the possibility of a French sculptor working on three Norfolk tombs is given further credence by the similar traditional Italian Renaissance styles, mixed with the smart revival of classical motifs in each case.

Tomb of the 3rd Duke of Norfolk

The first tomb to be examined is considered by experts such as by S.J.K.Wright to be one of the finest examples of early French Renaissance art in Europe. It is the tomb of Thomas Howard, third Duke of Norfolk, and (probably) his wife, Elizabeth. There is a possibility that in the same tomb, Thomas, second Duke of Norfolk, and his wife, Agnes, are also buried. The third Duke had an eventful history. At the end of the reign of Henry VIII, after many years of friendship, he fell from favour and was attainted with his son, the Earl of Surrey, for high

A History of Framlingham   Subjects   CHURCH

Viewed from top to bottom: Left:-   Roof, Thamar organ and High Altar.
                                  Right:-   The Trinity and the Font.

treason. Both were condemned to death and the sentence on his son was carried out. The Duke escaped the axe because Henry died the night before his decreed execution; he remained imprisoned during the reign of Edward VI, but was released and restored to favour by Mary Tudor. The collar on his effigy on the tomb bears the inscription *Gracia Dei Sum Quod Sum* - 'By the Grace of God I am what I am', a motto which he is said to have adopted to commemorate his deliverance.

The effigies are remarkable for their craftsmanship and detail, and it is of interest to notice the contrast between the effigies and the base of the tomb, which is Florentine in its style. The identification of the figures is most probably as follows: reading from left to right, north side: S. Philip, S. Jude, S. Simon, S. Matthias: west end, S. Peter, an Old Testament prophet, S. Paul: south side, S. Andrew, S. Bartholomew, St. James the Great, S. James the Less: east end, S. Thomas, an Old Testament figure, S. John.

In the north chancel aisle the beautiful painted alabaster tomb is that of Henry, Earl of Surrey (eldest son of the third Duke of Norfolk), and his wife Frances, daughter of John Earl of Oxford. He was convicted of high treason with his father under Henry VIII and was beheaded on 21st January 1547. He was a man of considerable culture, and then, as well as today is recognised as a poet of ability. This tomb was set up by his second son, the Earl of Northampton, in the reign of James I, when his remains were brought from the Tower to Framlingham.

Surrey's eldest son who kneels at his feet became the fourth Duke of Norfolk, and the tomb in the corner of the north chancel aisle commemorates with effigies his two wives with a vacant space between them. He was beheaded in 1571 because he was implicated in a plot by which Elizabeth was to be dethroned by Mary, Queen of Scots, who was then to marry him. His first wife was Lady Mary, daughter of Henry Fitz-Alan, Earl of Arundel. She has the hart at her feet. It is through this marriage that the Norfolk family transferred to Arundel. Lady Mary was the mother of the Blessed Philip Howard, who was imprisoned in the Tower for thirteen years by Elizabeth for refusing to abandon his allegiance to the Pope. The second wife of the fourth Duke was the Lady Margaret, daughter and heir of Thomas, Lord Audley, Baron of Walden and Lord Chancellor of England. She too had a famous son in Lord Thomas Howard, who commanded the fleet when Sir Richard Grenville overcame the Spanish Fleet single-handed in the 'Revenge'. It was his son who sold the Framlingham Estates to Sir Robert Hitcham.

The fourth Duke then married Lady Elizabeth Dacre from Cumberland, a widow with four children who, like the first two wives, died in childbirth. The children were brought up at Kenninghall Palace with the children of the second Duchess. Though her funeral was at Framlingham, there is no record of her having been buried there. From these three marriages stem the many branches of the present Howard family, and with each marriage the fourth Duke acquired large estates and great wealth.

The small tomb in the north wall is that of Elizabeth, the infant daughter of the fourth Duke and the Lady Margaret. It is probable that an effigy was formerly in the niche.

The last tomb to be noted immediately north of the High Altar is the most interesting. It is that of Henry Fitzroy, Duke of Richmond, a natural son of Henry VIII by Lady Elizabeth Talbois. His companion in studies and travel was the Earl of Surrey, whose sister, the Lady Mary Howard, he married. He died in 1536 at an early age. The carved panels from the Old Testament are:
(1) the creation of Eve, (2) the Garden of Eden, (3) The Temptation, (4) the expulsion from the Garden, (5) Adam and Eve with Cain and Abel, (6) Cain and Abel sacrificing, and Cain killing Abel, (7) Noah's

Ark, (8) Noah drunk, (9) Abraham's heavenly visitors, (10) The destruction of Sodom and Lot's wife being turned into a Pillar of salt, (11) Abraham- sacrificing Isaac, (12) The Decalogue and the Golden Calf.

The chancel once had three doors; the one on the south side, under a buttress is still used; a corresponding door on the north wall, west of the earl of Surrey's tomb, has been blocked off and the buttress extended to the wall. A doorway in the north aisle of the East wall, possibly used by the Dukes from the Castle has been walled up. Brackets were placed on the walls of the chancel for banners and helmets, and upon one of these, on the south side, hangs the Flodden Helm. Experts from the Tower of London and the Victoria & Albert Museum state it is in two sections, dated 1500 and 1520, and that it is a fine example of a tilting helm, probably carried in the funeral processions of the second and possibly the third Duke of Norfolk.

A sundial was placed on the south-east corner buttress in 1638, at a cost of 4s. 0d.

The church suffered some despoilation in 1644 at the hands of the employees of the Earl of Manchester. Mr. Francis Verdyn, one of William Dowsing's deputies, was entertained and given a half fee of 3s. 6d. and a pint of sack costing 8d.; possibly on

The Floddon Helm

this account, the Church suffered only minor damage, notably to the distinguished font cover, which, it is thought, was thrown into the churchyard, where it remained until after 1660. This treatment was the cause of the damage from damp and subsequent destruction of its base. The organs were destroyed for they were anathema to the Puritans, who held that the New Testament made no mention of their use in connection with worship; furthermore, because their sound is polyphonic the Name of God is sounded simultaneously three or four times, suggesting that there might be more than one God... so making the organ a blasphemous instrument. There were, moreover, suggestions of idolatrous ceremonies connected with pagan pipes.

Hitcham's Tomb

Following the Commonwealth era the Sir Robert Hitcham Will was put into operation. Almshouses were built and the unusual bench which stands in the chancel was made for the twelve alms persons who should attend Services at 8 a.m - and 4 p.m daily, taken by the Reader, for whom the provision of £20 per annum had been made. The black marble tomb supported by kneeling angels was erected, to the south of the tomb of the third Duke of Norfolk, in memory of Sir Robert Hitcham, the attorney who bought the Howard estates in 1635 and left them to Pembroke Hall in 1636.

It is thought that when Richard Golty, the sequestrated Rector, was restored to his living he rescued what he could of the font cover and caused a base to be fixed to the once fine conical top, so that it could stand on the font. He also was responsible in May 1661 for the erection of

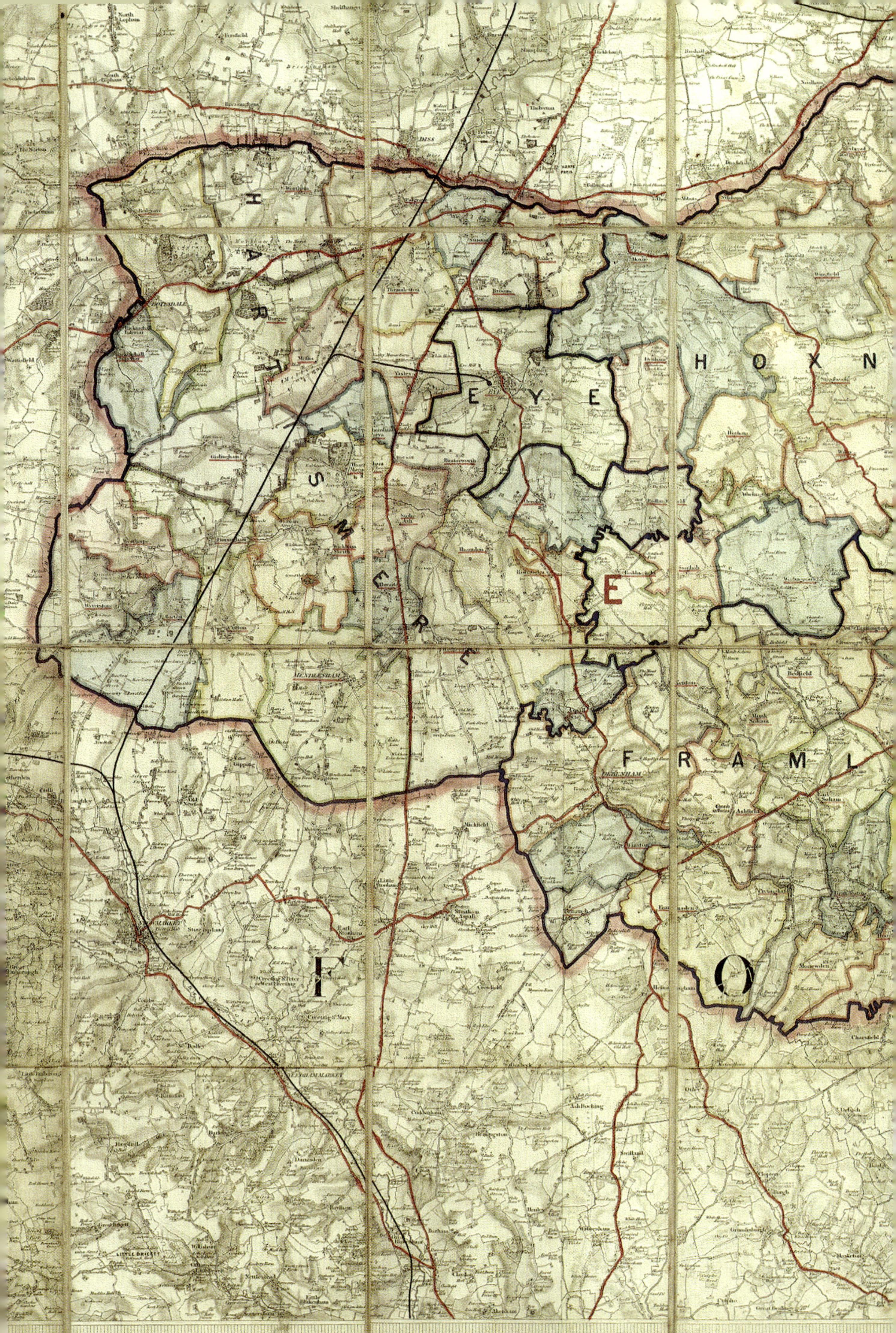

EYE
HOXN
E
FRAML
F
O
DISS

Map issued to Lawyer Read in 1915 in case of invasion.

the King's Arms made by Mr. Hugh Ludson for £8. 10s. 0d., and for the citation of 4s. 4d. served on Mr. Ireland, once a churchwarden, for refusing to contribute towards the King's Arms. In 1662, a 'Booke of Common Prayer' was bought for the church for 10s. 0d.

Fashions were changing and provision was made for an eye-catching trompe l'oeil: we read in Hawes & Loder (pp. 294/351), 'over the entrance into the chancel there is a spacious piece of architecture painted a stone colour in perspective 1700. It consists of three columns with their pedestals, entablatures, and compass pediment, of the Corinthian order; the inter-columns are the Commandments done in black upon yellow; over the Commandments and under the arching pediment, is a Glory, with, unusually, the word JEHOVAH, in Hebrew characters; above the said pediment are the figures of two Celestial Beings in a reposing posture, holding in one hand a trumpet, and with the other, sustaining a Crown of Glory; denoting, that all those who keep inviolably those Divine Precepts contained in the Two Tables of the Decalogue, shall be rewarded with a Crown of Immortality and Glory. And on each side, are painted two pedestals, on which are placed as many pots, replenished with flowers. ' This would seem to have been a trompe l'oeil, fashionable in the early eighteenth century, which at one time stood in the chancel arch. The fixing marks on the second and third pair of pillars in the chancel may indicate that first it was fixed to the third, and then to the second pair of pillars, in order to accommodate the box pews. Apart from the remains of the fixings, there is no sign of this 'screen'.

Hawes & Loder continue (on p. 295) that 'at the west end, within the Nave and the Chancel, on the partition between that and the church, are the Arms of King Charles II, painted in their proper colours'. 'And opposite thereto, the Altar-piece, which is only the Institution, between the Lord's Prayer and Creed, depicted in black letters on a sanguine colour, adorned with compartments of fruit and cherubims, with separate frames; the work is painted in imitation of wainscot thirteen feet high, above which is a cornice of the Corinthian Order; the whole is placed under a very noble and spacious six light window. The Communion Table is positioned on an Arabathrum of white pavement, advanced three steps above the area of the choir, and encompassed with rails painted of a light colour. All erected (as well the iniquity of the times would bear) in the year of our Lord 1700.'

These descriptions do not refer to any extant screens, but in the footnote [on p. 297) Mr. Hawes continues, 'the pillars of the Church are painted of a stone-colour. A new pulpit wainscot was made, in uniformity with the seats; and the Arms and Ornaments of the old one taken away'. He then refers to the first screen with its glory as 'the piece of Architecture with its ornaments over the entrance into the Chancel, [which] is taken away. On the sides of the Altar, the Ten Commandments are depicted in gilt letters upon a purple ground, framed and adorned with compartments of flowers and cherubims; in the centre of which is a glory with the letters IHS; all handsomely embellished. ' This last note throws light on the substitution of the glory as we know it today for the trompe l'oeil glory which at one time stood in the chancel arch. The painted wainscot was covered by genuine wainscoting of fine oak panelling keeping to the thirteen foot height of the painted altar-piece and finished with two pairs of decorated Ionic columns. Strangely, the new East window of 1743 which replaced an earlier one, extends below the top of the glory and the Ten Commandments, now without any floral embellishments. It seems this glory was soon covered by a curtain embroidered with a cross. It may be supposed that all three glories were abstract paintings devised to lead the thoughts of the viewers to contemplate the wonders of heaven and eternity. They are rare, one other is known in Babington Church, Somerset and a simpler one worked in velvet in 1753 , hangs on a pulpit in Shobdon Church, Herefordshire.

The Church underwent further change in 1700 when the Rev. Marcus Anthony was Rector; lengthy sermons and box pews being in fashion, scant consideration was paid to the sixteenth century pews with their carved ends. These were cut and used to support the new box pews, and a three-decker pulpit was fitted into the twelfth century pillars on the south side of the chancel arch.

Music, again, became an integral part of church worship. In 1701 Pembroke College gave to St. Michael's Church the organ that had been built for them in 1674 by Thomas Thamar. This was erected in 1708 on its 22' gallery at the west end of the church, behind the font. It has one of only eight known pre-Cromwellian church organ screens, and has the distinction of having some original sixteenth century painted pipes. The screen possibly of the sixteenth or seventeenth century may have been designed in part by Sir Christopher Wren, or part may have been 'found in the Church, and incorporated into the organ'.
(See J. Blatchly, Proceedings of the Suffolk Institute of Archaeology & History, Vol. xxxvii, Part 1, 1989.)

In the early eighteenth century, church bellringing had become popular, with the need to have an octave of bells. John Stephens added two treble bells to the earlier ring of five, and recast the tenor bell and No. 3 in 1720. Framlingham became the second or third in the county to have a ring of eight bells; Horham was the first in 1672 or 1673, and Bungay and Framlingham followed suit in 1718. This ring of bells all swing east and west.

The Thamar Organ

The church was again receiving gifts and memorials in the eighteenth century and the Rector, the Rev. James Brookes, set up the large six-light window over the high Altar in 1743. Over the south door in the chancel is the Roubiliac memorial, in the late Baroque/Rococo style, to Jane Kerridge, widow of Thomas Kerridge, and heir to Richard Porter, and put up by Richard Porter's friend and beneficiary, William Folkes. It is noteworthy that one of the leading sculptors of the day was employed, for Louis François Roubiliac, a Huguenot, was the sculptor of the statue of Handel in Vauxhall Gardens. In the mid eighteenth century gifts of outstanding artistic beauty were made by wealthy gentlemen. The fine brass chandelier for twenty lights which now hangs in the chancel bears this inscription: 'This is the gift of John Coggeshall gent 1742 John Giles fecit' Mr. Coggeshall also gave a silver flagon in the same year.

Viewed from top to bottom: *Left:-* Earl of Surrey's tomb and Richmond's tomb.
Right:- Niche of the blessed Virgin Mary and part of the third Duke of Norfolk's tomb.

Roubiliac Memorial

In the eighteenth century the Framlingham parishioners felt it necessary to have a porch for their greater comfort when fulfilling their legal and other commitments. The battlemented porch was built on to the south wall of the nave c. 1780, covering the existing doorway and its weathered corbels.

The church was somewhat neglected from 1813 to 1837, for the Rector, John Norcross, was not content with the tithing system and was not resident in the parish, leaving the care of souls to his curates, first the Rev. Edward Davies and then to the Rev. William Greenlaw. During these years there was strengthening of non-conformity in Framlingham, led by the Rev. Samuel Say Toms from the chapel in Bridge Street, which became Unitarian under his leadership, causing other non-conformist groups to form, which prospered. During George Attwood's rectorship, May 1837 to 1884, there was a growth of population in the town, and a concentration on music, for the Rev. George Attwood's father was the organist at St. Paul's Cathedral in London; but little was done for the fabric and furnishings of the church, apart from the installation of the Rev. George Attwood's gift of the window at the east end of the chancel, which in 1837 was put in place by Henry Clutton, a local stonemason, and of a clock in 1872 on the south face of the tower, given by a celebrated surgeon, Sir Henry Thompson, in memory of his father, the successful shopkeeper and Congregationalist, Henry Thompson.

CHURCH CLOCK

Responsibility for the structure of the church was undertaken by the new Rector and the P.C.C. in 1884 when the Rev. Edward Bickersteth, shortly to become the first Anglican bishop of Japan, found the church in much need of repair. In the following year a detailed survey and report, conducted by a London architect, Mr. E.S. Prior, was presented to the P.C.C. Major work was put in hand by 1888 when the Rev. James Pilkington was Rector. A temporary partition wall was erected in the chancel arch, and services were conducted in the chancel. During 1888 the belfry floor, the box pews and three-decker pulpit were removed, the organ was dismantled, and the walls were re-plastered without, however, the discovery and exposure of the fourteenth century Trinity which is painted on the south side of the north wall of the nave. The wood from the box pews was used to clad the north and south walls of the aisles, the stonework of the windows of the aisles was repaired and the windows were glazed with 'cathedral' glass fitted by Mr. Woolnough of Framlingham. (There was a Plumber and Master Glazier, E. Constantine Woolnough, listed in the 1851 census as aged 56, so unless his three sons were glaziers living away from home, he would have been too old to do this work in 1888.) The Coggeshall chandelier was rehung from the roof towards the east end of the nave.

By October 1889 the organ was erected between the first two pillars of the nave on the south side of the church, and 500 chairs were arranged for the congregation. The font was removed from the west end of the north aisle and placed in the centre aisle of the nave, near the arch to the tower, which was screened off as a vestry. The High Altar was placed in front of the temporary wall. Because of lack of funds, work on the chancel was halted until c. 1907, when a Cambridge architect, Mr. Morley, was called in to supervise. The roofs were releaded and made sound, and round the roof above the clerestory windows, about 1907, metal decorative bands with angels and words in gothic lettering were placed; these bands are a copy from a church in Paris. On the south side the message is 'Behold the tabernacle of God is with men and He will dwell with them and they shall be His people and God Himself shall wipe away all tears from their eyes and there shall be no more death' (Revelation 21, v. 3 - 4). On the north side, the lettering reads: 'Except the Lord build the house they labour in vain that build it + 0 pray for the peace of Jerusalem + They shall prosper that Love Thee + Peace be within thy walls + The Lord shall be thy everlasting light and thy God thy glory' + (Psalm 122: v. 6-7 Isaiah 60: v. 19).

A new oak roof was established in the main chancel; this roof and the chancel walls were decorated by Messrs. Leach & Son of Cambridge; the walls were stencilled with pomegranate/pineapple design taken from a green silk velvet exhibit of the late sixteenth century found in the Victoria & Albert Museum and copied by Auguste Pugin, (This exhibit has a silk border with the Medici insignia in the corners, and was probably earlier used as a pall for Pope Leo XI's coffin in 1605.) The main area of the chancel was stencilled in greens, and red was used as a canopy of honour around the carved wooden reredos of the Altar given by the Rector, the Rev. James Pilkington. The brick floor was removed and relaid with marble terrazzo apart from the choir stall area, and the aisles, where the floor was laid in eborite. Four windows of the south aisle were put in with a type of 'cathedral' glass. The organ was cleaned and removed to the first bay of the north aisle of the chancel, and choir stalls constructed from the old sixteenth century pews were set east-west, and balustrades were arranged around the tombs. A low wall with a pair of wrought iron gates separated the chancel from the nave. A hot water heating system and radiators were installed.

The whole church was finished and reopened on St. Michael's day, 29th September 1909; the sermon was preached by the Rev. H. C. O. Lanchester, Fellow and Dean of Pembroke College, Cambridge, later to become Rector from 1917-1947.

Between 1913 and 1954 twelve faculties were submitted for minor changes to the church. These included approval for a memorial window to the two Miss Edwards, sisters, at the east end of the north chancel aisle, and another for Mrs. G. M, Lanchester, the Rector's wife, in the west window of the north aisle wall.

In 1919 the Pilkington altar was removed, and replaced by an altar with riddle curtains. The carved Masonic Pilkington reredos was fixed to the west wall of the north chancel aisle. This area was surrounded by a screen and is now used as a vestry. In memory of Mrs. Greene Carley , a Lady-chapel with a curtained altar was established between the Richmond tomb and that of the fourth Duke of Norfolk, with fixed altar rails in line with the west of the Surrey tomb, effectively obstructing passage to the tombs.

Electric light was installed in the church in July 1928 at a cost of £87. 10s. 0d. by Mr. Charles Garrard. Chairs were replaced by benches in 1935, the gift of T.T. Buckmaster and others.

In 1948 a pulpit was installed by the north chancel arch by the Parishioners in memory of Canon H.C.O. Lanchester, probably designed by M. Cautley, it replaced a part of the old three decker pulpit.

In 1950 Canon Bulstrode and the P.C.C. invited a thorough survey and report to be made by a London architect, Mr. Alban Caroe, and plans were approved for major structural repairs. In 1951 approval was given for the repair of two buttresses of the church tower, and also in 1951 repairs were undertaken to the roof of the church. In 1959 the chancel three foot wall was removed, and a chancel step was constructed. Further plans were presented in 1966 for the replanning of the chancel in order to give prominence to the Glory and the High Altar, and access to the tombs. The Mills chest was brought from the Thomas Mills almshouses and placed against the south wall to the west of the church porch.

The organ was removed from the chancel and replaced on a shortened version of its gallery at the west end of the nave, in the tower arch. The choir stalls were also removed and placed to the east of the organ. The font was removed from its central position and re-sited east of the north door of the north aisle. The Glory was revealed behind the High Altar, and its eighteenth century table altar was discovered in the vestry and restored to its original position. The Lady-chapel altar was removed and rails were arranged around the High Altar as far as the second pillars, and across the chancel. A moveable Laudian altar with its large carpet was placed between the west arches of the chancel so that the priest could face the congregation at a nave altar, when westward facing communions were introduced in the wake of the liturgical movement. Space was achieved between the altars, and access given to the tombs. The William Allen small organ of 1797, acquired by St. Michael's in 1982, stands between the first of the western pillars on the south side of the chancel. A children's corner occupies the west end of the north aisle. In 1967 the medieval wall painting of the Trinity, on the south side of the northern pillars in the nave, was restored, In 1991 a lightweight and moveable lectern was made for the south side of the chancel step.

The bells, last overhauled in 1892, were restored and rehung in 1992, following a report by Mr. R.W.M. Clouston, when the ringing floor was replaced. The chiming hymn tune apparatus of c. 1800 which was weight driven and designed to be started by the clock, was put out of action.

In 1985 the altar rails had hassocks depicting the insignia of the Dukes of Norfolk made by Robin Gray, and kneelers in designs depicting the insignia or symbols of many of the clubs and organisations in the town were worked by members of the parish.

THE CHURCH BELLS

In 1553 the Church had five bells and a sanctus bell, three of which remain. In 1657 a sixth bell was bought, probably from John Bread II of Norwich. In 1718 the octave was completed.

<blockquote>

Bells 1 & 2.   John Stephens added two trebles and recast the tenor 1718
Bell 3.   John Stephens recast in 1720
Bells 4 & 5.   From the foundry of Richard Brasyer I or II, between 1423 and 1513.
Bell 6   An early bell by William Bread, cast in 1583
Bell 7.   Cast with John Bread in 1622
Bell 8.   Recast the tenor 1718 by John Stephens. Again recast, 1902, at the London Whitechapel Foundry.

</blockquote>

The bells were rehung in 1892 and had central holes drilled through the crowns of the seven older bells to permit the fitting of independent clapper staples. The bells all swing East - West and have inscriptions on them:

<blockquote>

Bell 1.   John Stephens of Norwich made mee 1718
Bell 2.   Prosperity to all my benifactors John Stephens *fecet* 1718
Bell 3.   John Stephens made mee 1720
Bell 4.   *Hac In Coelave Gabriel Nue Pange Suave*
Bell 5.   *Virginis Egregie vocor campna Marie*
Bell 6.   *Onnis sonus laudet dominum anno domini* 1583 RG
Bell 7.   *Anno domini* 1622 W I B
Bell 8.   *Vivat Rex Edwardus VII.* Recast 1902.
          Rev. J. Pilkington, (Rector), E.G. Clarke. M. Taylor. C.W.

</blockquote>

A chiming hymn tune machine of c.1800, has not been in use since the 1930s. It was designed to be started by the clock, and was weight driven when wound up, using a type of winch from the ringing chamber below. It consisted of a barrel 3 inches in diameter and 16 inches wide, with slots for pegs. To vary the tune, the pegs had to be re-slotted by hand.

ST. MICHAEL'S FRAMLINGHAM with ALL SAINTS, SAXTEAD

RECTORS

Henri de Vallibus	22nd March	1311
Adam de Stonore	24th December	1318
William de Newport	23rd May	1326
Richard de Burghstede	18th October	1328
Thomas de Brewonse	17th May	1354
William Mewryk	4th December	1361
John Dytton	19th February	1367
John de Harlysdon	23rd June	1374
Walter Amyas	4th August	1387
John Sylby	13th September	1387
Reginald Banham	27th February	1388
John Bury	24th April	1432
John Grimesby	11th January	1453
Edmund Albon	11th December	1476
Robert Oswestyr	5th September	1482
William Peller	7th October	1485
John Nettilton	September	1492
Reginald Calle	4th February	1501
William Hedge	5th August	1509
Thomas Seman	24th February	1536
Roland Cotney	14th April	1545
Richard Underwood	-	-
Richard Hoggart	27th February	1571
Nicholas Lock	-	-
Thomas Dove, Bishop of Peterborough 1601-1630	29th January	1584
Richard Golty, Suspended 1650-1660	16th September	1630
Henry Sampson, Nonconformist Minister	-	1650
Richard Golty, re-installed	-	1660
Nathanael Coga	18th November	1678
Marcus Anthony	18th April	1694
Francis Draper	15th March	1703
Philip Osbaldeston	26th May	1705
Christopher Selby	20th November	1728
James Jeffery	31st January	1734
James Brookes	11th April	1735
William Wyatt	4th July	1782
John Norcross	8th May	1813
George Attwood	1st May	1837
Edward Bickersteth, 1st Anglican Bishop in Japan	21st October	1884
James Pilkington	15th December	1885
Henry Lanchester	6th November	1917
Martin Bulstrode	18th March	1948
David Pitcher	27th May	1976
Richard Willcock	27th June	1992

EDUCATION & SCHOOLS

At least as early as the sixteenth century some education was provided for the children of Framlingham, for from Richard Green's *History, Topography & Antiquities of Framlingham* Page 187, we read that "in 1564 Simon Pulham built a new house on the site of the Guildhall and the School House [an adjoining tenement]" and in the footnote he hazards this was a 'Parochial or some other foundation school' (possibly connected with the guild of St. Mary) 'which was in existence as late as 1632', the year that Baldry was paid 4s.6d from the Churchwardens' Accounts 'for removing the old seates into the school-house'.

Perhaps Sir Robert Hitcham's school, that was held in the upper room of the Market House from about 1670 made the old school unnecessary, for we read that in 1692, the Rector, the Rev. Marcus Anthony, with the concurrence of the local inhabitants, gave orders for the unsightly building to be pulled down and for the present red-brick wall to be built along the southern boundary of the churchyard. Sir Robert Hitcham, through his Will, provided for 'a school for 20 or 30 or more poor children, inhabitants of the said town to be educated in reading, writing and casting accounts'. Under this Will the children were accommodated in the upper room of the Market House, which had no sanitary facilities. The residents from their distinguished properties that bordered the Market Place objected to boys using the outer walls of the building, but it was not until 1788, when permission, in answer to a request from the Rector, the Rev. Willim Wyatt and senior parishioners, had been given by Pembroke Hall for the Market House to be demolished, that a new school, with lavatories, was built adjacent to the Hitcham almshouses in New Road.

Following the first Regular Poor Law of 1601 a Town House, Nos. 19 and 21 Double Street, was built to provide accommodation for the infirm, and raw materials for work for the more able. As a result, a spinning school was started for girls and women to be taught the trade in a number of registered houses, and four pence a week was paid for each child. This school lasted until 1796.

In about 1705 a second free school was built on part of the late Thomas Mills' land at Brook Farm. This school for boys and girls was run until 1879, when following the 1870 Education Act, it was incorporated into the Hitcham elementary school in a new building on *White Horse* meadow, land between the Hitchams almshouses and College Road. In this school boys were taught on the ground floor and the girls and infants upstairs. (The old Hitcham School later became the Masonic Hall, and Thomas Mills school was used as a reading room for the people of Framlingham, before being sold early in the twentieth century to A.G. Potter for a bicycle workshop).

The East Suffolk Prize Scheme.

The **East Suffolk Prize Scheme** was founded in 1881 by A.J. Swinburne Esq., H.M.I. At that time elementary education was very backward, owing to many causes - the schools were maintained by voluntary subscriptions and a meagre grant from the Education Department; the schools were badly staffed, and the apparatus was very limited. Isolation prevented, in many cases, any advancement; teachers knew no other methods but their own; there was no meeting of teachers; no learning from one another; each went on ploughing his lonely furrow. Mr. Swinburne knew of the vast difference that existed between a good school and a bad school - how could he raise the one to the other? it was impossible to get all the schools or all the scholars together; but the teachers could meet and examine the work from all the schools. This must have been in H.M.I.'s mind when he issued his letter in December, 1880, saying it was proposed to start a scheme for the encouragement of plain sewing. The Duchess of Hamilton consented to become patroness, with the following Ladies as a committee: Miss Colbeck, Fressingfield Rectory; Miss Caroline Lacon, The Godrood, Ipswich; and Miss Raven, Leiston Rectory. The Scheme was heartily taken up, amongst those taking an interest in the

The East Suffolk Prize Scheme.

establishment being The Countess of Stradbroke, Lady Carolina Kerrison, Lady Blois, Mrs. Lomax and Mrs. Pelly. An examination was held in Needlework at 50 Schools and the work was exhibited at the first Meeting of the Scheme, on November 7th, 1881, at Saxmundham. The Countess of Stradbroke distributed the prizes, and a varied programme was carried out successfully. Mr. Hall, of Aldeburgh School, read a paper on English History; Mr. Lockwood, of Leiston, gave a model lesson on geography, which was followed by a paper on "good results of examinations, and how to get them," by Mr. Rix, of Somerleyton School, Miss Smeed, of Framlingham, gave a lesson on "Coal" to a class of Infants, and the Rev. B. W. Raven, read a paper prepared by Miss Bird, of Melton Schools, on the best methods of teaching Needlework. Thus the first meeting gave great encouragement for the future, teachers separated and wondered why such a meeting had not been held in the past. The year following, the annual meeting was again largely attended, when Professor D'Orsey gave a lecture on "Reading in Schools". This year the Needlework was judged free of charge by the London Institute for the Advancement of plain Needlework. The Scheme became known in other parts of the Country, and enquiries were made as to its management, &c., from Educationalists. Miss Jones, the Needlework Inspectress of the Education Department, in the following year judged the Needlework "because she considered the Scheme a good one." In her report, Miss Jones stated that "there is more method in the teaching, and the quality is much better." Thus H.M.I.'s statement "that what schools needed was to raise them, was to be brought together" was proved to be true very early in the life of the Scheme. Penmanship, Essay Writing, Recitations and Cookery were added to the Competitions. A Teachers' Library was now added to the Scheme, Sir Richard Wallace contributing £10 towards the initial expense. This Library has been and is now of great utility to the teachers; the books are sent to a depot, from whence they are circulated each month to the teachers, each school passing the books on to the next school. The teachers pay the small sum of 2/- per year, and for this they each receive 24 books. Mention must also be made here of Mr. Justinian Pelly, of Yoxford, Mr. Richard Proctor, Archbishop Benson, and Archbishop French, of Dublin, who presented to the Library a large number of books of standard authors. Mr. E.G. Warren, Framlingham School, became the Secretary to the Teachers' Library, and has continued to hold that position since the time it was started.

In 1884, the time of Meeting was changed from October to July, and Col. W. B. Long, of Hurts Hall, kindly granted the use of his grounds for picnics. The entries this year were considerably on the increase, and a very large amount of the work fell on Mrs. Swinburne, who has always taken such an active interest in the Scheme. Teachers know and appreciate the work which Mrs. Swinbourne has done, especially in the Needlework and Cookery sections. Mr. J. G. Fitch, Senior Inspector of the Eastern Division, attended the Annual Meeting and gave an address on " Reading as taught in the Schools."

In 1887, the Rev. F. Synge, Senior Inspector of the District, visited the Annual Meeting, and in his address spoke highly of the excellent work the Scheme was doing. Mr. Girling, President of the National Union of Teachers, addressed the meeting this year, principally upon the advantages of the Teachers' Circulating Library. It was in this year (1887), that one of the London papers in its leading article "lamented that the trade in fine Needlework was passing out of the hands of Englishwomen, and being absorbed by foreigners, and it was such a scheme as the East Suffolk Prize Scheme that was happily designed to rectify this mistake, by giving practical direction to the current demand for technical instruction by promoting healthy competition in Needlework of all kinds among children of all ages."

In 1888, Her Royal Highness the Princess Christian became a Patroness, being "pleased to give her name to the good work." The *Queen* newspaper said of the Scheme this year that "it was marked by much success," and Lord Carlingford said "the work has his Lordship's warmest sympathy."

In 1891, East Suffolk was honourably mentioned in *Circular 297* (Training of Pupil Teachers), issued by the Education Department, "in the establishment of a Prize Scheme for encouraging the efforts of Teachers, and the friends of Education." Sir Joshua Fitch wrote that the work of the Scheme " gives teachers a higher ideal of their work." The *School Guardian* the same year in its leading article said " The East Suffolk Sewing Scheme has been a very efficient agency in producing a spirit of wholesale emulation amongst the various schools in the district over which it extends."

1893 saw a further extension of the work of the Scheme, not only in Needlework and Cookery, but

The East Suffolk Prize Scheme.

in singing lessons by Teachers; the chief speaker at the Annual Meeting being Mr. Scott-Coward, Chief Inspector of Training Colleges. The Rev. J.F.A. Hervey, Chairman of the Technical Instruction Committee, also gave an address on Evening School work." Mr. W. Scott-Coward's address on "Knowledge comes, but wisdom lingers," will never be forgotten by those who heard it. No less than four of the leading London papers gave excellent reports of the meeting of 1893, a fact which speaks for itself.

At the meeting in 1894, the large amount of work sent in for exhibition, a publishers' exhibition and a larger attendance, made it imperative that arrangements should be made for larger premises for Exhibition in 1895. Accordingly, as the work of organization had increased considerably, a Committee of Teachers and Managers was appointed to assist Mr. and Mrs. Swinburne, who had borne the "burden and heat of the day" for 14 years. They saw that their "infant" had grown up a credit to themselves, and dearly loved by all, so they welcomed this voluntary assistance. The Scheme was divided into two parts, Mrs. Swinburne being Secretary of Part I. (Needlework and Cookery), and Mr. Pleasants, Metfield School, Secretary of Part II (Writing. Drawing, Singing), and Mr. T. H. Bryant, Laxfield, as General Secretary. In consequence the 1895 Exhibition was held in the Saxmundham Schoolroom, and the Singing &c. competitions were held as usual in the Market Hall. Letters were read at the Meeting from the Duke of Devonshire, Sir George Kekewich, Bishop Hills, the Archdeacon of Suffolk, and Rev. Cannon Lawrence, all speaking from their own knowledge of the valuable work which the Scheme was doing. *The Queen*, the lady's newspaper of November 9th, 1895, said "It is a great gratification to the promoters of this good work to know that the educational value of the Scheme has been fully recognized by the Education Department at Whitehall. A most unusual but deeply gratifying episode was that of the managers, masters and mistresses of the various schools insisting upon having the photograph of their Inspector (Mr. Swinburne) in the centre of the Certificate, and presenting him with a "First Class," in recognition of his 15 years arduous work at the Scheme."

In 1897, Sir George Kekewich, H.M. Secretary Education Department, came as a visitor, and heartily applauded the admirable work which was exhibited. Canon B. W. Raven, of Leiston, in his *Parish Magazine* July, 1897, said "It was decidedly the most interesting and successful Meeting that has hitherto been held." In 1898, the Exhibition was extended over two days, the Scheme being enlarged by Musical Drill, Military Drill, &c., competitions. Swimming was added this year, the competitions taking place at Lowestoft.

In 1899, Mr. W. B. Currey, H.M. Chief Inspector of Schools for the Eastern Division of England, delivered a valuable address upon Education. He said "It was most encouraging to find that so many people were willing to take the pains necessary for carrying on an organization of that kind. The purpose which struck him most was the opportunity given to persons interested in education for meeting one another, and learning from one another." Shields for singing and drill, having been given by kind friends, made the competitions keener, and the entries became so many that preliminary tests had to be taken. Mr. J. J. Steele, H.M. Sub-Inspector (who had helped the Scheme considerably since coming into the District), kindly acted as a preliminary judge. Mr. C. S. Hudson, the Drawing Inspector for the Eastern District, also assisted by revising the Drawing section and examining the hundreds of exhibits sent in. In 1900, Mr. Rider Haggard attended the Annual Meeting, and gave a splendid address on the "Book of Nature".
101 saw the 21st Anniversary. The Duke of Devonshire promised to attend the Annual Meeting, but was prevented from coming. The town of Saxmundham was decorated for the occasion. The Duke was represented by Sir George Kekewich, and the programme as arranged for the reception of the Duke was carried out in its entirety. Children with banners lined the route from Saxmundham Station to the School. There were present the Earl and Countess of Stradbroke, Mr. E. G. Pretyman, M.P. (Civil Lord of the Admiralty), Mr. F. S. Stevenson, M.P., and Sir Brampton Gurdon, M.P. The Leiston boys Church Lads' Brigade formed a guard of honour under the command of senior Lieutenant Garnett, Staff-Sergeant Cutt and the Chaplain (Canon Raven). The tent was crowded in every part with managers and teachers from all-parts of the County. Mr. Bryant, the General Secretary, in the names of managers, teachers, and friends of the Scheme, presented Mr. Swinburne with two volumes, one containing the signatures of 9,000 friends of Mr. Swinburne and the Scheme, while the other contained a series of photographs of schools and groups of managers, teachers and schoolchildren. Mr. Swinburne, who was evidently speaking under the influence of strong emotion, thanked them"

The East Suffolk Prize Scheme.

from the bottom of his heart. "Excellent speeches were afterwards given by Mr. Pretyman and Mr. F. S. Stevenson, and the 1901 Annual Meeting closed a day always to be remembered in the History of the Scheme. This year too, saw a larger number of entries in the Swimming competitions, due to the energy of Mr. F. J. Ratcliffe, Hon. Sec. of the Swimming section.

1902 saw a change in the Gen. Hon. Sec., Mr. Busby, Yoxford, taking the place of Mr. Bryant, Laxfield, who had worked with great energy during his years of office. The following also became assistant secretaries :- Mr. W. Smith, Henham; Mr. F. J. Ratcliffe, Lowestoft; Mr. Pleasants, Metfield; Mr. T. Rice, Earl Soham. Notwithstanding the great year of 1901, the Annual Meeting was a decided success, the Drawing section particularly showing great improvement. Mr. J. C. Colville (H.M.I. Surrey) gave an address, and said that "the work he had seen that day was creditable and instructive to any body of teachers in the world."

1903 saw the taking over of the Schools by the East Suffolk County Council, under the Education Act, 1902. The area of the Prize Scheme District being enlarged by all the Schools coming under one Education Authority, the Ipswich District was added to the Beccles District, and schools were invited to compete from the whole of the County of East Suffolk. Many of the subscribers to the Scheme now thought that the County Council should take over the Scheme, and carry on its useful work. Accordingly, application was made in June, 1904, to that body that they should take over the Scheme. In July, before the result was made known, came the Annual Meeting, when Mr. Swinburne gave his farewell address as President, the final words upon a movement which had engaged his unceasing attention and sympathy for 24 years, through many and varied vicissitudes. It was marked by characteristic geniality, a veneer of jocularity, which, one feared, cloaked a heavy heart on the severance of a life-long effort on behalf of education. The Rev. C. J. Steward Chairman of the Education Committee and Mr W. E. Watkins, Secretary, addressed the meeting. The Education Committee after several months consideration, decided in March 1905, not to take over the Scheme, and the Committee of the Scheme had thus two alternatives, to allow the Scheme to drop, or work it as before relying on the kindness of their former subscribers. Lord Stradbroke was invited to become President, and he replied by telegram, " Scheme has Lord Stradbroke's warmest support, and he accepts Presidentship unhesitatingly." Accordingly in July, 1905, the Exhibition was held at Ipswich, in the Higher Grade School. Old friends rallied round the flag and many new ones were found in the new District. The new President took an active interest in its work, and with the help of a strong Committee, Mr. Swinburne and the Sub-Inspectors, Mr. J. J. Steele and Mr. T. Hunt, all worked with untiring energy to secure the success of the Annual Exhibition. The Countess of Stradbroke distributed the prizes. Mr. A. Rankine, Chief Inspector, gave an address, and to give some idea of the way in which the organisation was supported, it is only necessary to mention that there was the largest attendance of school managers that has ever been experienced.

Since 1905, the Scheme has held its Annual Meetings at Ipswich, the entries have increased considerably, and greater interest, if possible is taken. The Scheme now possesses the following Shields:-

1. Boys' or Girls' School Singing Trophy.
2. Mixed School Singing Trophy.
3. "Pleasants" Boys' or Girls' School Musical Drill Trophy.
4. The "Adair" Mixed School Musical Drill Trophy.
5. The "Heywood" Military Drill Trophy.
6. The "Long" Cricket Trophy.
7. The "Lucas" Swimming Trophy.
8. The " Swinburne " Needlework Shield.
9. The "Lady Gooch" Swimming Trophy.
10. The "Tollemache" Shield for School Gardens.
11. The " Beauchamp" Shield for Life-Saving (Boys).
12. The "Crossley" Shield for Life-Saving (Girls).
13. The "Swinburne" Swimming Trophy for Girls.

Another Shield for next year's (1908) competitions, is offered by Mr. C. S. Hudson, Drawing Inspector, for excellence in Drawing and Manual Work.
The success of the Scheme through all these years may be summed up in the following advantages

The East Suffolk Prize Scheme.

which it possess: (1) Managers, Teachers, Parents and Scholars are brought together; (2) The children are stimulated to do their work well; (3) Teachers are helped to form a good standard of work; (4) Teachers are enabled to pick up many valuable hints which could not be gained in their isolated positions; (5) Children and Teachers are encouraged; (6) It improves the Children physically by encouraging drill, swimming, etc.; (7) Encourages and aids domestic training, e.g. needlework, cookery, etc. (8) Affords a splendid opportunity of comparison with a view to a good all round standard, and offers facilities to carry out the same; (9) Infuses new ideas by the visits of experts and others distinguished in education, e.g. Sir Joshua Fitch, Sir George Kekewich, Captain Scratchley, etc.; (10) The Scheme is a voluntary one; no School is compelled to compete in any or all of the competitions.

In the late eighteenth and nineteenth centuries private fee paying schools were to be found in Framlingham. Important among them was the school run by James Hill, who in 1798 bought the present 42 Double Street property and built, within the garden, a school-room for his 20 or 30 boarding and day pupils (See plan). William, his son, taught in the school and on the death of his father in 1829 became Headmaster. He was a member of the Unitarians and a man much respected for his integrity, morality and for his generosity to the poor of the town.

Another two such schools, one in Double Street, and the other in Church House, were run for boarding and day girls, the first by Miss Boult and later by Miss Goodacre, and the other by Miss Maria Marshall. Besides these three schools, five others are listed in White's Almanack of 1844, including one for local girls who were taught in the poor house within the castle. In 1864 the Albert Memorial College for Middle-class Boys was founded by Royal Charter, built on the hills to the south of the town within 15 acres of land belonging to the Hitcham Trust, and opened for the first 145 pupils in April 1845. (See Section 4.0).

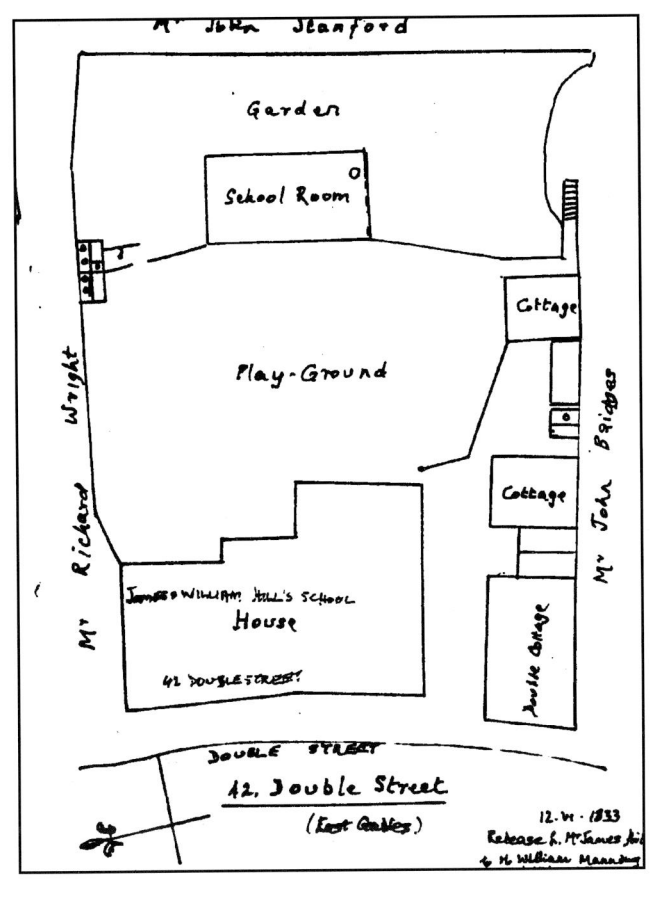

Plan of School Site 1833

Besides this school and the two in Double Street, only three others are listed in the 1874 White's Almanack. The Nesling-Webber school for girls opened in 1885 on the Market Hill and ran into the twentieth century, but there was no establishment for girls comparable to Framlingham College until 1902. For more than ten years there had been plans for such a school, to be funded from the Thomas Mills Trust, but the poor harvests from the Trust lands had prevented until 1902 the foundation of the Mills Girls Grammar School, on land between Fairfield Road and Fore Street.

From 1896 the Local Education Authority ran further education evening classes in mathematics, science, history, and also in woodcarving. Regular lectures were given to the farmers club on a variety of subjects, varying from farm management topics to world wide matters of interest.

The 1902 Education Act empowered the County Council to establish a local secondary school from the earlier elementary school, which had been forged from the two free schools set up from the gifts of Sir Robert Hitcham and Thomas Mills, two local donors. This secondary modern school was to be administered by the County Council, who invited one county councillor and one parish councillor to be on the controlling board, to replace the three parish councillors who had served on the old board. This produced an outcry from the people of Framlingham, who were exasperated by the removal of so much local responsibility for the education of its children. Many opposed the Act and its effects, six of whom became 'passive resisters' and had their goods disstrained by the Magistrates and were being repeatedly brought before them (See Section 5.0). In 1935 the Local Education Authority built the new Council Area Modern School on the north side of the road leading from Framlingham to Saxtead, and in 1937 the old elementary school known since 1902 as the Hitcham elementary school was rebuilt and run as a Church of England Junior School for pupils from Framlingham and neighbouring villages.

Framlingham College

The Old Hitcham School

In 1950 the Hitcham's Trustees and the school managers agreed to apply for voluntary aided status for the Junior school, which was granted. The £26,000 building project to remodel the school was approved, two classrooms were added in 1955 and two more in 1969. A casualty of the transaction was the name 'Sir Robert Hitcham's' primary school; this was remedied in 1979.

The 1944 Education Act offered secondary education to all and its effect was to raise the school leaving age from 14 to 15 years. The County Council proposed closing Mills Girls Grammar School and building a new secondary school in Saxmundham, but the householders rose as a body against this suggestion, and were supported by the local M.P. for Eye. The Mills Girls Grammar School, with its boarding house at Cransford Hall, became a grant aided school and admitted boys in 1975. The County supported the Modern Area School, the Mills School, the Church of England Hitcham's Junior school, known since 1979 as Hitcham's Primary school, which had two new classrooms added in 1969 and formed a Parent-Teachers Association in 1970, and increased the play area in 1972.

The Modern School was significantly extended in 1971 to accommodate pupils to the compulsory school leaving age of 16 and the East Suffolk County Council agreed that a comprehensive school would incorporate the Modern School with the Mills Girls Grammar School where numbers were increasing and being accommodated in new portable classrooms. This would be established in Framlingham with an increased acreage of land at the Modern school, and be called the Thomas Mills High School.

From the Chairman's report in 1974 to the Annual General Meeting of the Parish Council we learn that the Hitcham Primary school had 119 boys and 104 girls, the modern school had 350 pupils and that 41 of them had enjoyed a Schools Mediterranean Cruise, and that the Mills School had 340 pupils, including 20 boys who would join in September, a good foundation for the new Thomas Mills Comprehensive High School. From February 1975 the County's Northern Area Education Authority, based in Lowestoft, had control of the three schools in Framlingham, and it was expected that the comprehensive school would be fully operational within two years. The Headmaster of the Modern School, John Ives, resigned and was replaced by Michael Brown and in April 1977 a new upper school with sixth form facilities was put forward in the structure plan, which would cater not only for pupils from Framlingham but would include Sixth Form pupils from Debenham, Eye and Stradbroke. When the Mills Grammar School was closed its land was used as a residential and day care centre for the elderly. The comprehensive school was established as the Thomas Mills High School and included a sports hall for its own and the general use of the people of Framlingham.

FAIRS

In 1285 Roger Bigod claimed to have a warren in Framlingham and permission to hold a fair there at Michaelmas. In 1313 Thomas de Brotherton procured a licence for a second fair to be held in Framlingham upon the Monday, Tuesday and Wednesday in Whitsun week. The early fairs were probably held in the Churchyard. Later, in fair field at the southern entrance to the town and here were held most important local events creating much trade for inhabitants.

Nineteenth century whitsuntide fairs were celebrated by the erection of many stalls and sideshows that were arranged in narrow lanes on the Market Hill. There were the Samuels, Richardsons and Stans shows, as well as old Mrs. Bude's show and plenty of stalls. There were sparring booths and 'Poor old Harvey of Wilby used to arrive early and offer 'rides on horses', His cry was 'who'll ride, who'll toss, who'll ride a wooden hoss !' Fried sausages were produced by Will Hearn and Flemming of Badingham, with *ad lib* beer to wash them down, and all to the tunes played by the blind fiddler Gibbs who also sang songs and encouraged others to join in by selling song sheets at a penny a piece.

FARMING

Framlingham is composed of about 5,000 acre gross measure of which about 4,026 is deemed to be profitable land (R. Green's, *History of Framlingham* Page 7). In Saxon times, this was a well-wooded area with many fine oak trees much of which was emparked by the Bigods, who caused about 3 miles of wooden palings to encircle about 650 acres of land. The castle was sold in 1635 and disparked, when the land was cultivated in comparatively small holdings. Richard Golty, the Rector of Framlingham from 1630-1687, kept a tithe account book from which it is clear that dairy farming and cattle rearing were the main functions of the farms, supported by small fields of wheat, barley and flax. By comparison with cattle, horses were a rare commodity. Some farmers kept geese and a few sheep and most had pigs, hens and bees (honey not sugar was used for sweetening). Farming methods were traditional and remained so until the development of machinery in the nineteenth century. Until then many men and boys were employed to sow and to mow the corn and to scare the birds at seed and harvest time. The corn was mowed with a scythe, collected and stooked, and later threshed in the large barns in the threshing area of cross draughts from the opposing two doorways. Although beer was the national drink, it was brewed at home in comparatively small quantities from the harvest haysel (malt barley seed), until the early eighteenth century when, in company with so much else, specialisation demanded the development of maltings to brew the beer in bulk, the demand for barley increased.

Framlingham, the market town and centre of a farming area, developed five maltings, the first was established by John Welton and sold to his son Stephen in 1723, the second was developed by George Brooke Keer from 1788, and the third by James Maulden from 1803: the fourth and fifth from 1889 by E.G. Clarke, requiring ever increasing demand for barley. (See Maltings).
This development coincided with the soaring grain prices occasioned by the Napoleonic Wars. Many of the pastures on clay were ploughed up until about 80% of farmland was under the plough, crop

yields were low and farming methods primitive, wooden ploughs with metal shoes were used. After 1815 corn prices dropped dramatically and many fields lay fallow. The Corn Laws were introduced to steady the price of corn yet there were riots and much poverty. By the 1830s threshing machines were introduced which further engendered antagonism of the farm labourers towards the farmers. The development of machinery and drainage, care of the land and the selection of strains of corn increased the yields and also reduced the number of farm hands required.

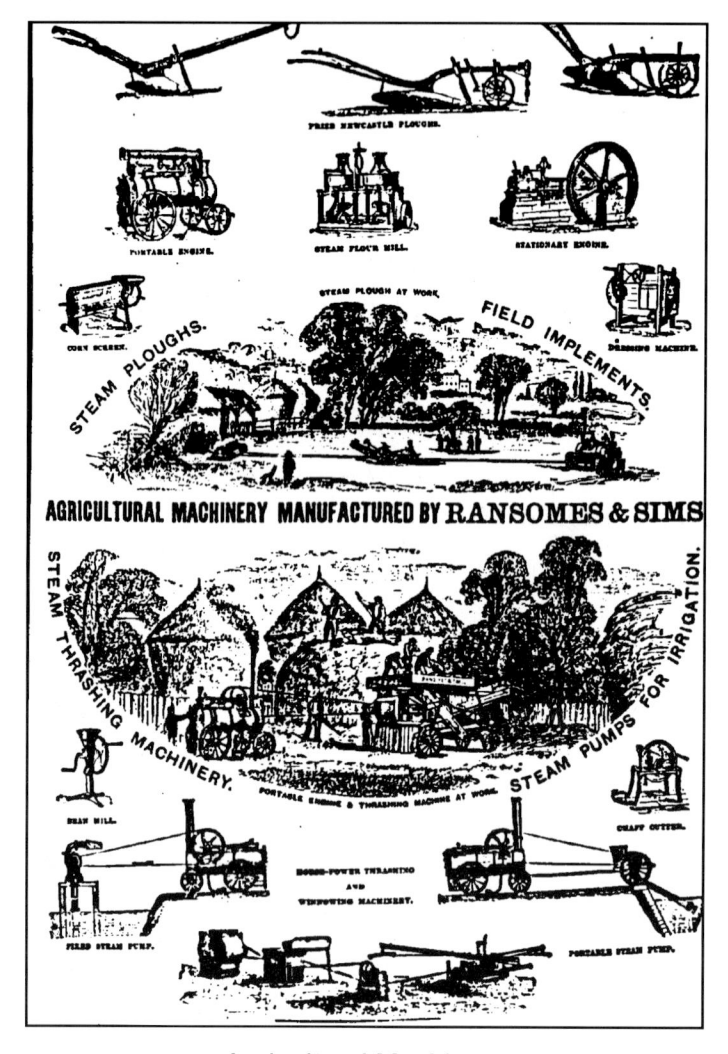

Agricultural Machinery

The demand for wheat for flour was growing. From 1847 Framlingham had its corn hall (See buildings) and its weekly corn market. From 1853 the local windmills were introducing steam to speed up their delivery of flour from the wheat, culminating in 1892 when the new Whitmore & Binyon processing plant was built in part of the Maulden maltings producing twenty sacks of flour each day (See mills). Farmers rose to the challenge and increased their supplies of wheat. This was done by developing more efficient ploughs. Ransomes made 86 different types of plough to suit differing conditions, and from 1843 the YL series of iron ploughs replaced the old wooden ploughs. From 1841 portable steam engines appeared on some farms, and in 1856 the single cable steam ploughing engine was available. From 1873 Ransomes made a straw burning apparatus, but the agricultural depression continued (see Section 4.1), until the first decade of the twentieth century, when steam threshing machines were employed, and from 1927 tractor mounted ploughs came into use. Also from the 1920's further attention was paid to improving drainage of the heavy clay fields; by piping and filling in ditches, uprooting hedges and increasing the size of the fields it was possible to use larger tractors, seed drills and notably sprayers. Combine harvesters were introduced in the mid 1950's and disc and reversible ploughs which were available in the mid 1960s all combined to produce increased yields.

The 1960's were of particular importance for pig farming in Suffolk. This had been a growing industry until 1939 when the pig population was 223,446 but there was a severe drop to 58,612 by 1944, and then steady growth so that by 1963 Suffolk had the largest pig population in any county in England and Wales, and 5.8% of the total production of the country. By 1968 the numbers were up again to 440,703. However, a disease caused pig production to falter in 1973 and arable farming again became predominant in the enlarged fields. This has been a gradual process over the past about eighty years, but one that has changed the look of the countryside from the tithe map of 1848 which showed the many small fields that have become the hundred plus acre fields that we see today. Framlingham today is the centre of arable farming, with only a few cattle and sheep, and with reduced, but highly efficient, pig production.

FIRE BRIGADE & APPLIANCES

Like Dennington, Framlingham was among the larger communities to have its own fire 'engine' manned by volunteers as early as 1703. Framlingham has preserved its first known fire engine; this appliance was designed to be pulled or pushed to the fire by four men; it was, in effect, a mobile pump. It was small, about 3' x 1'6" x 2' deep, with a 'chimney', built of wood with small solid wooden wheels with metal tyres (see drawing). Water from a pond or river was pumped by two men and sucked into the lower part of the machine through leather hoses, which were rivetted together, and projected towards the fire by another volunteer through the hoses from the top of the 'chimney'. This 1703 engine has been restored by Mr. David Grant, a fireman, who claims to have painted it in its original colour - a strange mauve. (This is the same colour that English Heritage has used for the bannisters in the Great Hall of the Castle). The engine is presently on view in the showcase of the 1974 Fire Station on the Saxmundham Road, Framlingham.

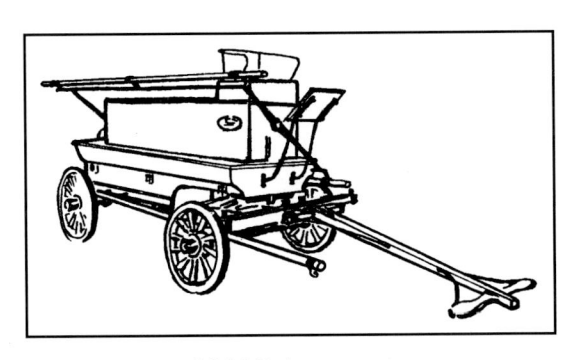

Four-man Manual Fire Ext. Bought by parish 1703, replaced 1844. Restored to original colour (Mauve/purple) by fireman David Grant, Ipswich.

1844 Bristows

The second fire engine, bought for Framlingham by public subscription in 1844 was built by Bristows of Whitechapel, a specialist firm of fire engine builders. It was designed to be horse-drawn by two horses and has room for 6 or 8 men aboard. It has a double action pump to be worked by three men on each side, and as before, water was drawn into its tank through leather and rivetted hoses to be fed from ponds and aimed at the fire, it has large spoked and metalled waggon wheels and was painted red. It is presently on show in the hall of Framlingham Castle Poor House. (See drawing).

Framlingham had a third fire engine, but its whereabouts are now unknown. From the Parish Council Minutes we learn that it was in use in the 1920s and before, that it could be horsedrawn or tractor drawn to fires, and that it was kept in Crown & Anchor Lane; and that, as before, it was manned by volunteers who only received money when they attended fires. It was one of the three that were handed over to the Parish Council by the Fire Brigade Committee, with a money balance of £45.1s.11d. in 1926, and it was one of the four that were paraded through the streets of Framlingham in December 1928. We learn from these Minutes that the third engine was loaned to Framlingham College in 1930 to augment their fire-fighting equipment, of four leather buckets to a corridor. No further records of this, the third fire engine, can be found.

When fire engines were horse-drawn there was much delay before the engine could be summoned to attend a fire. In the days before 1926, first the key to the Church must be found and the Church bells clanged by pulling all eight bell ropes in a particular order known as 'firing the bells'. The bells would be 'fired' differently for fires occurring in the town or in the country. This alerted the volunteers; then the horses must be caught (latterly they were kept in a field along the Dennington Road) and taken to Crown & Anchor Lane and harnessed to the engine, and only then could the fire-fighters attend the fire. Certainly a delay of at least half an hour! However from 1928 when Framlingham Parish Council bought for £145 a second hand motorised Dennis fire engine, complete with canvas hoses and ladders, matters were much improved. The 'Dennis' was a sophisticated piece of equipment, as may be seen from the drawing, and it served Framlingham well from 1928 until it was called upon to attend the blitz in London, from where it never returned. Additionally, by arrangement with Plomesgate Rural District Council, from 1931 the Framlingham Fire Brigade was to be called upon to extinguish fires in neighbouring villages at charges issued by the Essex & Suffolk Fire Brigade offices. In 1936 regular uniforms, including tin hats, were issued and standards were imposed for accredited drivers and for sirens and the hoses. The siren supplied was found to be 'unsatisfactory' and volunteers were alerted, as of old, by the 'firing' of the Church bells.

Following the Fire Brigade Act of 1938 operative from 1st January 1939, Framlingham's Brigade was governed by Blyth Rural District Council and under the Emergency Fire Brigade measures in rural districts it had responsibility for nineteen surrounding villages, covering 281 farms and a population of 8,107 persons. More equipment was provided to an enlarged force of men between the ages of 45 and 55.

From 1939 to 1942 the Fire Brigade was part of the Air Raid Precaution Service and known first as the Auxiliary Fire Service, and then from 1942, as the National Fire Service. It was given professional status with new uniforms and specialist training for its members, including First Aid training which was given free by the local St. John's Ambulance men.

In 1941 the Fire Brigade and the Auxiliary Fire Service were included in the Fire Service scheme, with a new 4-6 ton truck and pumps added to their equipment. Once the Dennis fire engine had gone to London, Framlingham was supplied with a Dennis hand-operated fire pump that was drawn at first by Mr. Hatcher's tractor and later by Mr. A.G. Potter's one-ton Ford truck, which was able to reach the fire more expeditiously, while the firemen were driven to the fire in his Bean motor car.

DENNIS D3 'BRAIDWOOD' BIG 4 PUMP-ESCAPE 1934

Fire hydrants were positioned around the town and an iron static water tank was erected outside the *Crown Hotel* on the Market Hill, along with an air raid shelter, and from 1943 an additional brick water tank was built.

In 1948 the fire services were returned from the National Fire Service to Local Authorities and the Framlingham Fire Brigade operated under the Suffolk and Ipswich Fire Authority, later to be transferred to the East Suffolk County Council. In 1964 Framlingham removed its Commer engine from Crown & Anchor Lane to a wartime building that had been connected with Parham Airfield in the Badingham Road (now the Guide & Scout HQ), and this was opened by Mr. John Self, chairman of the Town Council.

The Surridge sculpture: 'Fire dragon attacking castle badge'.

From January 1971 the East Suffolk County Council, encouraged by Mr. W. Allen, the Superintendent, proposed that there should be a new fire station at a cost of £27,000, which the town council thought was unnecessary and extravagant, and that the Badingham Road Fire Station was adequate; but in March 1971 plans for the new fire station to be built on the Saxmundham Road were approved by East Suffolk County Council, and on Monday 16th December 1974 Mr. K.L. Holland, H.M. Chief Inspector of Fire Services opened the building. Every operational and training facility, including a 40 ft. drill tower for ladder practice was in place, with a lecture room, a fire prevention office, and facilities for social functions. On the front of the building is a bronze sculpture of a fire-dragon attacking the castle badge, made by Mr. B. Surridge. Each of the 12 firemen carries a portable telephone and in answer to a call the fire engine, now a smart Volvo, is manned and on its way to the fire within three minutes. So different from the arrangements before 1928 already described.

INNS

Framlingham, the centre of an agricultural district, has always had a number of Inns. They were the natural gathering places for farmers and agricultural workers, who followed their strenuous occupation for long hours, engendering a tremendous thirst. This often could not be quenched with water (as it was polluted), while tea and coffee were beyond the means of all but the wealthy. Ale and beer were the staple drinks for the masses. Home brewing was common practice, for 18 gallons of beer at a cost of approximately 1/2d. per pint could be made from one bushel of malt and 1 lb. of hops; but for many the public house was the place not only for a drink and for doing business and striking bargains, but for gathering and exchanging ideas.

Railway Inn

Within the Borough, Framlingham has supported inns of three categories.

Those with accommodation and stabling, licensed premises and beerhouses. In the first category we may place the fifteenth century *Crown* and *Griffin*, on the Market Hill, the *King's Head*, later re-named the *Black Swan*, which gave its name to Swan Street, and probably the *Blue Boar*, later named the *Queen's Head*.' *The White Horse*, without the Borough, also comes into this list. The second category covered licensed premises, and may have included the *Bull* and the *Dove*, later the *Hare & Hounds* in Double Street, the *White Lyon* on the Market Hill and the *Black Horse* at the upper end of Bridge Street. The third category probably included the *Duck & Mallard* and the inns which were established later, such as the *Marlborough Head*, the second *Griffin* on the Market Hill, and the *Farriers Arms* in Double Street, along with several other beerhouses established more recently without the Borough. These include the *Mill House* on the Saxmundham Road, the *Castle Inn*, Fairfield Road by the Kettleburgh Road Gate crossing, later disused and the name transferred to the inn by the town pond, the *Railway Inn* established about 1863, opposite the Mills Almshouses, the short-lived *King's Arms* Beerhouse in Well Close Square (see Chap. 1832-63) and the *Cherry Tree* at the top of Brook Lane. *The Station Inn*, built about 1860 was a residential commercial inn with stabling for 16 horses.

The White Horse Inn

The Queen's Head

It may be that between 1660 and 1760 several substantial citizens set aside part of their dwelling houses for public drinking, as was the custom elsewhere. There was an overtone of disapproval of licensed houses during the period of Puritan domination. Ale houses on licensed property were visited by government 'conners'. These were men wearing leather breeches, and carrying a small oak board, who entered the premises and ordered a pint. A little of the liquid was poured on to the board, which was placed on a stool and sat upon. After some time, the conner stood up; if the board stuck to his breeches the ale was pronounced good; if the board fell away, it was 'small beer'!

Public Houses

Crown	Cherry Tree
Bull	Duck & Mallard
Dove (Hare & Hounds)	Marlborough Head
Black Horse	Castle
King's Head (Black Swan)	Wagon & Horses
Queen's Head (Blue Boar)	Shoulder of Mutton
White Hart (Crown & Anchor)	Mill Inn
Farriers Arms	Railway Inn
White Horse	Station Inn

MALTINGS

Framlingham has had five maltings on different sites and at different times. The first was owned by Peter Parham, Gent., Charles Clarke, Mercer, and Alpe Ward, Apothecary, and worked by John Welton who owned the *Black Swan* and *White Horse* Inns. It occupied the triangular island site of 3 roods, bounded by the River Ore, Millbridge Road and Well Close Square, with a kiln and a malting house, offices, outhouses, a barn, stables, buildings and gardens. It was bought in 1723 by John Welton's son, Stephen, who also became the owner of the two inns. In turn, these properties were left in 1777 to Lydia, his widow who, in February 1788, sold them to George Brooke Keer for £1,000. In 1820 the *Black Swan* was mortgaged to Mr. Charles Clubbe for £525, and the Welton maltings site was leased by George Brooke Keer Snr. to his son, George Brooke Keer, and his partner, William Barthrop, for 15 years. Now free of this responsibility, George Brook Keer Snr. bought three cottage properties and set up his maltings site in the centre of the Borough. He developed this area, bounded by White Hart Lane, Back Street, part of Bow Street and Church Street, into a well planned maltings and brewery with two kilns, a tunn house, brew house, spirits rooms, a coopers' shop, stables, gardens etc. (see plan). From this complex he supplied his evergrowing empire of inns and public houses in and around Framlingham, numbering 21 by 1832. He was probably the largest employer of labour in the Borough, having at least 10 men on the site. He also built himself a fine Georgian mansion on Bridge Street, with a 46 ft, long vinery and a heated greenhouse in the extensive garden, on land stretching from Church Lane to the Unitarian Chapel; and he built the Manor House for his son, in Church Street, with a tennis court in the garden abutting the maltings. (See drawing).

George Brooke Keer had built up his business by borrowing heavily, and in 1832 he was confronted with heavy customs and excise taxes on malt, which he could not meet. Alas, the crash came when George Brooke Keer was declared a bankrupt and his empire was put under the hammer and sold in 31 lots by William Butcher, Auctioneer of Norwich on 21st June 1832 before a great company of people assembled on the Bowling Green by the Castle. The sale realised about £21,000 and George Brooke Keer was spared a prison sentence, (See details of the sale). The third site was a small maltings on Station Road bought in 1879 and owned by Edwin Clarke, who also developed George Edward's malting on the corner of Castle Street and the Badingham Road and used part of George Brooke Keer's old malting, becoming by the 1920s the largest supplier of malting barley in the country.

Check-House

The fifth site, that known as the Maulden maltings, was established in 1801 on the N.E. side of the River Ore in Bridge Street. It had one kiln, a steep, a mill house, storage barns and sheds, and was run with various owners and maltsters until 1879 when James Maulden, who was both a maltster and a miller, bought the property for £600. (See plan). This was a time of development and expansion. There was a growing demand for flour as well as for animal feed, and by 1885 James Maulden had installed a steam rolling mill for flour, bran, pollards and meals. He also distributed corn, coal, coke. and cake. By 1888, additionally, he dealt in tea and in Wills tobacco and cigars. In 1891 he advertised that he had installed a complete roller flour plant ... capable of producing 20 sacks of flour per day. By 1893 he had invested in one of the new Whitmore & Binyon steam roller flour plants for the greater control and improved standard of flour. This thriving business, with its additional buildings became the largest employer of labour for nearly 60 years until 1946 when production stopped. In 1955 the property was sold to Col. E.G. Clarke for storage only.

MILLS

It is not known precisely where the earliest of the two mills stood, but it is known from the Manorial Accounts that one of them was a six-sailed mill. Remains of the oldest known extant mill, a smock mill, now known as the Round House, has been converted into a dwelling. It stands to the S.W. of Station Road, near to the new Victoria Mill Road. This must have been known as a good area for mills, as a post mill, No. 284630, owned by Andrew and Mary Bedingfield, was sold to Edmund Cocking, baker of Framlingham, in 1714; this mill passed through several hands until it was sold in 1825 to Mr. Jasper Peirson for £500 and occupied and worked by Edmund Kindred, and later his son John, who on 19th September 1842, with Mr. William Collins, Millwright, and Mr. Newson, a workman, attempted to raise it on screwjacks to extend the round house for further mechanism. Tragically it was blown over and wrecked. Mercifully, the three men survived. John Kindred, before falling into severe financial straits in 1853, bought the site for £400 and built a brick tower mill, known as the Victoria Mill.

Roller Flour Mills (1893)

Smock Mill

In 1853 John Peirson erected the first steam mill in Framlingham for Edmund Kindred Jnr. on part of the old Welton Maltings in Well Close Square. It was built by Messrs. Mallows, with Mr. William Collins and Mr. J. Barton as the millwrights and engineers, using second-hand machinery from Ipswich. After Mr. John Peirson's death in December 1861, Mr. Crisp of Butley Abbey bought much of the machinery at an auction, while the building was purchased by the Framlingham Peoples' Hall Company, who had it converted into the Peoples' Hall. (See Non-Conformity).

Tower Mill   Post Mill

The Victoria Tower Mill, No. 284634, was bought in 1889 by Thomas Twidell Buckmaster for £610. Within this mill he installed steam which he ran himself, and which was later run by his son John. Subsequently he bought some adjacent land upon which the Railway Terrace Cottages were built, as well as a house for himself.

There were three other mill sites in 'greater Framlingham'. One was on the Saxmundham Road, on the corner of the old road to Peasenhall, where the mill was worked by Mr. John Smith. The second mill site was in Station Road, 1896-1910, and is now probably used as a store. The third site was at Mount Pleasant, where there were two mills owned and worked by Mr. Philip Aldrich. These were sold by auction in 1837 for £890 to Mr. Woods and finally a Parish Councillor and the author of Weather Notes, a Mr. Whitehead, ran the mills until about 1900. The post mill had come from Apsey Green, and stood on a round house. On this second site stood a brick tower mill, which was burnt down in 1837 as a result of a mishap with Mr. Aldrich's son's lighted pipe; The son was smoking in the mill, and when ordered by his father to return to the house, in his haste to obey, the boy hid his lighted pipe in a desk which smouldered and caught fire. This mill was replaced by a second post mill bought at Woodbridge, and moved intact to Mount Pleasant. It was later sold to Mr. Sutton of Tannington, then owned by Mr. Ostler, until it was blown down and destroyed. The mills were corn mills, used for grinding flour and animal feeds.

NON-CONFORMITY

At least as early as 1630 Non-conformity was practised clandestinely, in Lincoln's Barn, on the south-western outskirts of the parish, where Thomas Mills, among others, was a Baptist preacher to a growing congregation. During Charles I's reign in the 1630s and 1640s Framlingham was affected by the groundswell of Dissenting activity that was later further increased by the Earl of Manchester's setting up of the Ecclesiastical Province of East Anglia, with fourteen precincts. The loyalist Laudian Rector, Richard Golty, was losing support; for example, in 1636 Nicholas Danforth, an influential inhabitant and one time Churchwarden, left Framlingham with his children aboard the 'Griffon', a ship carrying Puritans to New England, where he became a Selectman. In 1650 Richard Golty, refusing to sign the oath to the Commonwealth, was sequestrated. Framlingham was without an Anglican pastor at a time when Non-conformity under the Protectorate was becoming intolerant, requiring the acceptance of dogma, morals and discipline, in turn shifting opinion towards the Independents and causing a blurring of the several sects of Non-conformity. It was at this time that Pembroke Hall, Cambridge, a dissenting College since 1644, now having the gift of the living of St. Michael's, appointed Henry Sampson, though not ordained, to take charge of the parish. He was a most able young non-conformist don who inspired his congregations with his teaching and preaching. We learn from the Woodbridge Quay Congregational Church Book of 1651 that he 'laid the foundation of the Congregational or Independent Church in Horn Hill at Framlingham', and we know that from 1654 he was commissioner for one of the fourteen precincts of the Ecclesiastical Province.

"Henry Sampson laid the foundation stone..."

Non-conformity grew in Framlingham during his administrations, coupled with those of his brother-in-law, Jonathan Grew, also a graduate of Pembroke Hall. Many of the successful businessmen and artisans of the district joined this congregation, and continued to worship in the little Chapel and in licensed private houses, when Richard Golty was restored as Rector in 1660. Henry Sampson then 'not being satisfied to conform' was removed from office, though he remained in Framlingham as a teacher and preacher until 1662 when he left the country to train as a medical doctor.

The Declaration of Indulgence of 1672 resulted in 1,609 licences being granted to non-conformist ministers, among them Austin Plumstead, who was licensed to be an Independent Teacher in the house of Ann Fenn in Framlingham. Additionally, the houses of Jonathan Fenn and Charles Churchyard were licensed as places of worship. It would seem that the Chapel on Horn Hill was served by Presbyterian/Congregational Ministers, among them the Rev. Samuel Baxter, M.A., during the 1690s. He was followed by the Rev.

Unitarian Church

George Smith until 1701 and Rev. Sidrach Simpson until 1705. When the well-known and influential Baptist preacher Thomas Mills died, he willed that he should be buried in linen, in front of his Garden House in a tomb. This request was carried out by his friend, executor, and chief beneficiary of his will, William Mayhew. Thomas Mills made a number of bequests, the most important being to provide six two-storey Almshouses for men and women. To this bequest William Mayhew added a further two, and supervised the building of the eight almshouses on Feak's pightle, across the road from Thomas Mills' Brook Farm and Garden House.

In 1703 Samuel Lodge, M.A. (Glasgow) 'a gentleman of figure and fortune and a considerable preacher', started his seventeen years' service as Presbyterian/Congregational Minister in Framlingham. (He was ordained on 20th April 1772, shortly before his death, but he never administered the Lord's Supper). He instituted the *Brief Book* in 1707, which was maintained until 1818. During this long incumbency the life of the borough was vibrant. Non-conformity was a motivating power with plans to build a larger chapel for Baptists and Presbyterians. This was made possible by the death of William Mayhew, who left money in his Will of 1713 for this purpose. From the Church Book of Dissenters of the year 1716 we read that Woodbridge Quay Congregational Church gave £8 towards this distinguished building in Bridge Street, which was completed in 1717. Samuel Lodge was assisted by two deacons, John Keer (a grocer) and William Hill, a Schoolmaster, and supported by Joseph Bird (a baker), Joseph Revans (a land owner), John Blomfield (a weaver), John Taylor, William Freeman, Thomas Bucke (who owned property including a maltings), Edward Keer, a land owner, and Thomas Keeble who owned part of Saxtead Woods, who were all leading members of the non-conformist community.

Framlingham dissenters, in company with dissenters elsewhere, were showing tolerance to local Quakers and combining with the worship of Baptists, Congregationalists and Independents.

Richard Chorley, a widower, succeeded the Rev. Samuel Baxter in 1723, and married his widow, Anne. During his ministry the Meeting House Trust was formed, and in February 1731, Mrs. Martha Smith bequeathed her property in Castle Street to the Trustees with a legacy 'for preaching of the Gospel as long as liberty shall be allowed to Dissenters to meet and preach'. Mr. Chorley's term of service in the Chapel ended when he became blind, and 'out of step' with his congregation, when he joined the Church of St. Michael. On 30th December 1757, the 'Clarke's' cottage (now No. 19 Bridge Street), next to the Meeting House, was bought by the Trustees for the Minister's residence. Eight ministers served for short periods (see list), until 1773, when Samuel Say Toms was appointed to care for the congregation of some 253 persons. Ordained in 1774, he served until his resignation and death in 1829. In 1783 the congregation founded its Benevolent Society, and in 1792 a burial ground for its parishioners was opened at the back of this Meeting House.

Congregational Church

The East Anglian Unitarian Society's institution in 1812 was attended by the Rev. Samuel Say Toms and Mr. Samuel Keer from Framlingham; in 1813, at Norwich, the Rev. S.S. Toms was elected President of this Society. This caused a split in his congregation, although he carried many with him and remained in charge of the building, which became the Unitarian Meeting House. Those of the Congregational persuasion were most critical of the Rev. Samuel Say Toms who had 'obtained, from one of the Trustees, the

Deeds of the Chapel, and had continued to hold possession of the pulpit, thus adding one to the multitude of instances of wilful perversion of property, charitably intended for dissent purposes' [*Suffolk Congregationalism* T.J. Hosken; p.302]. In spite of this rift, Framlingham honoured the Rev. Samuel Say Toms on 22nd August 1823, the 50th anniversary of his ministry, with a dinner at the *Crown* and gifts of a silver teapot, cream jug and basin, with the following inscription: (From Green's 'History of Framlingham', P.237).

> From the Congregation of
> Unitarian Christians and Friends
> at Framlingham, Suffolk.
> To The Reverend Samuel Say Toms
> 22nd August *Anno Domini* 1823

This piece of Plate is presented by them ... in testimony of their high estimation of his enlightened liberality of principle. The Church bells were rung, and Framlingham was *en fête* for the occasion.

The Wesleyan movement had been growing from c. 1739, with John and Charles Wesley and George Whitefield holding their open-air meetings and bringing the Christian faith to the poor; by 1744 regular circuits for preachers were established. The movement reached Framlingham after 1784 by which time the Wesleys had broken from the Anglican Church, and in 1794 a small society of Wesleyan Methodists established themselves by preaching in licensed houses. A chapel, erected opposite the Thomas Mills Almshouses, was opened for worship on 25th November 1808. The number of Wesleyans grew, and a gallery to accommodate them was built within the Chapel. Although Green reports 'there is no burial ground', when the Chapel was pulled down, to make way for the site to be used for the *Railway Inn* and its bowling alley, graves were found in what was to become the inn yard. (A list of preachers from c. 1808 to 1833 is attached). The last sermon heard in this Chapel was preached by the Rev. J. Renshaw on Sunday 15th March 1868 [Green p. 238 & 239) after which date the congregation removed to the People's Hall in Well Close Square. This neat pseudo-Gothic red brick building of 1867 was once Framlingham's first steam flour-mill, built in 1853 by John Peirson for John Kindred. Bought and adapted at a cost of £1,200 by the Framlingham Peoples' Hall Company, a limited liability company made up principally of Framlingham Old Wesleyan Chapel worshippers, it was converted into the Peoples' Hall. In 1874 Robert Lambert reports 'Here the Independent Wesleyans worship on Sundays, and the Hall is let on certain other days for moral, literacy, scientific, social or political purposes'. It is now known as the United Free Church.

In 1817, Samuel Dale, a member of Rendham Independent Church, started a local prayer meeting, and some of the congregation formed a missionary society of Independents and Congregationalists, served by visiting preachers and using a small cottage beyond Hermitage Place. John Fruer was elected Secretary and Henry Thompson Treasurer.

John Fruer converted and gave a cottage of his own as a place of public worship for 300 persons. This was opened on 4th May 1819, The growing congregation raised at first £15 per annum for securing preachers on Sundays from the Suffolk Itinerant Society. This sum was doubled in 1819 and Mr. Muscott, a regular preacher, was present when on 7th December 1820, a Church was formed with eight members united into Church fellowship. They were Samuel Dale (from the Rendham Church), John Fruer, Samuel Dale jun., Henry Thompson, John Fruer Jun. (from the Woodbridge Church), Francis Runnacles, Francis Bush and May Taylor. In April 1821 John Fruer enlarged the building to accommodate a further 40 hearers and 60 children, and a Sunday School was founded with 15 children and three teachers.

In September 1822 the Rev. Thomas Quinton Stow was invited to the pastorate and during this time a piece of land was purchased for a new church; on 6th April 1823 Rev. Thomas Stow laid the foundation for the building in Fore Street, which was completed by John Fruer and opened for worship on 6th August 1823. Thomas Stow resigned in 1825, the first duly recognised agent to Australia to the Colonial Missionary Society, formed in 1836. The congregational Church, known as the 'New Meeting' by the older local inhabitants, celebrated its golden Jubilee on 24th September 1873, with the Rev. C.E. Gordon-Smith as its Pastor. This Church was then served by several Ministers (see list in Appendix), until 1959. From 1962 to 1968, the Rev. A.S. Fincham, who was the County Minister and Secretary of the Suffolk Congregational Union, preached in the Church. The Congregationalists then merged with the Presbyterians, and from 1972 the Church became the United Reformed Church.

United Reformed Church

THE SALVATION ARMY

Evidence of the Salvation Army in Framlingham is scrappy, but a 'Barracks was established at No. 17 Double Street in March 1892 and enlarged possibly in 1896'. It was closed some time between May 1900 and November 1905 but re-opened in May 1913, and closed between 1916 and July 1921.

THE PLYMOUTH BRETHREN

The Plymouth Brethren first met in Framlingham in 1877 and from 1880 have used the wooden building at the back of Albert Place for their meetings.

THE CHRISTIAN SCIENCE SOCIETY

The Christian Science Society started in 1956 in Framlingham in a limited way, with an informal group of Christian Scientists. In 1964 a move was made to rent rooms in Bridge Street with a display window, and in April 1971 the group was recognised by the Mother Church as the Christian Science Society, Framlingham. In 1973 the Society was sufficiently well established, and bought the freehold of a studio in Fore Street which was adapted to form the present Church, first used on 26th October 1975; and added the harness maker's shop, 21B Fore Street, to be used as a reading room with display windows.

MINISTERS OF THE CONGREGATIONAL (Since 1972 UNITED REFORMED) CHURCH

Thomas Rutton Morris	Jun. 1821-1822
Thomas Quinton Stow	1822-1825
James Goodeve Miall	c.1826-Apr. 1832
Henry Hollis	1834-Nov. 1842
Samuel Alexander Browning	1843-1870
C.E. Gordon Smith	1871-1875
Henry Goddard	1876-1877
Rowland Mark	1878-1887
Edward Keen	Jan. 1888-Jul. 1896
Henry Alfred Todd	Dec. 1897-1904 as Evangelist
	1904-1911 as Minister
Enoch Thomas	Oct. 1912-1913 A student pastor for a year; he declined to serve longer
Charles Waring	Dec. 1915-1918
William George Lambert	1919-1933 Evangelist: at Brandeston also from 1913
David Thomas Scotland	1934-1942 [Also Brandeston]
William Hugh Walker, B.D.	1942-1947 [Also Brandeston]
John Marshall Vick	1950-1953 Evangelist. [Also Rendham]
Rudolph Naish Davies	1956-1959
Algar Samuel Fincham	1962-1968 [Secretary, Suffolk Congregational Union, and 'County Minister
Arthur Edward Simmons	1982- [Part time, with Saxmundham]

MINISTERS OF THE "OLD MEETING"

Presbyterian/Congregational:

Samuel Baxter	-1698
George Smith	to 1701
Sidrach Simpson	1701-1705
Samuel Lodge, M.A., Glasgow	1705-d. 20th Apr.1722 [Buried in parish church]
Richard Chorley	1723-c.1732
Thomas Cooke	ord.1735 d. July 1739
Matthew Jackson	1739
Samuel Wood, Jun.	1740-1756 [Ord. 13th July 1744]
Andrew Bennet	c. 1756
Jeremiah Longfield	1756-c.1760
John Walker	Oct.1760-1767 [settled with church, 2nd April 1761]
William Stuck	c.1768-9
Henry Post Williams	c.1772

UNITARIAN MINISTERS from 1813:

Samuel Say Toms	Aug.1773-27 Aug. 1829
William Clack] assisted	1823-1828 } Clack & Bowles,
Henry Bowles] S.S. Toms	1828-1829} and at first, Esdaile, were
John Esdaile	May.1829-1836} co-pastors
Alfred Hardy	1837-1842
Charles Case Nutter	1842-1847
Michael Castle Gascoigne	1848-1853
Thomas Cooper	1854- d. 25th Oct. 1880
William Annetts Pope	1874-1879 Co-pastor
William Fielding	1882-1884
James Henry Cliffe	1885-1886
Henry Lee Baker	1886-1888
Alfred Amey	1889-1902
Richard Newell	1903-1910
Herbert Charles Hawkins	1910-1913 Lay pastor
William Henry Sands	1914-1925 Lay pastor until ordained 1925
Wright Broadbent	1925-1937 Lay pastor 1937-1959 Minister
Nicholas John Teape	1959-1974 [Minister at Ipswich]
Clifford Martin Reed	1976- [Minister at Ipswich]

ROMAN CATHOLICISM
(With acknowledgements to Commander O.Sitwell, R.N.)

Roman Catholicism was not openly practised in Framlingham from Tudor times until the 1939-1945 War, when some Masses were said in the old Corn Market in the *Crown* by a travelling Missioner. Following 1947 when the Hon Peter Rous and his family came to live at Bruisyard Hall, Father Gabriel Reidy. O.F.M., came weekly to say a Mass in Framlingham, in the *Crown & Anchor Inn*, by courtesy of the Landlord, until it was possible, in May 1952, to buy a plot of land at the bottom of Fore Street and to erect a temporary wooden building. The Church was dedicated to St. Clare and consecrated on 22nd July 1952, (the 400th anniversary of Queen Mary's Proclamation in 1552). Furnishings were provided and arrangements were made to collect Father Gabriel each week for a Service. In 1966 Father Gabriel died, and Masses were said by one of the Friars from East Bergholt.

Gradually improvements were made within the Church, including the gift of a harmonium. In about 1972 the Framlingham Council of Churches was formed, and the Anglican, Roman Catholic, Methodists and the Congregationalists, now the United Reformed Church, agreed to join together in a Procession of Witness on Good Friday, and for certain other combined Services, so forwarding the ecumenical movement.

In 1973 the Friary moved from East Bergholt to Canterbury. Without the Friars, the Church was served by Priests from Ipswich, Stowmarket and Woodbridge in turn. The congregation grew, the fabric of the building was materially improved and the Church was granted permanent status. Father William Jolly, who had in 1947 given vestments, and whose father had made some of the furniture for the new Church, returned to say a weekly evening Mass. He was a diabetic and almost blind, but survived until 1982, and was responsible for suggesting that Oswald Sitwell be given a Papal Medal for his share in re-establishing a Roman Catholic Church in Framlingham, which he received in 1981.

The Church then had Father Seeley to minister to them, and from 1985-1992, the Church was served by the Vicar General, Monseigneur Drury, and now 1994 by Father Wynekus, a priest from Woodbridge (who was created a Dutch Knight) and, assisted since May 1991 by a deacon, celebrates for a congregation of some 110 souls.

PARISH COUNCIL

CENTENARY OF FRAMLINGHAM PARISH COUNCIL

The Parish Councils Bill introduced in 1894 during Mr. W.E. Gladstone's leadership, became law as the Local Government Act of 1894. It enacted that Parish Councils be established in Parishes with powers:
- (1) of carrying out certain Acts; the Burial Acts and Public Improvement Acts among others,
- (2) of dealing with parish property,
- (3) of raising certain rates and
- (4) with powers to acquire and manage land for allotments.

The Framlingham Parish Overseers accordingly called a public meeting for 4th December 1894 at the Castle Hall at 6.00 p.m.. This meeting was well attended. It was proposed by Mr. Henry Mallows, seconded by Mr. Charles Goodwin, and carried nem con., that Mr. T.W. Read, who was clerk to a number of school boards and to the Governors of the Hitcham's Charity, be the Chairman of the meeting.

In answer to Mr. Read's request for nominations, a list of 15 names was presented to him. They were proposed by the Fellmonger and leather merchant Mr. Francis Read and seconded by Mr. Robert Lambert, the Printer and proprietor of the *Framlingham Weekly News*. After the prescribed 15 minutes, during which time no other names were submitted, the Chairman found the 15 names valid, and none withdrawn. The following 15 men were declared the first elected Councillors:

John Bridges	of Albert Place, Tailor
Thomas Twidell Buckmaster	of Station Road, owner of the Victoria Mill, corn-miller, farmer and benefactor to the Town. He built the Railway Terrace, his house and store-house in Victoria Mill Road.
Samuel Green Carley	Grocer and Italian warehouseman, supplied wine and spirits in his shop on the Market Hill. He built 'Winston House' in Double Street.
Charles Harper	Labourer,
John Howard	Tailor, living in Station Road.
Dr. George E. Jeaffreson, J.P.	12 Market Hill; he also farmed.
John Martin, Managing Clerk	of the County Court, Agent for Liverpool, London & Globe Fire and Life, Agent for Imperial Offices, Clerk to the Magistrates. Lived in Double Street. (Tony Martin's Grandfather)
Benjamin Norman	Gun-maker, Cutler and mechanical iron worker, lived in Church Street.
Rev. James Holme Pilkington	the Rector
William Pipe	a Farmer, of Rose Farm.
Joseph Savill	Farmer (not in the White's 1892 List)
Calvin Denny Smith	Farmer, of Hatherleigh Farm
John Robert Watson	Farmer, of The Oaks, Herbshaw Green.
Reuben Whitehead	Miller, merchant and keeper of the weather reports; wrote annually in the *Lambert Almanack*. Lived at Hill House, Mount Pleasant.
Samuel Wright	Piano Tuner and musical instrument dealer, in charge of the Territorial Band.

The first meeting of this Council was held in the Boys' School on 14th December 1894, when all 15 signed the Declaration of Acceptance of Office, and when Dr. J.E. Jeaffreson was unanimously elected Chairman, and Mr. John Martin was elected Vice-Chairman. After a vote, Mr. F.G. Ling was elected Clerk to the Council and invited to continue his duties as Clerk to the Burial Board, and to bring those books to the Council.

The responsibilities of the Lighting & Watching Committee set up to fulfill the Lighting & Watching Act of 1833 were transferred to the Council, and the area of the Town to be lit by gas-light was established.

The Council then turned their attention to the water supplies to the Town, which included water from springs and wells; these were listed:

> A spring on Horn Hill (later College Road)
> An artesian well at the College,
> A well at Mrs. Dickson's stables,
> A pump on Adcock's premises
> A well in Barrack Cottage and in Newson's garden
> A spring at the Back of Harris & Mobbs premises
> A spring in the Hermitage property
> A pump on Larner's property at the corner of Vyces Road
> From 1897/8 the Jeaffreson pump to a bore 500 feet down

Framlingham was not connected to a public water supply until 1945, when complaints were made of the hardness of this water.

PRINTING

Printing was introduced to Framlingham in 1810 by John Ludbrook (the gentleman of the paper shirt-front See Section 3.1). He was succeeded by Richard Green, the author of the *History of Framlingham*, whose printing works were in Church Street, probably on the corner with White Hart Lane, lately the Cooperative Society building, before he moved to 13 Market Hill, where in 1861 Robert Lambert was working for him. William Dove Freeman had a small printing works in No. 9 Double Street from 1841 to 1867, the year that Richard Green sold 13 Market Hill. Robert Lambert bought William Freeman's printing works in 1869 and produced the *Framlingham Weekly News* and the *Lambert Almanack* there until 1897 when he sold his printing business to H.B. Maulden who installed a steam printing machine. In 1901 Arthur Fairweather took over the printing and issuing of the Almanack from his Woodbridge works.

The following advertisments have their dates of printing shown.
Those below are 1907 and 1908 respectively.

A. T. WICKS

THE
Leading
House

IN THE DISTRICT FOR

KEEN AND THRIFTY BUYERS

Of all kinds of

Millinery, Drapery,

Ready-made Clothing

Outfitting, Boots, &c

All Goods marked in Plain Figures at Lowest City Prices

**LONDON HOUSE,
MARKET HILL, FRAMLINGHAM.**

T. J. Wright

THE SQUARE,
Framlingham.

PIANO & ORGAN TUNER

NEW AND SECOND-HAND

Pianos, American Organs and Harmoniums

Always in stock by Best Makers

For Sale or Hire.

THOMAS BUCKMASTER,

Coal and Coke Merchant,

Station Road, FRAMLINGHAM.

PRICES ON APPLICATION.   TERMS CASH.

Orders will receive Prompt Attention.

E. MIDDLETON

WHOLESALE & RETAIL

PASTRY COOK,

CONFECTIONER, FRUITERER, &c.

Bride, Christening, and Birthday Cakes

TASTEFULLY ORNAMENTED.

MADERIA, POUND, SPONGE, LUNCH & GENOA CAKES

ALWAYS IN STOCK.

ICES, JELLIES, CREAMS

ETC., MADE TO ORDER.

Talbot & Co's. Mineral Waters, Soda Water
Lemonade, Gingerade, Seltzer & Potass Water

DEALER IN BRITISH & FOREIGN WINES.

Cooked Hams (Home Cured) always on cut

WEDDING BREAKFASTS, BALL SUPPERS

— AND —

PARTIES OF ALL KINDS CATERED FOR

Orders by Post will receive Prompt Attention.

MARKET PLACE, FRAMLINGHAM

1892

1906

A. G. POTTER,

(TOMB HOUSE), FRAMLINGHAM.

"SWIFT" CYCLES, The World's Best Fully Guaranteed

Prices from £8 8s. to £16 16s.

New Hudson Cycles
(The Cycle for hard wear)
From £6 15s.
To £10 10s.

Accessories of Every Description.
Bags, Bells, Lamps, Pumps, Outfits, Clips, Tyres, Covers, Tubes, Valves, &c. All at Lowest Cash Prices.

THE Sun Cycles
Fitted with Dunlop Tyres and guaranteed for TWO YEARS.
From £8 8s.

Replating, Enamelling, & all kinds of Repairs carefully and promptly executed.

PRICES TO SUIT ALL.

Estimates and Price Lists free on application. Personal attention given.

BASKETS AND WOOD GOODS OF EVERY DESCRIPTION.

Note Change of Address:—
A. G. POTTER, Tomb House, FRAMLINGHAM.

A. & W. HUNT,

REGISTERED

Practical & Sanitary Plumbers

Double Street, FRAMLINGHAM.

Plumbing, Painting, Graining, Paperhanging and General House Decorating, Glazing, Gas-fitting and Bell-hanging (electric and pull).

JARVIS SCOGGINS,

NEW AND SECONDHAND

Furniture Dealer,

Cabinet Maker, Upholsterer, Ironmonger

China, Glass, and Earthenware Dealer,

TOBACCONIST, &c.,

Well-Close Square, FRAMLINGHAM.

New and Secondhand Furniture of every description, bought, sold or exchanged
Carpets taken up, shaken, and re-laid
All kinds of Furniture repaired, Polished and upholstered
Pictures Mounted and Framed on the shortest notice
Iron and Brass Bedsteads, Mattresses and Bedding
Carpets, Floorcloths, Mats and Matting
Bassinettes and Mail Carts
Paper Hangings in great variety, and Paper hung, ceilings whitewashed
Household Furniture carefully packed and removed
Men's Leather Gloves. Tin Trunks, and Cart Lamps always in stock
All kinds of Flower Pots and Saucers, Seed Pans, Cream Pots, Pork Pots, Bread Pans, Milk Bowls
Adkin and Sons' Loose and Packet Tobaccos
Cigars and Cigarettes from the leading makers
Walking Sticks and Tobacconists' Fancy Goods of every description

ALL GOODS DELIVERED FREE.

PONY AND TRAP TO LET.

For Cleaning and Renovating Furniture,
Use the New . . . .
Furniture Polish,
In 3d. and 6d. Bottles.

Prevents the worm from eating the wood. Unsolicited Testimonials. Made and sold only by—

JARVIS SCOGGINS,

Well-Close Square, FRAMLINGHAM.

1903

1903

Teeth. ARTIFICIAL TEETH of superior quality
Unequalled for Durability & Natural Appearance.
EVERY CASE GUARANTEED.

MAY BE HAD OF   Excellent Unsolicited Testimonials.

EUSTACE D. GIBBS, Manufacturer of Artificial Teeth, Fore St., Framlingham.

Established 40 Years.

GEORGE FISK,

CHURCH STREET, FRAMLINGHAM.

HAS ALWAYS A

Large stock of Boots & Shoes

READY-MADE CLOTHES, &c.

Suitable for Working Men

AND AT THE

Very Lowest Prices.

1906

JOHN HOWLETT,
Plumber and Glazier,
House, Sign & Ornamental Painter,
CASTLE STREET, FRAMLINGHAM.

Estimates given for all kinds of Repairs.

Ye Olde Curiosity Shop.

H. H. LANMAN,
Watchmaker, Jeweller, &c.,
DEALER IN ANTIQUES AND CURIOS,
CASTLE STREET,
& DOUBLE STREET, FRAMLINGHAM.

Wanted to purchase in any condition:
ANTIQUE
Furniture — Coins — Clocks
Silver — Carving — Brass Work
China — Curiosities — Iron Work
Pictures — Watches — Inlaid Work

Good Prices Given. **Distance no object.**

C. CLEMENTS,
STATION ROAD, FRAMLINGHAM,
Respectfully begs to intimate that he has

Horses & Traps to Let on Hire
on most reasonable terms

C. C. has received the highest testimony from Patrons
TERMS GLADLY FURNISHED ON APPLICATION

1907

CASH CLOTHING STORES,
Church Street, FRAMLINGHAM,
JAMES FREEMAN
(LATE GEO. FISK).
Large and Well-selected Stock of
OUTFITTING, DRAPERY AND BOOTS
At Lowest Cash Prices.

C. W. WRIGHT,
Complete House Furnisher,
Station Road, FRAMLINGHAM,
And High Street, Aldeburgh-on-Sea.

NEW AND SECOND-HAND FURNITURE DEALER.
Sideboards, Cheffoniers, Couches, Tables, Chairs, ...
Bedsteads, Bedding, &c., of every description, in best quality.

Pianofortes, Mail Carts, Bassinettes
OF LATEST DESIGN.

MANGLES, WRINGERS, &c., from Best Makers, for
Cash or by Easy Payments.

A Good Variety of
ANTIQUE FURNITURE, CHINA, GLASS, CURIOS, etc.

Furniture repaired, upholstered and polished
MATTRESSES RE-CORDED AND RE-MADE.

SALES ATTENDED ON COMMISSION.

1908

Ladies' Costumes.

COATS and SKIRTS a speciality.

A choice selection of
TWEEDS, SERGES, & HABITS.

Liveries
Equal to the production of any London House.

Livery Hats, Gold & Silver Bands, Laces, etc

The Ladies' and Gents' Tailor

Gents' Tailoring.
Lounge Suits, Dress Suits, Shooting Suits.

STYLISH
Riding Breeches
Of Scotch and West of England Tweeds.

Overcoats.
Fancy Vests.

Prefection in
Fit, Style, Finish.

Largest stock in the district for selection
PATRONS WAITED ON AT OWN RESIDENCE.

JOHN SELF,
FRAMLINGHAM.

GET IT AT
WAREINGS'!
High-class General & Fancy DRAPERS

The well-known
Dressmaking & Millinery
Establishment

FUNERALS FURNISHED.

LADIES' & GENTLEMEN'S BOOTS & SHOES

It is always our endeavour to give the highest value to our customers, and our Stock being always replete with newest Seasonable Goods, Ladies will have no difficulty in meeting their requirements at

Wareing Bros.,
GENERAL & FANCY
DRAPERS,
Market Hill, Framlingham.

Everything Farmers Use at Rock Bottom Prices.

We can quote you cheaper than the Stores for Prompt Cash.

G. and A. BRIDGES,
— General Smiths and —
Agricultural Ironmongers
FRAMLINGHAM

GIVE US A TRIAL IT WILL PAY YOU.

Ransomes', Bentall's, and Roberts' Ploughs and Fittings.
Chaff Cutters and Food Preparing Machinery.
Ransomes', Edlington, and Martin's Cultivators.
Cook's Champion Sack Lifters.
Bean Drills fitted on any Plough.
Jointed and Cambridge Rolls.
Harrows for all purposes.
Separators, Churns, and all Dairy Accessories.
Forks, Spades, Shovels, Bolts, Nails, Screws, Galvanized Roofing, Hammers, Lanterns, Axes, Hooks, Hatchets.
Wire Netting, all sizes, Sheep Netting and Stakes.
Furnace Pans, Feeding Skeps.
Eaves Troughing by length or fixed.
Estimates Free.
Root Cutters repaired with New Knives and Plates.
All kinds of Smithy Work by Experienced Workmen.

ALL 1915

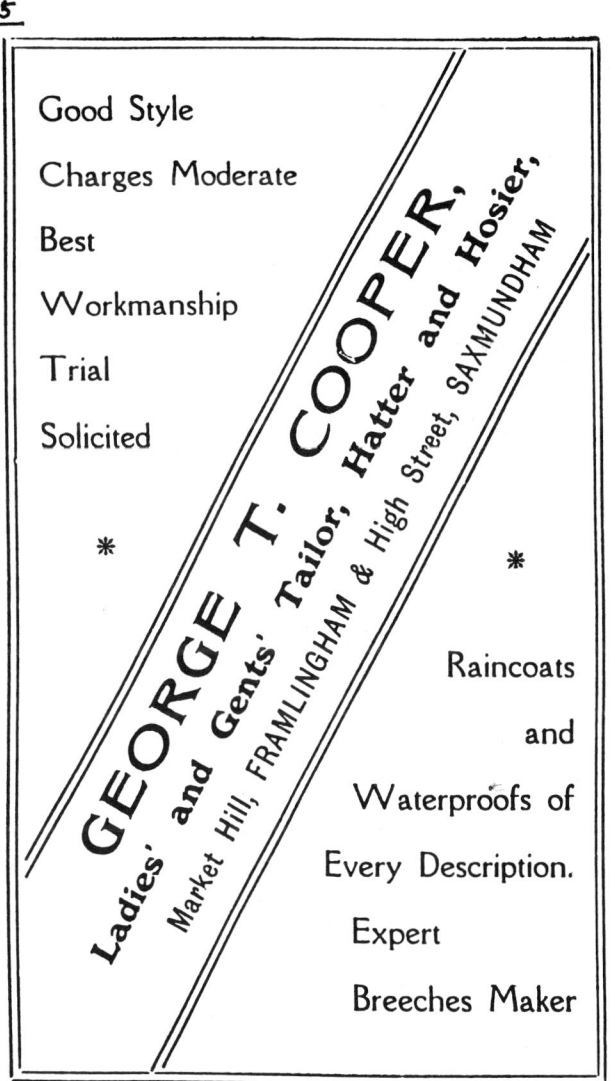

After all said and done you can't possibly get better Value for CASH in the following Departments than can be obtained of me—
JAS. FREEMAN.

Drapery,
Heavy and Fancy

Clothing,
Ready-made and To Measure.

Outfitting
in all its Branches

Boots
Shoes and Overshoes
WHOLESALE and RETAIL

ORDERS BY POST CARRIAGE PAID

Club Tickets Taken.
Working Parties Supplied

Jas. FREEMAN,
CASH CLOTHING DEPÔT,
Church Street, FRAMLINGHAM

Good Style

Charges Moderate

Best Workmanship

Trial Solicited

*

GEORGE T. COOPER,
Ladies' and Gents' Tailor, Hatter and Hosier,
Market Hill, FRAMLINGHAM & High Street, SAXMUNDHAM

*

Raincoats
and
Waterproofs of
Every Description.
Expert
Breeches Maker

S.G. CARLEY & Co.

GROCERS

Tea and Coffee Dealers

and

ITALIAN WAREHOUSEMEN,

Wholesale and Family Buyers are assured that the greatest care is taken to supply the very BEST PROVISIONS at the —LOWEST POSSIBLE— PRICES.

AGENT FOR

W. & A. GILBEY'S WINES and SPIRITS.

Bass's Burton Ales.

Guinness's Dublin Stouts.

and Ind Coope's AK Ale always in Stock.

MARKET HILL,

Framlingham

THE Ladies' and Gentlemen's TAILOR

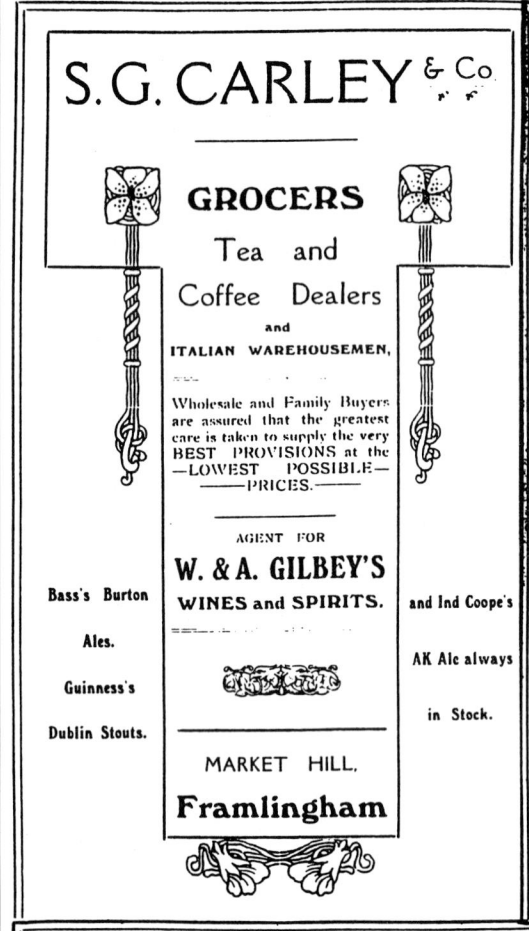

LADIES' SUITS & OVERGARMENTS.
Choice ranges of Patterns made up in the Latest Styles. Perfection of Fit. Quality Unsurpassed. :: :: Satisfaction Assured.

GENTLEMEN'S TAILORING ..
Of Every Description. Business and Sporting Suits. Perfect Fitting Breeches and Overcoats. Stylish, Durable . . . . . . Moderate Prices.

LIVERIES
Chauffeurs' Complete Outfits

Depot for—
"N & C" Nicholson RAINCOATS and OVERCOATS -
For Ladies' and Gentlemen. These Coats have achieved a world-wide reputation and are Second to None.

The Latest Production in
"CHRISTY'S
HATS and CAPS
Always on Hand.

JOHN SELF,
Tailor, Hatter & Outfitter,
FRAMLINGHAM.

F. HOLMES,
Family Baker and Confectioner,

ICES, TEAS, AND LIGHT REFRESHMENTS.
WEDDING, BIRTHDAY, & all kinds of CAKES
:: :: MADE TO ORDER. :: ::

MARKET HILL, FRAMLINGHAM.

PRINTING! PRINTING!
OF EVERY DESCRIPTION
Artistic, General and Commercial,
AT LOWEST PRICES.

NOTHING TOO LARGE.—NOTHING TOO SMALL

Read these Spontaneous Testimonials.
The Originals can be seen on application.

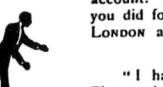

"I enclose cheque in settlement of your account. I was very pleased with the Printing you did for me—JUST AS GOOD as I can get in LONDON and MUCH CHEAPER."

"I have pleasure in enclosing you cheque. The work was WELL and QUICKLY DONE, and we are very grateful to you for charging so very cheaply."

STATIONERY.
Large stock of Military Notepaper, Envelopes, Writing Pads, and all Commercial Stationery.

A. FAIRWEATHER,
"REPORTER" PRESS, WOODBRIDGE.

Everything Farmers Use
AT ROCK BOTTOM PRICES.

Ransomes', Bentall's, and Roberts' Ploughs and Fittings.
Chaff Cutters and Food Preparing Machinery.
Ransome's, Edlington, and Martin's Cultivators.
Cook's Champion Sack Lifters.
Bean Drills fitted on any Plough.
Jointed and Cambridge Rolls.
Harrows for all purposes.
Separators, Churns and all Dairy Accessories.
We can quote you CHEAPER THAN THE STORES, FOR PROMPT CASH.

G. & A. BRIDGES

Forks, Spades, Shovels.
Bolts, Nails, Screws.
Galvanized Roofing, Hammers.
Lanterns, Axes, Hooks. Hatchets.
Wire Netting all sizes, Sheep Netting and Stakes.
Furnace Pans, Feeding Skeps.
Eaves Troughing by length or fixed.
Estimates Free.
Root Cutters repaired with new knives and Plates.
All kinds of Smithy work by experienced workmen.
GIVE US A TRIAL IT WILL PAY YOU.

GENERAL SMITHS
AND
AGRICULTURAL IRONMONGERS
FRAMLINGHAM.

RAILWAY

As in many other parts of the country, railways came to Suffolk in a haphazard and piecemeal fashion.

Particular lines were promoted by individuals in local areas, for example, Samual Peto, who also built Lowestoft harbour, planned with John Cobbold (an Ipswich brewer and banker) and a director of the Eastern Union Railway, to link Yarmouth to the Pitsea Junction north of the Tilbury and Southend railway. It was left to the East Suffolk Railway under its initial title of the Halesworth, Beccles and Haddiscoe Railway, to open a line to passengers on 4th December 1854. This line (initially run by the Eastern Counties Railway) was extended in the north to Norwich and in the south to Wickham Market and Woodbridge, where it was joined by the Eastern Union Railway from Ipswich.

Framlingham Railway

The growing prosperity of Framlingham in the 1850s and the need for transporting particularly cattle and grain in bulk, encouraged the East Suffolk Railway to build a line from Wickham Market (Campsey Ash) to Framlingham. This development of 5 miles and 5 furlongs proved to be both expensive and difficult to engineer and to run, and there was considerable criticism of the siting of the terminal station. There were many delays but eventually the railway line was opened for trading on 1st June 1859, only to be involved within two months in a fatal accident of Edward Plantain, a railway worker. However, at the inquest in the *White Horse*, Framlingham, on 27th August 1859, the Coroner Mr. C.C. Brooke apportioned no blame to the Railway Company. From 1862 until 1923 the line was run by the Great Eastern Railway, when it was incorporated into the L.N.E.R. and British Rail from 1948.

In 1883 there were five daily services but this was not a profitable line. There had to be speed restrictions and there was competition from road traffic and the rivers and sea trade proved rivals for the Eastern routes. In spite of these limitations the Railway had a character all its own, and its trains fulfilled many duties. For example, there were Sunday excursion trains to London, run from Framlingham to Liverpool Street Station and drawn by the big J-class engines; then there were the Suffolk Hunt specials, when L.M.S. coaches and horse boxes were used, with converted coaches, and L.M.S. special cattle vans for the foxhounds; and signalmen used much initiative to enable the train to follow the fox. There was much camaraderie among the nine Framlingham Railway employees who held a social meal together each year.

Cheap fares to Yarmouth were arranged through the Summer of 1859 when First Class return fares cost 5s.0d., Second class 4s.0d. and Third Class 2s.0d. The number of daily services from Framlingham to Wickham Market and return was increased from four each day in 1859 to 6 each day in 1938, and daily freight trains served all stations but Parham until 1965. Trade increased through the years. In 1893 and 1895 the platforms at Framlingham Station were extended, but by 1961 the population of Framlingham had dropped from the 1851 numbers of 2,450 to 2,005 and in 1952 provision for passenger traffic was stopped. When this passenger service from Wickham Market to Framlingham was stopped, a local Framlingham citizen, Mr. Gerald Needham, persuaded British Rail to run a special train, usually drawn by a B-class engine, for the Framlingham College pupils at the beginning and end of their terms. This continued until 1958 when the J15 engine took so long to 'blow up steam' that the train missed all its connections and a B.R. official visited the College the next day, to confirm that no further specials would be run for the School. The line finally closed to goods traffic in 1965.

ROADS

The road pattern in Framlingham is most unusual and probably stems from Saxon times when, it is conjectured, the castle stood at the confluence of present day Castle Street and the road leading to the Rectory, with Church Street and the way to the castle, Double Street and Fore Street being the inner and outer fortifications to the east; and the mere forming their protection on the west. The market area is triangular in shape on a direct route to the Norman castle thus confirming its medieval constitution.

The oldest houses in Framlingham are to be found in Church Street and Castle Street with several in Double Street displaying shop fronts of the eighteenth and nineteenth centuries. Framlingham, the market town for the area, has roads leading to it from Badingham, Saxmundham, Parham, Kettleburgh, Saxtead and Dennington.

The way to Framlingham from the southwest from Woodbridge via Hacheston and Parham, used in the eighteenth and nineteenth centuries by carts and carriages, was via a steep hill called Holgate (Hugget) Hill, and on up Fairfield Road to the *Crown Inn*, or via White Hart Lane (now Crown & Anchor Lane) to the Market Place. Present day Station Road probably did not come into existence until the early nineteenth century; for it is recorded on Hosskinson's map of 14th August 1783 as a lane to Kettleburgh, but it is shown on the first edition Ordnance Survey map of 1837 as a road.

The present day brick built bridge that joins Station Road to Broadwater and Holgate Hill may have supplanted a 'winding bridge' mentioned in a nineteenth century description of a runaway horse, and giving credence to the legend that stones for the castle were brought by water from Orford.

The way from Norwich was probably via Fressingfield and Dennington, round the Castle Park and into Framlingham via Horn Hill (now College Road). A lane came into this road from the right, known as Red Rose Lane (now Pembroke Road) - the name may be connected to an annual payment of a red rose as rent for the adjacent Red Rose Meadow (as recorded in R. Green). A short distance further down the hill on the left, is a right of way from present College Road to New Road, this right of way follows the earlier Sheepcoat Lane; towards Well Close Square on the right, Love Lane joins Brook Lane, via the old Hermitage. Well Close Square, the area at the foot of the hill, was so called on account of its several wells.

Fore Street

Present day Fore Street was earlier known as Lurke Lane or Back Street; the name Back Street recalls that the houses on the east side of the Market Hill, and the houses on the south side of Double Street, backed on to this lane. Only when houses fringed this road was it renamed Fore Street. The lane running south from Back Street was called Infirmary Lane, for it reaches the farm house on the hill, once the 'sick house' or pesthouse (bought by the feoffees for the town in 1725).

Riverside was formerly called Millbridge Road, as the water mill owned by the inhabitants of the castle probably stood on the corner with Bridge Street.

Travellers to Framlingham from Kettleburgh came via the present footpath that skirts Lampard Farm or Lampard Brook Farm, and Hill Farm and into Brook Lane. Later they used the Kettleburgh Road, now Station Road. The old road from Earl Soham, now but a track, joins Brook Lane by Lincoln's Barn.

Coldhall Lane (earlier Coldhaugh) leaves the road to Saxmundham on the right, and (now only a track) branches left and right. Left to St. John Grove, and Parham North Green and Parham Mill Green, and right to Cole's Green. The green road to the north of the Saxmundham Road is the old road to Peasenhall.

Double Street was earlier known as Bow Street, when its north side supported the gardens from the south side of Swan Lane (Castle Street). It earned the name Double Street, so it is said, when houses were built on each side of the road.

Cat Alley joined Swan Lane to Bow Street; now part of it is a privately owned passage leading to 30 Castle Street. Swan Lane (earlier Castle Ditch) was so called when the large *King's Head Inn* became the *Black Swan* in the seventeenth century.

The side of the Market Place, on which the *Crown Inn* stands, was formerly known as 'Crosse Street', probably because the Market Cross stood there.

Church Street

Riverside

Castle Street

38 Castle Street

Moat House

Double Street with the Town House

11 & 13 Double Street

27 Double Street

31 & 33 Double Street

42 Double Street

Bridge Street

Regency House

SERVICES

LIGHTING:
The lighting of Framlingham was reviewed each year in accordance with the Lighting & Watching Act of 1833. The town had from 1828 oil lighting of its main streets. Gas lighting was introduced by Joseph Barker Senior in about 1845, and had both increased the quality of street lights and the number of lamp standards from 40 to 70 lamps as the town expanded. The practice was for payment for lighting from sunset to 10.45 p.m., later extended to 11 p.m., from October to April, with no lighting during the four days of the full moon. During the first world war the power was at first reduced and then no lighting was provided. In 1935 the East Anglian Electricity Company applied to erect poles on the Market Hill for domestic electricity and were required to put the wires below ground, but they were not ready to light the town. In 1937 tenders were invited from the Gas Company and from East Anglian Electricity Company. At that date the Electricity Company could not compete with the Gas Company, but in 1945 they outbid the Gas Company which was prepared to light 70 lamps for £311 while they offered a 7-year contract at £247.5s.0d. per annum, and their tender was accepted.

From 1st April 1967 the Highway Authorities became responsible for lighting 60 lamps on the main roads, leaving the Parish Council responsible for 37 lights. Gradually fluorescent lighting was introduced and from 1969 the County Council became responsible for all the lighting.

SEWAGE:
By 1897 problems of sewage disposal from the recently built houses in the Freehold and similar problems from the 1898 development of Pembroke Road and the College Hill estate and drainage problems from the Railway Terrace, caused the Parish Council to consider improving the inadequate old disposal methods that included individual bothies and an outflow into the river. By 1903 Framlingham Parish Council approached Plomesgate Rural District Council and asked that they should provide a main drain for Pembroke Road. In 1904 Plomesgate R.D.C, delegated their powers for sewage to Framlingham P.C. and in June of that year an 'inefficient survey of sewage and its increases' was made. In November the East Suffolk County Council was appealed to because

Plomesgate R.D.C. had done nothing. This brought some action, but it was not until 1909 after Suffolk County Council had been 'criticised for sloth' that in October Mr. Miller prepared a report for the R.D.C, which resulted in the setting up of a committee of 8, 4 from the R.D.C. and 4 from Framlingham P.C., to consider Mr. Miller's proposal. Mr. Mackenzie Richards was empowered to spend £550 loaned by Plomesgate R.D.C. and action was taken. This was the quasi-satisfactory situation until 1925 when 1 acre, 1 rod, 3 poles in the Kettleburgh Road was sold for £120 for the present sewage works, with a sewer to connect the new council houses on the Saxtead Road, built by Mr. F. Baldry. This was further extended in 1930 with a new sewer for Fore Street and the Saxmundham Road, to cater for the nine bungalows that had replaced the stables of the first World War.

In 1948 plans for public lavatories to be built in Crown & Anchor Lane by the R.D.C. were made and approved, and realised by 1950.

Plans for the installation of a satisfactory new sewage system were further delayed by the setting up of the Regional Water Authority with responsibilities for the supply of water and the disposal of sewage in place of the R.D.C. In March 1974 Framlingham's sewage scheme at a cost of £29,000 was submitted to the new Authority, to learn that there was a one year delay before any action could be taken. In October 1974 the sewage plans were passed to the newly formed Anglian Water Authority and in October 1975 this body recommended that £174,000 was required to extend the sewage system which would be undertaken within the current five year plan. Extensive sewage works were put in hand in 1978 which made possible a housing development scheme with an increase of the population in the extended borough of Framlingham.

TELEPHONE:
In 1906 a telephone exchange was opened in Bridge Street with 22 subscribers who could use the telephone between 7 a.m. and 9.30 p.m.

From 1926 until 1937 the local exchange was run by Mrs. Mabel Gladwell from 'Glenview', Fore Street. It became automatic in 1961 since which time it has been expanded to S.T.D. The telephone building in Fore Street was erected in 1968.

WATER:
Water for Framlingham was a constant problem and expense to the Parish Council. There were three main public sources of supply; the spring pump on Riverside, the Jeaffreson pump situated at The Haynings, given in 1898 by that family to the town, and the College Road pump; in addition to several wells in the town to be found in the castle, in Well Close Square, in Double Street, and in several private properties. In 1914 the Jeaffreson's Well was fitted with a portable steam engine by the army, to supply those who were billeted, with their gun carriages, in Gun Park (later Pageant Field) with stables for their horses along the Saxmundham Road. Various schemes for piped water were promoted from 1908 onwards. In 1920 at a general Parish Meeting, 43 inhabitants were in favour of piped water and only 2 against; but it was found to be too costly and the matter was dropped, in favour of a current sewage scheme, until 1945 when at last the pumps were pronounced obsolete and piped water was provided, only to be criticised for its property of hardness.

Spring Pump

TANNERIES

Framlingham is known to have had three tanneries. Probably the earliest (recorded by Hawes & Loder called 'York') belonged to Samuel Wightman. This was let to and run by Loveless Wilson. It stood on the corner of present day Riverside and Fore Street, and may well have used the buildings lately standing on present day Ipswich & Norwich Co-operative Society Ltd. land, as the York tan office, worth half a Burgens. The hides were soaked in the River Ore and dried on surrounding railings.

Tannery

The second sizeable tannery belonged to Mr. Edwards, who owned the thatched cottage by the old smock mill to the S. of Station Road. Within this property is a pond, supplied by an active spring, in which Mr. Edwards' employees soaked the hides, which were dried in the garden.

The third, (recorded by a photograph in J. Bridges' *Framlingham', Portrait of a Suffolk Town'*) was owned by Frank Read of Fore Street, and worked by his son and John Wesley Bridges. It occupied the site across the Ore from the Maulden maltings.

Additionally, in 1840, James Cooper owned field No. 904, called Tanner's Meadow, but detailed records of the use of this site are not forthcoming. Possibly it may be connected with Thomas Smyth, Tanner, who died in 1528.

TRADES

YEARS 1600 -1649

1	baker	1	chapman	1	labourer	1	plumber
2	blacksmiths	1	cooper	1	maltster	1	spinster
1	bricklayer	4	cordwainers	1	millwright	4	tailors
4	butchers	9	husbandmen	1	pailmaker	3	weavers
2	carpenters	1	innkeeper	1	pewterer	2	wheel-wrights
						26	yeomen

Between the years 1650 - 1699 the lists include:

2	apothecaries	1	chapman	1	knacker	1	tailor
2	bakers	1	clerk	1	labourer	1	tallow-chandler
1	blacksmith	1	cooper	2	linenweavers	1	tanner
3	bricklayers	2	cordwainers	4	maltsters	1	thatcher
2	butchers	1	grocer	1	mercer	15	yeomen
1	carpenter	2	innkeepers	2	spinsters	+1	yeoman (in the Castle)

The Parish Register, between the years 1697 and 1705, adds:

2	apothecaries	2	drapers	3	ironmongers	2	saddlers
1	barber	9	farmers	1	joiner	3	shoemakers
1	bricklayer	1	farrier	1	knacker	9	tailors
3	butchers	2	gentlemen	1	locksmith	2	thatchers
4	carpenters	1	glover	1	maltster	1	turner
1	com{b}er	1	grocer	1	mason	7	victuallers
3	coopers	1	hosier	1	miller	1	weaver
2	Doctors, physic	1	huntsman	2	molecatchers	2	wheel-wrights
						1	woolpicker

CLASSIFIED LIST BY TRADES: 1724

APOTHECARY	Thomas Turner	INNHOLDERS	Thomas Doughty
BAKERS	Joseph Bird		Thomas Fuller
	Moses Berry		Edward Kell
BLACKSMITHS	Christopher Turner		James Kemp
	Sylvester Bridges		John Newson
BREWERS/	Thomas Buck		Francis Newson
MALTSTERS	Sarah, Welton		John Newark
BUTCHERS	Andrew Smith		Thomas Woods
	John Sawer	KNACKER	Josiah Mulliner
	John Steel	LOCKSMITH	Henry Warden
	Thomas Woods	MASON	John Spink
CARPENTERS	Francis Baldry Richard Baldry	MILLER	John Smart
	Hammond Doughty	OUTSETTERS	(Those who lived outside the
	John Read		Borough, probably farmers)
	John Smith		Michael Barker
COOPER	Josiah Raymer		Robert Bowen
CORDWAINERS	John Doughty		Robert Baker
	Thomas Wightman		George Chappell
CHIRURGEONS	Charles Moor		Thomas Keeble
	James Stud		Richard Verdon
DRAPERS	Francis Kilderbee	PERUKEMAKER	Abraham Javelleau
	James Moor	POTASH OFFICE	Richard Waynforth
	Robert Rope	SHOPKEEPERS	James Butcher
GLAZIERS	John Leverland		Mathias Berry
GLOVER	Valentine Gobbett		Benjamin Brown
GROCERS &	Robert Green		William Clark
CHANDLERS	John Keer		George Clark
	John Wilgress		George Chappell
	George Woolnough		

SHOPKEEPERS (contd.)	James Davy	TANNERS	Loveless Wilson
	Henry Wells	TURNERS	Francis Baldry
	Thomas Wells		Thomas Howell
	Stephen Bootman		Daniel Packard
	Henry Warden	WEAVERS	Benjamin Keer
		WHEELWRIGHT	Daniel Waller

John Keer, ... tenant of house & shop in the Street, Grocer (2 + 1 burgens)
Edward Kell, ... tenant to Buck, Innkeeper of Blue Boar Inn (now the Queen's Head)
Charles Moor/More, ... tenant of house & shop, Chirurgeon
John Newson, ... tenant to Buck, Innholder of The Crown
John Newark, ... tenant to Wightman, Innholder of the Marlborough Head, Market Hill
Francis Newson, ... tenant to Welton, Innholder of the Black Swan
James Studd/Stodd, ... tenant to Robert Stodd, house & shop in the Street, Chyrurgeon
Andrew Smith, ... tenant of house & shop in the Street
George Woolnough, ... tenant of house & shop and Chandler's Office in the Street
John Wilgress, ... tenant of house & shop in the Street, Grocer, 8 Castle Street, bake office.
Loveless Wilson, ... tenant of Wightman, Tanner & Tan Office on Riverside
Henry Warden, ... tenant of Leverland, house & shop in the Street, Locksmith

OWNERS AND TENANTS from the 1724 SURVEYOR'S REPORT

Thomas Buck, ... owned Malting & Brewing offices? Mount Pleasant, Red Rose Meadow, Shop in the Street (several burgens)
Joseph Bird, ... owned dwelling house and baking office
James Butcher, ... owned a shop in the Crosse (half burgens)
Moses Berry, ... owned a baking house and rented much land.
Matthias Berry, ... owned a house and shop Castle St, (Kirby's)
Benjamin Brown, ... owned a house and shop
Edmund Cocking, ... owned a house, shop and baking office (burgens)
George Chappell, ... owned a house and shop
John Doughty, ... owned a house and shop, Cordwainer, Castle St. (two burgens)
Thomas Doughty, ... owned the White Horse Inn in Well Close Square
Hammond Doughty, ... owned a house and shop, Carpenter
James Davy, ... owned a shop in the 'Crosse'
Robert Calleen, ... owned a house and shop, Grocer
Valentine Gobbet, ... owned a house, a Glover (one burgens)
Abraham Javelaw/Javelleau, Owner of house & shop in the Street,* Perukemaker
Francis Kilderbee, ... owner of house & shop in the Street, Draper worth £50 per annum
Janes Kemp, ... owner and Innholder of the White Lyon, Market Hill
James Moor, ... owner of house & shop in the Street, Draper
Daniel Packard, ... owner of house & shop in the Market, Turner
John Spink, ... owner of house & shop in the Street, Mason (half burgens)
John Sawer, ... owner & tenant of house & shop in the Street, Butcher, Castle Street, (¾ burgens)
John Smart, ... owner of house & shop in the Street, and a Windmill
Thomas Turner, ... owner of house & shop in the Street, Apothecary
Christopher Turner, ... owner of house & shop in the Street, Blacksmith
Henry Wells, ... owner of house & 2 shops in Castle Street, Tailor, (and barber ? Deeds 1721)
Thomas Welles, ... owner of house and shop in the Street, Tailor
Thomas Woods, ... owner of White Hart Inn, and Butcher in White Hart Lane
Sarah Welton, ... owner of Malting Office in Well Close Square
Daniel Waller, ... owner of house & shop in the Street, Wheelwright

Francis Brown, ... was tenant of Malting Office etc.
Francis Baldry , ... was a tenant, a Carpenter
Silvester Bridges, ... was tenant of a house and shop in Double Street, Blacksmith
William Clark, ... was tenant to Gawain Till for house and shop
George Clark, ... was tenant for a house and shop
Thomas Fuller, ... was tenant to W. Clark, as Innkeeper of the Dove Inn (now the Hare & Hounds) in Double St.
Thomas Howell, ... tenant of house & shop in the Street, Turner
Samuel Keer, ... tenant to Buck, house & shop in the Street, Baker

* It is believed that 'the Street' refers to Castle street, or Church Street, but with the growth of the town (the Chapel built 1651) it could have been Horn Hill/College Road.

TRADES   Subjects   A History of Framlingham

HEADS OF FAMILIES, TRADES: 1851 CENSUS

ACCOUNTANTS	Margaret Stewart	COLLARMAN	Frederick Leathers
ATTORNEYS (Law)	William Edwards	COOPERS	Charles Waters
	Charles Clubbe		William Vice
AUCTIONEERS	Thomas Baldwin	(Retd.)	David Whayman
& ESTATE AGENT		COUNTY COURT	Charles Gibbs
BAKERS	John Aldous	BAILIFF	
	Thomas Gravlin	CURRIERS	Robert Smith
BANKERS	Thomas Cage		Elizabeth Read
BASKET MAKER	Samuel Major	DOCTORS	William Jeaffreson
BLACKSMITHS	Edward Bridges	DRAPERS	William Nichols
	George Rogers		Mary Larner (wife)
	Edward Smith		Henry Thompson (Retd.)
	Fruer Bridges	DRESSMAKERS	Emma Measeries
	James Everett		Elizabeth Fisher
BRAZIERS	William Harding		Adelaide Pipe
BRICKLAYERS	Robert Drake		Elizabeth Newson
	Robert Fulcher		Alethea Woolnough
BUILDERS	William Hall		Harriet Quinton
BUTCHERS	Robert Bloss	DRUGGIST	Sarah Manning
	John Kerridge		Henry Clutton
	Francis Bilney	DYER	Thomas Wells
	John Dixon	FARMERS	Robert Wightman
CABINET MAKERS	William Leech		Goodwyn Goodwyn
	Edward Crowfoot	FARM	Norman George
	Daniel Waller	BAILIFFS	Benjamin Rackham
	Enoch Golding	AGRICULTURAL	Samuel Drane
	John Wightman	LABOURERS	William Taylor
	William Bridges		William Page
	Samuel Dale		Robert Lambert
	Henry Clutton		Abraham Read
	John B. Smith		Philim Catchpole
	John Scotchmer		George Potter
	Mark Webb		Charles Botwright
	David Smith		Samuel Fairweather
	Mathew Newson		John Gooding
	Charles Goodhorn		Jasper Newson
	Henry Dallestone		Henry Drane
	Charles Goodhorn		Josiah Markham
	Job Bridges		Charles Watling
CARPENTER	James Waller		Robert Sheldrake
CARRIERS	John Stannard		Lionel Smith
	William Mann		Thomas Howard
CARTER	John Bishop		John Lord
CHARWOMEN	Maria Button		James Nichols
	Harriet Coe		Samuel Barrett
	Sarah Newson		William Fuller
	Rebecca Smith	FISHMONGERS	Susanna Smith
	Rhoda Drarve	GARDENERS	Samuel Pratt
CLERGY	George Attwood		John Nichols (& Groom)
	(Rector)		Henry Carr
	Thomas Brereton		Henry Hall
	(Curate)		William Hearn
	Michael Castle	GLOVERS	John Row
	Gascoigne		Mary London
	(Unitarian)	GREENGROCER	James Gilen
	Samuel Brunning	GROCERS/DRAPERS	William Robinson
	(Independent)		Jonathan Hart
COACH MAKER	Samuel Wightman		Hatsell Garrard
COACHMAN	James Watson		Jesse Wightman
	Sophia Etridge (Wife)		Samuel Smith
COAL SELLER	Benjamin Exworth		Jonathan Seaman (Retd.)

HEADS OF FAMILIES, TRADES: 1851 CENSUS (cont'd)

GROCERS/DRAPERS	Hezekiah Middleton		Mary Barrington
(cont'd)	Josiah Middleton		John Oakley
GUNSMITH	William Burrows		Mary Bloss
HAIRDRESSERS	Richard Laye		Mary Cook
	John Moyse		Louisa Bevington
HARNESS	Job Bridges		Mary Hunt
MAKERS	Thomas Fisk	RELIEVING OFFICER	John Cottingham
	Thomas Scotchmer	SCHOOL TEACHERS	William Hill
HORSE DEALER	Henry Bloomfield		Rachel Boult
HURDLE MAKER	James Leech		Samuel Lane
INLAND REVENUE	John Gray		Margarett Tate
INN KEEPERS	Samuel Bloss		(Music)
	William Collins		Thomas Sharman
	George Thurston		Ann Hadcock
	Samuel Sheppard		Diana Tucker
IRONMONGER	Josiah Barker	SERVANT	James Warne (Footman)
LAUNDRESS	Hannah Vice	SHOEMAKERS	James Fedman (& China)
MALTSTERS	George Edwards		John Read
	William Noble		James Field
	Robert Grimwood		Henry Goodman
	William Brown		John Garbett (& Stationer)
	James Maulden		George Mayhew
MILLERS	Robert Sheldrick		Samuel Newson (& Grocer)
MILLINERS	Elizabeth Barker		Henry Johnson
	Matilda Oxborow		Frederick Harsant
	Anne Leek (Straw)		William Scotchmer
OSTLERS	Lodger		George Smith
	with E.Hammond		William King (Retd.)
	Alfred Read	STONE MASON	George Clutton
PARISH CLERK	Robert Carr	SWEET SHOP	Susan Dalleager
PLAIN	Sarah Coots	& GENERAL	Daniel Ludbrook
NEEDLE-WORKERS	Susan Gee		Robert Middleton
	Maria Carnfoot	TAILORS	Charles Dorling
	Sarah Gooch		George Allused
	Martha Wells		Samuel Wright
PLUMBERS	William Fisk		Josiah Larner
& GLAZIERS	Constantine Woolnough		Stephen Newson
PAINTER &	Fred Newton		Jonathan Capon
GLAZIER			George Hall
POLICE	John Creassey		Stephen Blumfield
POSTMAN	John Read		William Robinson
POST	James Rowland		George Clodd (& Draper)
MESSENGER			James Newson
PRINTER &	John Olding	TALLOW CHANDLER	Josiah Baxter
BOOK-BINDER	William Dove	TINMAN	Henry Seaman
	Freeman		James Pratt
	Richard Green	WATCHMAKER	Samuel Barker
PROPRIETORS OF	Henry Larrett		Samuel Taylor
HOUSES & FARMS	Matilda Stanford		Benjamin Gostling
	Mary Day	WHEELWRIGHTS	John Leggett
	Maria Cooper		Henry Leggett
	Eliz. Fairweather	WINE	Edward Lancaster
	Elizabeth Wyatt	MERCHANTS	Manning Keer
	Samuel Fover (Architect)	WOOLCOMBER	James Marshall

TRADES: 1871 CENSUS

Population 2,509. Inhabited houses: 334 (635M, 755F) total 1,390. Ellis Gleed, Registrar.

AGRICULTURAL LABOURERS	John Leggett		Daniel Smith
	George Potter		George Tillett
	James Fuller		Isaac Packard
	Rebecca Smith	BUILDERS	Charles Turner (+2)
	William Fevyear		Robert Drake (Retd.)
	William Fuller		Henry Mallows
	George Mayes	BUTCHERS	William Wolton
	Charles Watling		Dinah Dickson
	Charles Smith		Fred Woods
	Francis Barham		Margaret Pratt (Pork)
	Enoch Clow		John Dixon
	James Leggett (Retd.)		Henry Everett
	Josiah Clow		Henry Hall
	George Goodwyn		Luke Price Major
	Henry Drane		John Kerridge
	Daniel Cousins	CARPENTERS &	James Friend
	James Cook	CABINET MAKERS	James Waller
	John Smith		James Smith
	Benjamin Bilney		John Scotchmer (Snr.)
	Robert Goodchild		Henry Clutton
	Josiah Middleton		John Scotchmer (Jnr.)
	Samuel Barker		Charles Goodwin
	John Smith		George Hammond
	John Morris		David Crowfoot
	John Garrard		William Goodwin
	William Coates		William Noy
	George Eade		John Wightman
	Geroge Potter		William Leech
	Samuel Ward		John Smith
	James Noble		Edgar Leech
BAILIFFS	Henry Wallace		Thomas M. Dale
(COUNTY COURT)		CARRIERS	Henry Sturgeon
BAKERS &	Thomas Gravlin	& PORTERS	John Fiske
CONFECTIONERS	Robert Middleton		P. Spirit
	Charles Gibbs		Samuel Mean (Rly.)
	John Rivers		William Fuller (Rly.)
BANK AGENTS	Jonathan Hart		Charles Dixon (Corn)
BASKET MAKER	Arthur Barker		George Kemish (Coal)
BILL POSTER	Henry Chandler		Robert Harper (Corn & Coal)
BLACKSMITHS	John Barker	CHEMISTS	Henry Gooch
	John Goddard		Henry C. Hutchins
	George Godbold	CHIMNEY SWEEPS	George Catchpole
	Fruer Bridges		Charles Catchpole
	Alfred Juby	CLERGY	George Attwood (Rector)
	Alfred Pratt		Thomas Brereton (Reader)
	Edward Bridges Snr.		Thomas Cooper (Unitar)
	Edward Bridges Jnr.		Samuel Browning (Ind.)
	William Neeve		James Cattlem (Curate)
BOOKMAKER	William Smith		Charles Smith (Ind.)
BOOKSELLERS	Richard Green (Post)		Joseph Hartley
& STATIONERS	Robert Lambert		(U. Methodist Free Church)
(Appr.)	Richard Bellingham	COACHBUILDERS	William Winter
	Richard Scott		Caleb Fosdike
BRAZIERS	Mary Pratt		Robert Canwell
	Frederick Pratt	COAL MERCHANT	Robert Wightman
	Henry Simmonds	COMMERCIAL	James Barham
BRICKLAYERS	Daniel Button (Retd.)	TRAVELLER	
	Stephen Mallow	COOPER	Charles Waters

TRADES: 1871 CENSUS (cont'd)

CORN MERCHANTS	Edwin Chandler		Jesse Wightman
	Alfred Creassey		Susasn Kindred (& China)
CURRIER DEALERS/	Francis Read	GROOM	James Watson
SHOPKEEPERS	George Green		James Airy
	James Freeman		Abraim Harman
	James Green	GUNMAKER	Benjamin Norman
	Joseph Templin	HAIRDRESSERS	George Gibbons
	William Oakley		Richard Lay
DOCTORS	George Jones LRCP		John Moyse
	George Jeaffreson MRCS	HARNESS MAKERS	George Rose
DRAPER	George Fisk		William Smith
DRESS MAKERS	Fanny Sherwood		George Upton
	Anna Clarke	HORSE TAMER	James Watson
	Jane Barnes	HOSTLERS	Robert Hawes
	Harriet Fisher (Asst.)		Robert Smith
	J. Taylor		James Hawes
	Sarah Newson		George Fox
DROVER	William Goodman	HURDLEMAKER	James Leech
E. INDIA MERCHANT	Frederick Jennings	INLAND REVENUE	Samuel Owens
-ENGINEERS	Charles N. Collins RN (Retd.)	INNKEEPERS	William Greenard
FARMERS	William Wolton		John Howlett
	John Miller		James Ling
	Francis Miller		John Clow
	John Bridges		James Hockings
	John Gray (Retd.)		Thomas Wright
	David Keer (Retd.)		William Sewell
	Francis Phillips (Retd.)		John Brunning
	William Groom		Abraham Clements
	William Rayner Sn.	LABOURERS	Jonathan Pottle (Retd.)
	William Rayner Jn.		Thomas King
	Goodwyn Goodwyn		Robert Cracknell (Retd.)
	(& Land Agent)		William Watling
	Francis Phillips (Retd.)		John Fairweather Snr.
FELLMONGERS	James Clutten		John Fairweather Jnr. (Coal Yard &
	William Neeve		local porter)
FISHMONGERS	George Smith	LAUNDRESS	Hannah Vyce (Retd.)
	Isaac Strowger		Hannah Smith
GARDENERS	Henry Fairweather		Emma Wright
	John Stannard	LEATHER	Elizabeth Read
	Robert Lambert	CUTTER	
	Samuel Pratt (Retd.)	MALTSTERS	William Noble
	William Harsant		George Edwards (& Farmer)
	William Hearn (& Corn Merchant)		Daniel Howard
	John Mann (& Coal Merchant)		Isaac Lambert (& Brewer)
GASMAN	Thomas Pearson (In Gasworks)		James Maulden
GLOVERS	Mrs. Warling	MILLERS	Arthur Hill (App.)
	John Row (Leather)		Henry Knights
GROCERS	Daniel Dallistone (Retd.)	MILLINERS	Mary Barnes
	Charles Dorling		Mary Catchpole &
	Samuel Carley		Deborah Capon
	Robert Carley		Anna Woolnough (Assts.)
	Betsy Carley	NURSES/SERVANTS	John Self
	George Belcher, (Asst.)		Ellen May (Hskpr.)
	George Keen, (Asst.)		Harriet Grisling
	Henry Wells Snr.		Rose Hearn
	William Ling (& Draper)		Susan Green (Companion)
	Alice Stoker		Mary Wright (Char.)
	Henry Lenny (Appr.)		Mary Ann Wade
	Edward Aldous (Appr.)		Elizabeth Button
	Benjamin Grice (& Draper)		Phoebe Kindred
	Hatsell Garrard		

TRADES   Subjects   A History of Framlingham

TRADES: 1871 CENSUS (cont'd)

NURSES/SERVANTS (cont'd)	Caroline Juby		Anne Newson
	Ellen Goddard (Nurse girl)		Jane Crow
	Margaret Holmes		Elizabeth Tillett
	Maria King		Maria Scales
	Elizabeth Clow		Mary Dale (Char.)
	Lydia Ann Edwards (Cook)		Mrs. Chandler
	Dorcas Stanford		Elizabeth Cone
	Myra Allman		Hannah Taylor
	Elizabeth Dorling		Alice Pendle (Nursemaid)
	Phoebe Barham		Mary Girling
	Sarah Dening		Emma Read
	Margaret Crane	PAINTERS	William London
	Susan & Mary Watson		James Freeman
	Emma Clow		Robert Turshill
	Elizabeth Kell (Companion)	PARISH CLERK	Samuel Lane
	Dorcas Noble (Governess)	PHOTOGRAPHER	James Wilkes
	Caroline Carter (Cook)	PIANO TUNER	Samuel Wright
	Hannah Wix	PLUMBERS	Henry Fisk
	Jane Stannard		John Hunt (Glazier)
	Elizabeth Ashford		George Hunt (Glazier)151
	Mary Ann Lambert (Cook)	POLICE INSPECTORS	Jonathan Cattermole
	Sarah Simpson		William Hammond
	Georgina Nichols		Jonathan Smith (Retd.)
	Sarah Fryett	POSTMAN	Jesse Smith (Rural)
	Sarah Linstead	PRINTER	Thomas Reeve (Appr.)
	Elizabeth Clarke	RAILWAY WORKERS	Frederick Ketcher
	Mary Ann Creasy		(Station Master)
	Elizabeth Carlton		Benjamin Exworth (Plate Layer)
	Emma Clow		William Mayhew (Engine Driver)
	Rose Goddard	RAILWAYMEN	William Stannard
	Harriet Smith	& PLATELAYERS	James Hall (Clerk)
	Harriet Bilney		Robert Steward (Engine Driver)
	Margaret Scotchmer		(Joseph Clarke)
	Alice Barker (Cook)		(Fireman)
	Emma Curtis		Anthony Grissing (Porter)
	Miriam Barber	RAT CATCHER	Francis Harvey
	Mary Sheppard (Cook)	RURAL MESSENGER	James Rowland (Retd.)
	Emma Toad (Cook)	SCHOOLMASTERS	Rev. A C Daymond
	Isaac Kindred	& MISTRESSES	George E Parly
	Caroline Stannard		Betsy Sherwood
	Maria Watson		Elizabeth Newson
	Jane Murbey		Samuel Nave
	Lucy Copping (Nursemaid)		Ellen Death
	Elizabeth Rivers		Mary Aldrich
	Mary Ann Battle		Alice Bruce
	Caroline Oxborrow (Char.)		William Hill
	Letitia Godbold		Mary Ann Fairweather
	Fanny Godbold		Elizabeth Goodman
	Maria Wells		Catherine Newport
	Maria Crowfoot		Sarah Dobbin
	Harriet Jolly		Sheppard Tucker (Tutor)
	Catherine Parmenter (Housekeeper)	SHEPHERD	Samuel Hannard
	Lawrence Heffer	SHOEMAKERS	-. Pratt
	Eileen Heffer		-. Smith
	Lydia Crawford (Ck)		James Lay
	Mary Ann Eade		James Butcher (Retd.)
	Maria Swann		James Vyce
	Anne Rowland		John A. Garbett
	Mary Mapleton		Joseph Smith
	Caroline Emerson		Thomas Thrower
	Elizabeth Mayhew		Charles King (& Postman)
	Louise Mills		Samuel Newson

TRADES: 1871 CENSUS (cont'd)

SHOEMAKERS (cont'd)	Francis Leggett		William Bone (Machinist)
	Charles Cone		John Thompson
	Henry Johnston		Thomas Rackham
SHOPKEEPER	Elizabeth Bacton (Retd.)		Thomas Dowsing
SOLDIERS	-. Vyce		George Hall (& Organist)
	John Merriot (Sgt. Instructor)	TALLOW CHANDLER	John Dorling
	Hales Dutton	THATCHERS	James Heffer Snr.
	William Revitt (Retd.)		James Heffer Jnr.
SOLICITORS	Robert Taylor (Retd.)	VETS	Joseph Smith
	Charles Clubbe		George Marjoram
	John Martin (Clerk)	YEOMAN	Henry Larrett
STONEMASON	George Dale	WAREHOUSEMAN	William Roxburgh
	James Bloomfield (Lab)	WATCHMAKERS	Obadiah Myall
TAILORS	Edward Wells		Samuel Barker (& Ironmonger)
	George Tillett		Charles Percy
	Julia Juby (Machinist)	WHITESMITHS	Joseph Barker Snr.
	Charles Dorling (& Grocer)		Joseph Barker Jnr.
	James Miller	WINE MERCHANT	Edward Lancaster
	John Newson (Cutter)	WOOLLEN DRAPER	James Larner
	John Howard	(& TAILOR)	Edward Wells

TRADES: KELLY, 1901

AUCTIONEER	A. Preston	COWKEEPERS	J. Hostler
BAKERS &	A. Bonney		J. Larter
CONFECTIONERS	A. Dew	CYCLE &	A. G. Potter
	L. Gibbs	MOTOR ENGINEERS	A. Shulver
	E. Middleton	DOCTORS	Dr. J. Breese
	G. Nicholls		Dr. Jeaffreson
	H. Noble		Dr. G. E. Jeaffreson
	W. Simpson	DRESSMAKERS	M. Daniels
BANKS	Barclays		J. Markwell
BOOKSELLER	H. Damant		M. Mobbs
BLACKSMITH	G. Bridges		S. Newson
BRICK/TILEMAKERS	P. Smith	FARMERS	J. Brown
	F. Baldry		C. Gibson
BUILDERS	S. Mallows		F. J. Cook
	H. Rudd		G. Crane
BUTCHERS	P. Allen		R. Dring
	W. Bowler (P)		E. Garrard
	J. Brownsord		W. Girling
	G. Canham (P)		H. Jeaffreson
	E. Carr		F. Kemp
	B. Durrant		A. J. Larter
	J. Hostler		M. Mann
CARPENTERS	T. Dale		G. Mannall
	F. Mallows		R. Nesling
CARTING AGT.	R. Scoggins		W. Pipe
CHEMIST	Holland		D. Shelcott
CORN & COAL	T. Buckmaster		J. Snell
MERCHANTS	E. G. Clarke		G. Taylor
	J. Fairweather		P. Wolton
	E. Gardner		W. Woodgate
	W. Hatcher	FELLMONGER	F. Read
	H. Manby	FISH MERCHANT	W. Barber
	J. Symonds	FRUITERER	H. Fairweather

TRADES: KELLY, 1901 (cont'd)

GREENGROCER	R. Oxborrow		J. Woodward
FURNITURE	C. Wright	REGISTRAR	H. Rogers
	J. Scoggins	ROPE/TWINE MAKER	C. Downing
GROCERS/DRAPERS	F. Barnes	SADDLER	S. Howard
	S. G. Carley	SHOEMAKERS	W. Bennett
	C. Cook		H. Coleman
	F. Doning		A. Cone
	H. Fairey		H. Cooper
	Wells & Co.		W. Hammond
GUNSMITH	B. Norman		H. Hunt
	D. Scase		G. King
HAIRDRESSERS	T. Mayes		J. Peck
	W. Moore	SHOPKEEPERS	J. Fisk
HORSE SLAUGHTERER	J. Read		J. Freeman
INSURANCE AGENT	E. Pritty		H. Lanman (Antiques)
IRON MONGER	C. Garrard		E. Mayhew
JOBMASTER	C. Clements		C. Simmons (Draper)
MARKET	H. Clark		M. Simmons
GARDENERS	J. Whiting		D. Watson (China)
MARBLEMASON	G. Dale Jnr.		A. Wicks
MILLERS	F. Button		T. Wright (Music)
	J. Maulden	SOLICITORS	F. Ling
MILLINERS	E. Crane		R. & F. Mayhew
	A. Gardner		G. Nicholson
PHOTOGRAPHER	C. Dowsing	STATIONER &	G. Summers
	J. Self	POST OFFICE	
PIG DEALER	G. Abbott	SURVEYOR	G. Dale Snr.
PLUMBERS	J. Howlett	TAILORS	G. Cooper
	W. Hunt		C. Dowsing
POULTRY	J. Fuller		C. D. Hall
PRINTERS	W. Maulden		H. Miller
PUBLIC HOUSES &	A. G Brackenbury		J. Self
BEER PURVEYORS	J. Browning	T.A. SGT	W. Finch
	W. Cocks	THATCHER	J. Heffer
	W. Hawes	VETERINARY	C. Nesling
	A. Heffer	SURGEON	
	H. Howlett	WATCHMAKERS	C. Myall
	A. Newson		C. Rose
	J. Reeve	WHEELWRIGHT	H. & C. Moore

TRADES: KELLY, 1916

ACCOUNTANT	T. W. Read	BOOTS & SHOES	W. Bennett
ANTIQUE DEALERS	H. H. Lannan		H. Coleman
	W. Redwell		H. Cooper
APPARTMENTS	Kate Austin		E. J. Freeman
	E & K Brown		W. Hammond
	E. Button		J. Self
	E. Lambert	BUILDERS	F. Baldry
AUCTIONEER	A. Preston		F. Mallows
BAKERS &	A. Bonney	BUTCHERS	F. P. Allen
CONFECTIONERS	A. Dew		J. B. Brownsord
	Miss L. Gibbs		Elizabeth Carr
	F. Holmes		T. S. Toy
	W. Simpson	BRICK MAKER	P. Smith
BANKS	Barclays	CARPENTERS	T. Dale
BEER	Ellen Heffer		F. Mallows
RETAILER	A. Newson	CARTING	W. Hatcher
BLACKSMITH	W. Girling	CONTRACTOR	R. Scoggins

TRADES: KELLY, 1916 (cont'd)

CHEMIST	H. Sara	HAY PRESSER	J. Orsler
CHINA & GLASS	Mrs. Simmons	HORSE	J. B. Read
	A & E Watson	SLAUGHTERER	
COAL MERCHANTS	T. Buckmaster	HOTELS	Crown
	E. Goodner		Crown & Anchor
	W. Manning		Hare & Hounds
	J. Symonds		White Horse
CORN MERCHANTS	E. G. Clarke	HOTELIERS	F. W. Ablett
	H. Manby		Joseph Hardy
CYCLE AGENTS	A. G. Potter		C. H. Howlett
	A. Shulver		A. Pendle
DOCTORS	E. J. C. Dicks		F. Pullen
	C. H. Vintner	INSURANCE AGENT	J. Williams
DRAPERS	C. Simmons		H. Maulden
	Wareing Bros.	IRONMONGERS	G & A Bridges
	A. T. Wicks		C. Garrard
DRESSMAKERS	Mrs. E. M. Markwell	JOBMASTER	C. Clements
	M. Mobbs	LEATHER SELLER	F. Read
	Agnes Thompson	MARKET GARDENER	H. S. Clark
FARMERS	C. Abbott	MILLERS	F. Button
	J. Abbott		W. Maulden
	J. Atkins	MILLINERS	Emma Crane
	J. Brown		Alice Gardner
	Mary Brunning		Grace Self
	E. G. Clarke	MOTOR CAR	W. J. Fairweather
	Mrs. E. B. Dring	PROPRIETORS	C. Garrard
	E. R. Dring	PHOTOGRAPHER	C. Dowsing
	C. Freeman		J. Self
	H. J. Johnson	PIANO TUNER	C. J. Wright
	C & A Larter	PLUMBER/PAINTER	H. Hunt
	E. Larter	PUBLISHERS &	
	J. Larter	PAINTERS	Maulden & Son
	W. Ling	REFRESHMENT	
	G. Mann	ROOMS	Charlotte Clow
	W. Mann	SADDLER	A. G. Brackenbury
	J. Moore		S. Howard
	R. Nesling	SCHOOLS	Mills Girls
	G. Read		Grammar
	H. Reeve		Framlingham College
	J. Robinson		Elementary
	A. Robinson	SHOPKEEPERS	J. Fisk
	R. Staniforth		H. Noble
	J. D. Wightman		H. Hearn
	P. Wolton		M. Mayhew
	W. Woodgate	SOLICITORS	F. G. Ling/Mayhew
	E. K. Warren		H. F. Ling/Reeve
FISHMONGER	J. Reeve	STONEMASON	G. Dale
FRUITERER &	H. Fairweather	TAILORS	G. Cooper
SEEDSMAN			C. Dowsing
FURNITURE	J. Scoggins		C. Hall
BROKER	C. Wright		J. Self
GROCERS	Addy Bros.		
	S. G. Carley	TOBACCONIST	
	C. Cooke	& GROCER	R. Oxborrow
	F. Dorling	VETERINARY	C. C. Nealing
	International Stores	SURGEON	
GUNMAKER	Norman	WATCHMAKERS	C. Myall
	D. Scase		C. Rose
HAIRDRESSER	W. Moore	WHEELWRIGHT	Moore Bros.

TRADES: KELLY, 1937

ANTIQUES	V. Finbow		C. Raven
	H. Lanman		H. Reeve
AUCTIONEER	Moore Garrard		A. Robinson
BAKERS &	S. Bonney		E. Rolfe
CONFECTIONERS	A. Dew		W. Sly
	Mullinder		G. Smith
	R. Simpson	FISHMONGERS	H & N Reeve
	G. Smith		W. Rushbrook
BANKS	Barclays, Lloyds	FLORIST	J. Heron
BUILDERS	F. Baldry	FRUITERER	R. Brackenbury
	A. Mallows		E. Eyre
	T. Rayner		T. Stebbings
BUTCHERS	P. G. Allen	FURNITURE	C. Wright
	J. Brownsord	GROCERS	Addy Bros
	F. Durrant		Carley
	C. Clement		F. C. Dorling
	A. Ruffles		S. Priest
CARPENTERS	J. B. Dale	GUNMAKER	Norman
	F. Mallows	HAIRDRESSERS	D. Hudson
CARTERS	C. Thompson		C. Moore
	W. Hatcher		D. Simpson
	E. Rolfe	INSURANCE AG.	N. Sullivan
CHEMISTS	G. Hales	IRONMONGERS	A. E. Bridges
	A. Last		C. Garrard
CLOTHIERS	Dowsing		A. Scoggins
& TAILORS	F. Eyre		C. Simmons
	J. Freeman	JOURNALIST	A. E. Dorling
	C. Hall	LIVESTOCK	
	J. Self	AGENT	J. Larter
CORN MERCHANTS	E. G. Clarke	MARKET	
	T. A. Manby	GARDENERS	F. Clark
CYCLES & GARAGES	Fairweather		F. Dickerson
	H. Fiske	MILK SALESMAN	T. Read
	A. G. Potter	MILLERS	W. E. Maulden
	L. Walne	NEWSAGENT	H. Heath
DENTIST	S. C. Beauchamp	OPTITIAN	A. Rivron
DOCTORS	Dr. Armstrong	PAINTER &	
	Dr. D. Craig	DECORATOR	S. Sturman
DRAPERS	T. Brand	PIANO TUNER	C. Wright
	A. J. Wicks	PRINTER &	
EGG DEPOT	F. Sainsbury	STATIONER	H. Maulden
FARMERS	C. Abbott	PUBLIC HOUSES	Castle Inn
	L. Barker		White Horse
	W. Boast		Crown Hotel
	A. Wolton		Farrier's Arms
	J. Brown		Crown & Anchor
	W. Woodgate		Hare & Hounds
	B. Birch		Queens Head
	W. Stanforth		Railway Inn
	G. Chambers		Station Hotel
	D. F. Clarke	PHYSIO-	Goodman
	C. Dring	THERAPIST	Turner
	C. Fulcher	REGISTRAR	L. Waddell
	W. Harvey	REGISTRY OFFICE	E. Farrow
	H. Howard	SADDLERS	G. Brackenbury
	C. Larter		H. Clements
	A. Moore		J. Howard
	A. Mulliner	SCHOOLS	C. Last (Kindergarten)
	R. Nesling		C. Lee (Prep.)
	P. Nickolds	SHOEMAKERS &	W. Bennett
	S. Priest	BOOT REPAIR	E. Bonney

Families

THE BROOKE KEER FAMILY

Jonathan Keer, who in 1772 bought Stair House, a property on the corner of Church Lane and Bridge Street, married Mary Brooke. They had a son, George Brooke Keer who married Dorcas Barthrop and had three sons and a daughter, George Brooke, Davie, Manning, and Mary Keer. Davie was a medical doctor and Manning was a wine merchant and for a time was agent for the Norfolk and Norwich Joint Stock Banking Company (See Banking). Mary, the daughter, married William Barthrop who became a partner in the brewing firm and inspired a theatrical company to come to Framlingham (See Section 4.0). George Brooke Keer married Mary Barthrop, William's sister.

George Brooke Keer senior was an energetic man who created a large and prosperous brewing firm which occupied the land from Church Street to Back Lane/Fore Street, and from Double Street to White Hart/Crown & Anchor Lane (See plan). He bought 21 Inns and Public Houses as well as 195 acres of land and property, and he built for himself a lovely Georgian house on to Stair House, with a pillared portico and an eighty foot capital iron palisade in front of it. He equipped the garden with a large vinery, a hot house, lawns and trees (See drawing). He borrowed money readily and when a new malt tax was imposed, he could not meet his commitments and was in 1832 declared a bankrupt. This was a great blow to Framlingham, for he was one of the largest employers in the town, employing 8 to 10 men in the brewery, as well as coopers, and his household staff, and he owned about 8 horses and 3 drays.

By order of the Assignees all the following were to be sold by auction;

> "Suffolk Chronicle, **Saturday, 19th May, 1832,** page 2, col. 1.
> Important sale of valuable **BREWERY PROPERTY AT FRAMLINGHAM,** in the County of Suffolk. Mr William Butcher will sell by auction at the Crown Inn, Framlingham, Suffolk, on **Thursday, June 21st, 1832,** in 31 lots, the undermentioned property by order of the Assignees of **Mr George Brooke Keer, a bankrupt.**
>
> Lot 1. The Brewery and Mansion adjoining
> Lot 2. The Malt Office and Premises adjoining
> Lot 3. The White Hart Inn
> Lot 4. Two dwelling houses occupied by Dixon & Williams
> Lot 5. The Waggon and Horses Inn
> Lot 6. Two stables and a walled-in garden adjoining lot 5.
> Lot 7. Mansion House on Market Hill.
> Lot 8. A farm called Saxmundham Farm containing 79A 9R 6P
> Lot 9. Bedingfields Farm containing 97A 9R 6P
> Lot 10 The Crown Inn
> Lot 11 The Queens Head
> Lot 12 The White Horse Inn
> Lot 13 The Hare and Hounds
> Lot 14 The Queens Head - Stradbroke
> Lot 15 Three Cottages adjoining - ditto
> Lot 16 Two stables and an orchard adjoining - ditto
>
> Lot 17 The White Hart Inn - Stradbroke
> Lot 18 The Willoughby Arms - Parham
> Lot 19 The Angel Inn - Woodbridge
> Lot 20 The Swan Public House - Alderton
> Lot 21 The Fox Public House - Hollesley
> Lot 22 The Elephant and Castle - Eyke
> Lot 23 The Bowling Green Public House - Badingham
> Lot 24 The Royal Oak Public House - Laxfield
> Lot 25 The White horse Public House - Sweffling
> Lot 26 The White Horse Public House - Rendham
> Lot 27 The Tuns Inn & Posting House - Yoxford
> Lot 28 The Chequers Public house - Friston
> Lot 29 The Ship Public House - Blaxhall
> Lot 30 The Red Lion Inn - Glemham
> Lot 31 Nuns land containing 20A 0R 22P (Framlingham)
>
> Full particulars of which, with lithograph plans of the Brewery and Farms, will be ready for delivery by 20th May and may be had of Messrs Bignold, Pulley and Maws, Solicitors, Norwich and at their office Bridge Street, Blackfriars, London; Messrs Carthew & Sons Solicitors, Harleston; at Mr Green, Bookseller, Framlingham; and of Mr Butcher Auctioneer & Surveyor, Norwich".

Market Hill. Left: Police House. Right: Step & Stair House, built by G.B. Keer.

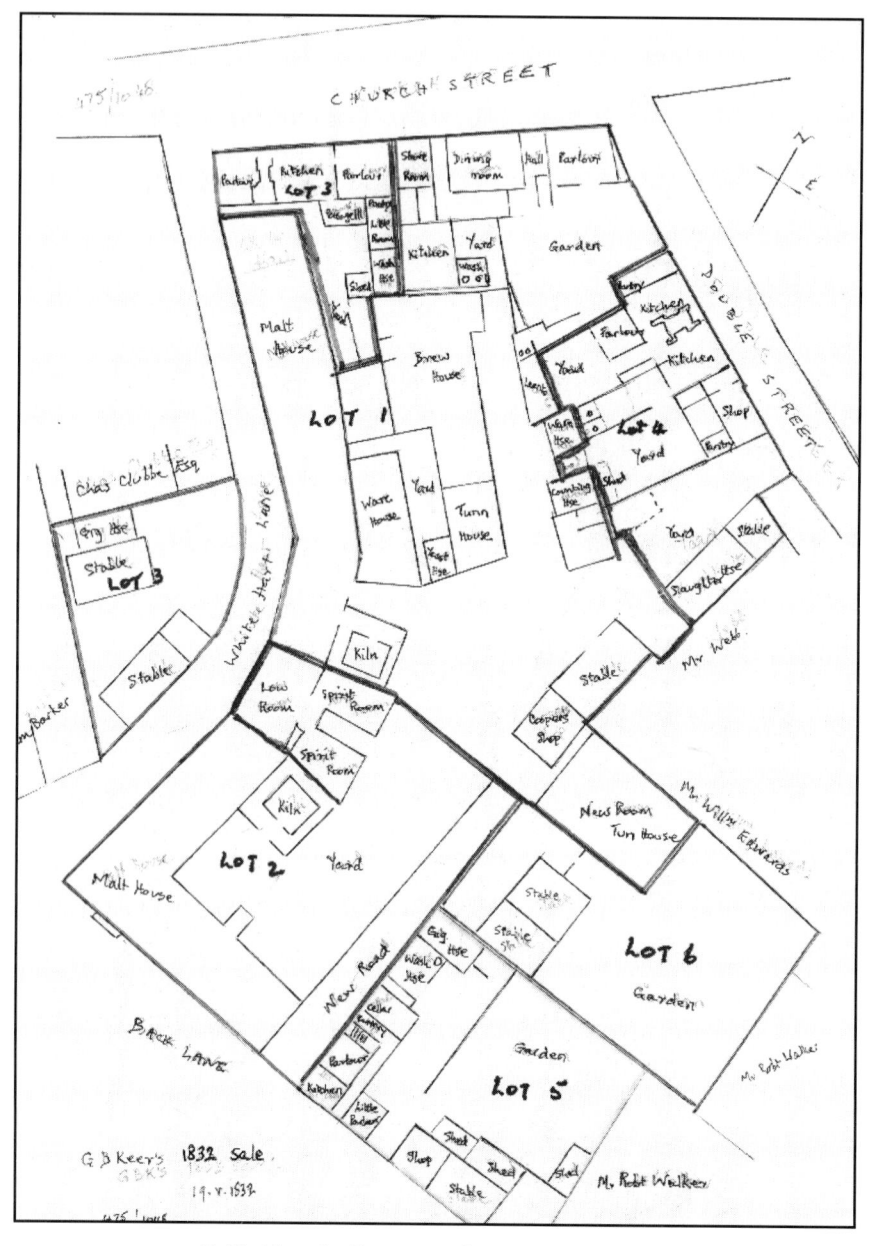

G.B. Keer's Brewery & Maltings, 1832

The auction sale was conducted by Mr. William Butcher of Norwich, on 21st June 1832 and although advertised to be held in the Crown Hotel was in fact held on the Bowling Green by the castle before a large concourse of people. The sale realised about £22,500. The beautiful mansion was bought for £1,000 by Mr. Mason of Ipswich who dismantled it and realised a considerable sum from seven further auction sales which were held by Joseph Abbott of Debenham for the building materials and valuable fixtures of the mansion house, with two sales in December 1832 and 2 in January and 2 in February 1833, the last in March 1833. Finally on 13th April 1833 J.W. Baldwin held a sale within the grounds of the mansion house for '1,000 bunches of tiling, rough cast and ceiling laths riven from the best Memel timber, in small lots, for convenience of purchasers'. E. Lancaster, a wine merchant, later bought most of the brewery and the manor house adjoining, from Abraham Thompson, a builder who had lent money to J. Dixon and had thereby himself become a bankrupt. George Brooke Keer's new tun house, the building approached up a new road from Fore Street (See plan) became Framlingham's theatre from about 1833 to 1874/5. In a modified way, the brewery continued until about 1879, when it was again sold in lots, part was used as shops and part as a garage which subsequently became flats.

THOMAS TWIDELL BUCKMASTER

Thomas Twidell Buckmaster was a man from Bedford who had recently bought the Letheringham mill. He came to Framlingham and bought land near to the railway terminal in about 1860, where he developed a brickworks and built the railway terrace of houses, his house, granary and store. He strengthened his position in Framlingham by buying from Mr. Kindred the adjacent Victoria tower mill into which he introduced steam. He was a regular attender at the London Corn Market, making his journeys to London by train. On one occasion the train was cancelled because of engine failure. T.T. Buckmaster chartered a special train for his journey and successfully recovered the costs for it from the Railway Company! He became a Parish Councillor and a much respected and generous figure in Framlingham, and a great supporter of St. Michael's Church. In 1937, with an anonymous donor he gave the oak benches that stand in the Church and he left the Church a large bequest.

EDWIN G. CLARKE

The coming of Edwin G. Clarke from Worlingworth in 1879 coincided with local agricultural demands; the surrounding area was changing from dairy farming to arable. Milled flour and malting barley were in demand. E.G. Clarke started in a small way by buying a modest malting in Station Road, and by sending a horse-drawn cart round the areas for orders for malt. He had noted that there was both a demand for wheat for flour by bakers and confectioners, and for malting barley by brewers, and that the surrounding farms were changing from dairy farming to arable farming to fulfill these demands. The Framlingham Corn Market Hall had been built in the Crown courtyard in 1867. Beer could be brewed from one bushel of malt and one pound of hops which could result in 18 gallons of beer, it was generally sold at ½d per pint. The employees and farm labourers came at the harvest for their gifts of bushels of malt until home brewing became illegal in the 1920s.

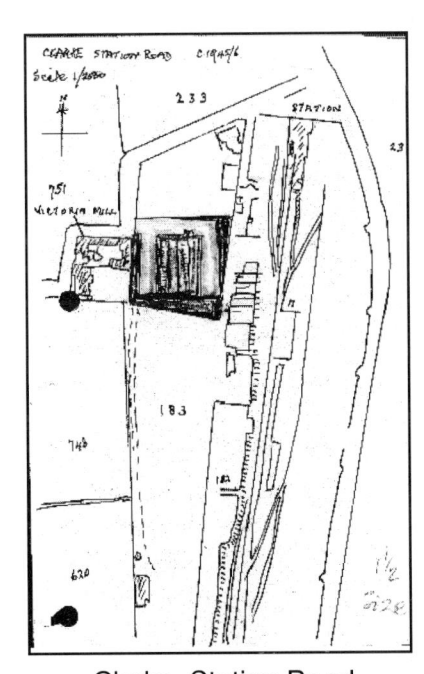

Clarke, Station Road

E.G. Clarke bought property near to the railway terminus and further along the track, where he later developed animal feedstuffs in his black granary. The family prospered and became influential in the community.

Mr. Clarke expanded his business by buying a malting at the corner of Castle Street with the Badingham Road and another in Fore Street. Towards the end of the nineteenth century he had also acquired a granary and another malting in Station Road alongside the railway tracks. He diversified by manufacturing animal feedstuffs in the black granary, at first by using two pairs of millstones that were driven by a horse driving a horizontal shaft, and then by an oil-fired generator, which on occasions augmented the electricity supplies to Framlingham. The ground grain was mixed on the granary floor then weighed and sacked up by his employees whose wages were about 14s. 0d. per week. Mr. Clarke's sons Percy and Donald joined the firm in 1901 and 1907, and served as soldiers during the War.

During the 1914-1918 War malt barley was sent by rail to Ipswich. In 1920 a branch of the firm was opened in Stradbroke, and also in 1920 the first one ton Ford lorry was bought, to be joined by two five-ton ex-army vehicles for delivering foodstuff. The horses were retired from the business by 1925. The small beginnings were bearing fruit.

By the 1930s this firm now in the hands of a grandson, Col. E.P. Clarke, was the largest supplier of malting barley in the country, and had won the Diploma of Honour in the National malting Barley Competition.

FREDERICK CORRANCE, J.P.

The Corrance family bought the Broadwater Estate, with its timber-framed house, and built the present Broadwater House, and owned and farmed much land in Parham as well as their holdings in Framlingham. These Framlingham properties were sold in 14 lots in 1862 by Mr. Frederick Corrance's executors and included;
Lot 1, Broadwater House in its surroundings with part of the Market Hill property with lands to the River Ore; this Market Hill property was sold to Mr. Hatsell Garrard in 1872.
Lots 8, 9, and 10 included the Riverside steam mill built by J. Peirson, and land opposite the lower end of Fore Street (see plan, page 170).
Lot 11 included land at the South and East end of Station Road between this road and the newly built East Suffolk rail track. Lot 3, a field (No. 335 on the Apportionment Map) was North of Pembroke Road, and
Lot 2 included the Regency House with No. 9 Double Street. Mr. Corrance's estate also included land in Parham with a brickworks lying between Parham and Framlingham.

THE FRUER FAMILY

Thomas Fruer, a Burgensholder, in 1755 married Sarah, and John, one of their seven sons, was a bricklayer. He married Anne and they had three sons and a daughter. Samuel, who lived in the Limes, married Barbara Goodwyn and Ann married Christopher Sparham of Castle Street (See the Griffin Inn) and their daughter married John Bridges, who had been apprenticed to Samuel Fruer in 1781. They also married into the Clodd family. It was John Fruer who built the Congregational Church in Fore Street between April and August 1823 and who developed Well Close Square in 1835. (See plan, page 170).

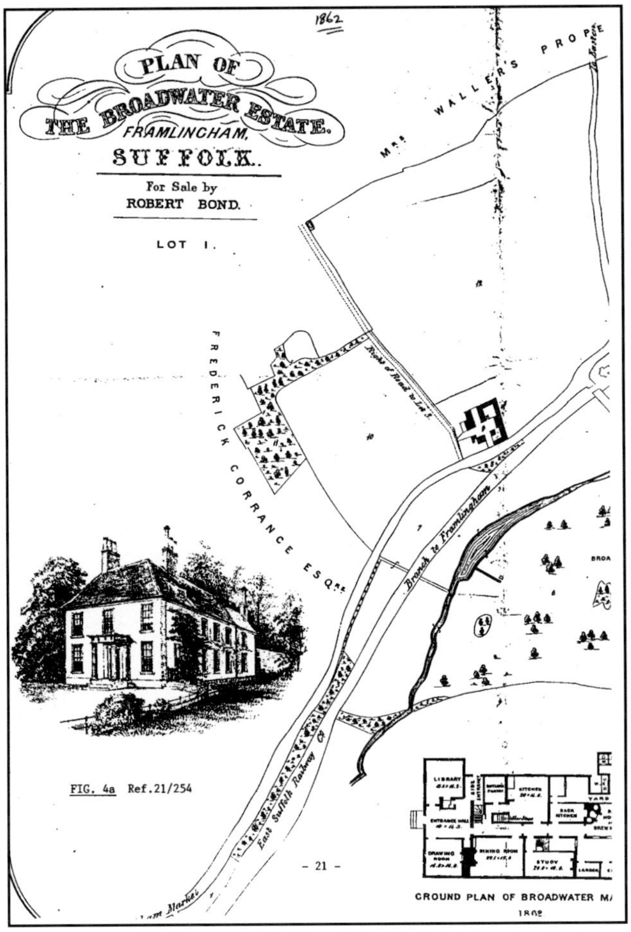
1862
PLAN OF
THE BROADWATER ESTATE.
FRAMLINGHAM,
SUFFOLK.
For Sale by
ROBERT BOND.
LOT 1.
FREDERICK CORRANCE ESQ.
Branch to Framlingham
East Suffolk Railway Co
FIG. 4a Ref.21/254
- 21 -
GROUND PLAN OF BROADWATER M
LIBRARY
KITCHEN
ENTRANCE HALL
DRAWING ROOM
DINING ROOM
STUDY

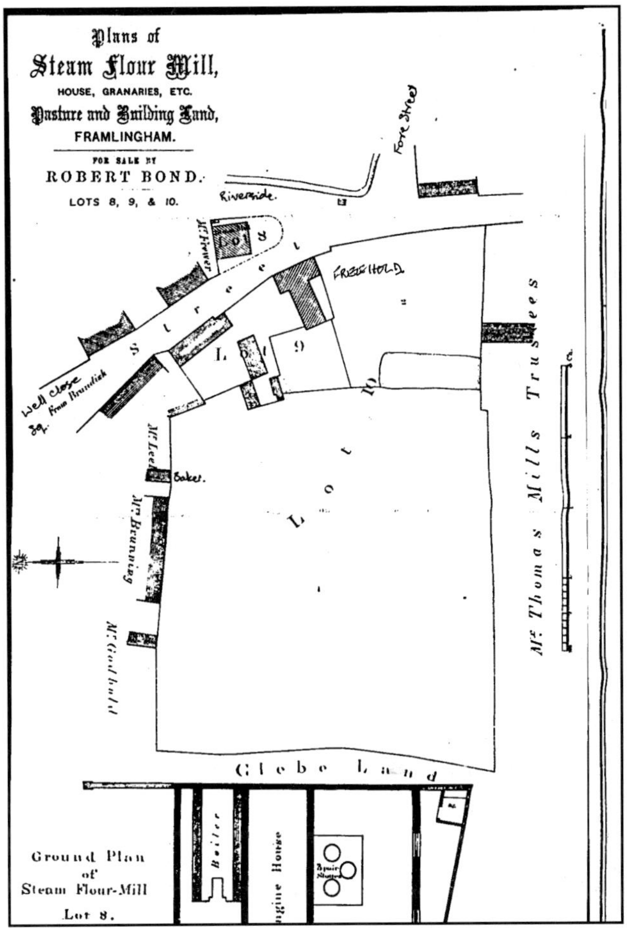
Plans of
Steam Flour Mill,
HOUSE, GRANARIES, ETC.
Pasture and Building Land,
FRAMLINGHAM.
FOR SALE BY
ROBERT BOND.
LOTS 8, 9, & 10.
Riverside
Fore Street
FREEHOLD
Street
Lot 9
Well Close Sq. from Brandish
Mr. Thomas Mills Trustees
Mr. Brunning
Baker
Lot 10
Glebe Land
Ground Plan of Steam Flour-Mill
Lot 8.
Boiler
Engine House

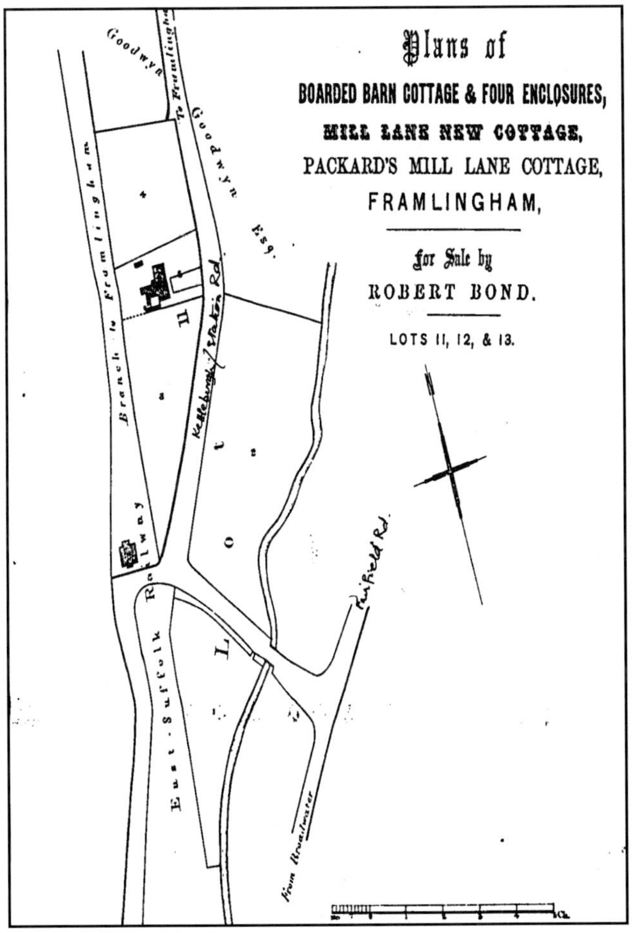
Plans of
BOARDED BARN COTTAGE & FOUR ENCLOSURES,
MILL LANE NEW COTTAGE,
PACKARD'S MILL LANE COTTAGE,
FRAMLINGHAM,
For Sale by
ROBERT BOND.
LOTS 11, 12, & 13.
Goodwyn
Goodwyn Esq.
To Framlingham
Branch to Framlingham Railway
Kettleburgh / Station Rd
Fairfield Rd
East Suffolk Railway
From Broadwater
Lot 11
Lot 13

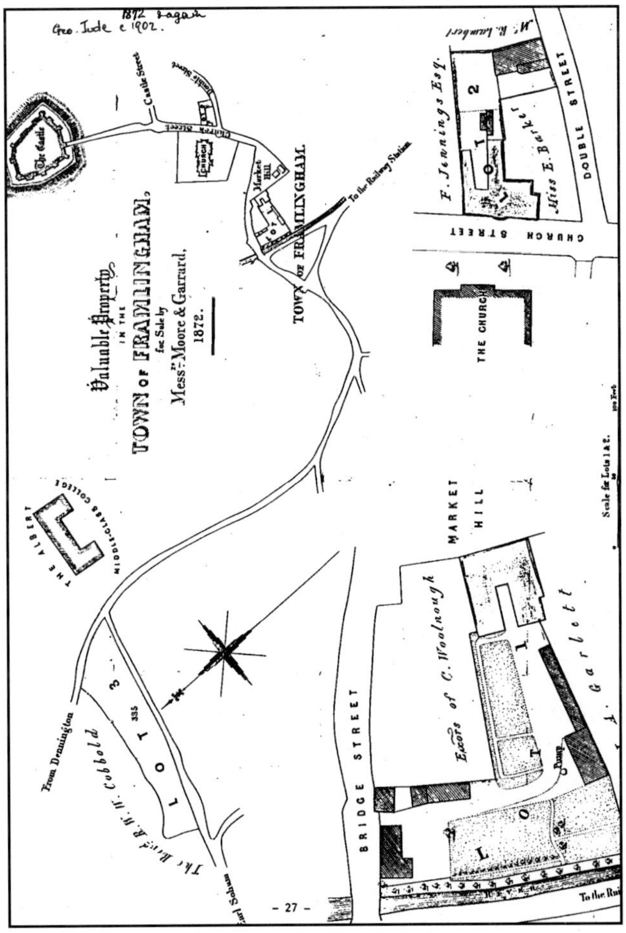
1872 Sagar
Geo. Jude c 1902.
The Castle
Castle Street
Market Hill
TOWN OF FRAMLINGHAM
To the Railway Station
Valuable Property in the Town of Framlingham for Sale by Messrs Moore & Garrard. 1872.
F. Jennings Esq.
Miss E. Barker
DOUBLE STREET
CHURCH STREET
THE CHURCH
THE ALBERT MIDDLE CLASS COLLEGE
MARKET HILL
From Dennington
Lot 3
The Revd. R. H. Cobbold
Exors of C. Woolnough
Garlett
BRIDGE STREET
Lot 1
Lot 2
Pump
- 27 -
To the Rui

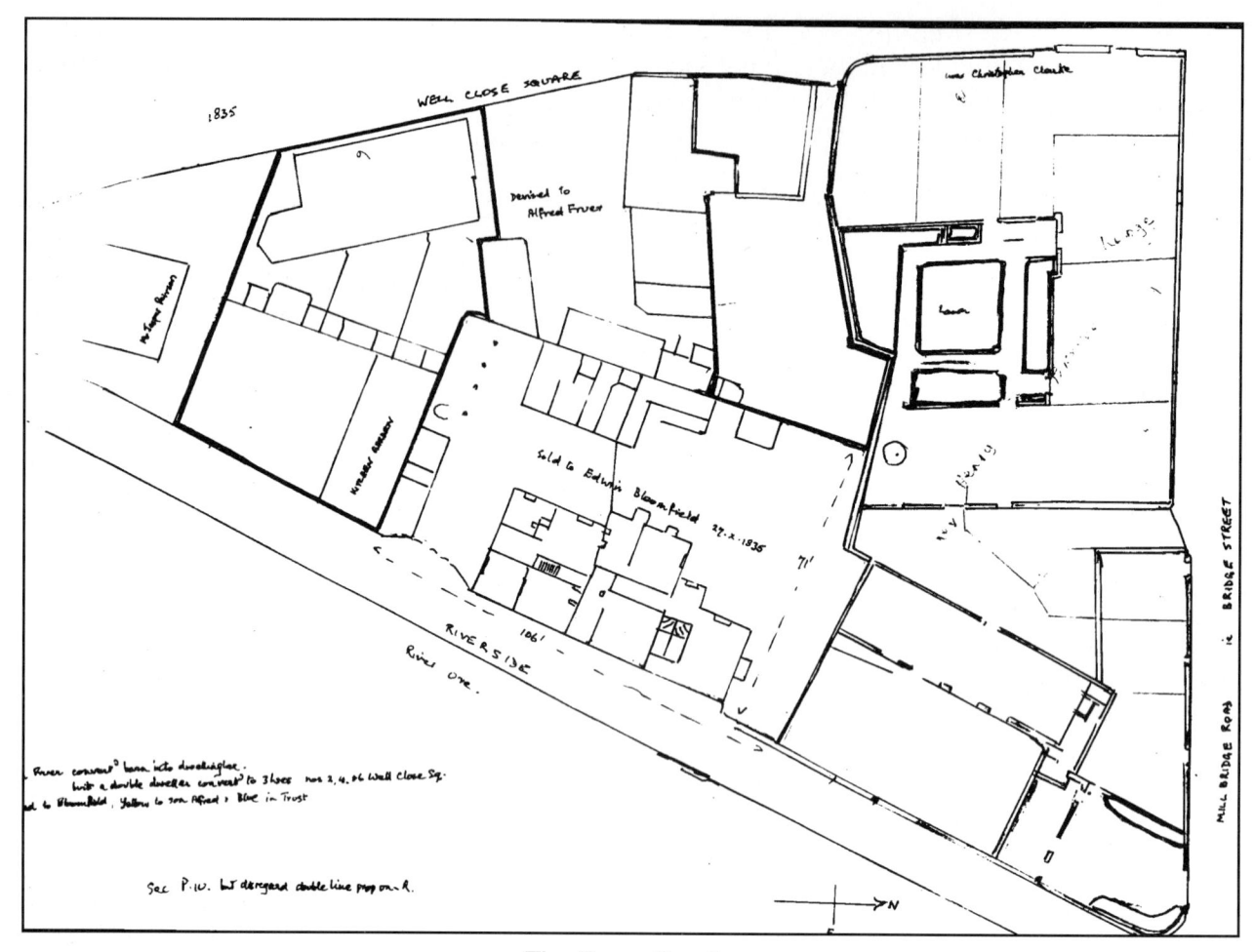

The Fruer Family

HATSELL GARRARD & HIS SON CHARLES GARRARD

Hatsell Garrard's father came to Laxfield from London, and his son Hatsell came from there to Framlingham in the 1840s where he set up his grocery and clothing business, buying in 1872 the distinguished property on the South side of the Market area with its land reaching the River Ore. He let this property to George Jude in the 1870s (see page 24) and it passed to Mr. Wareing, a clothier, in 1902, and then to the Barnes Brothers.

Hatsell Garrard set up his son Charles in William Barker's premises in Church Street in about 1886 where he traded in hardware. At the turn of the century Fruer Bridges joined Charles Garrard, and his son, Alfred G. Bridges, was responsible for the business until about 1935, when this business was finally bought by Mr. Woods, a senior employee. In 1960 three directors, Alban Hills and his wife Joyce née Bridges, and John Bush, bought the business which was run by John Bush until it was sold in 1981 to Mr. Hayward. Following his bankruptcy of 1982 the firm, still trading under the name Bridges & Garrards, was bought by Mr. Turley of Tunbridge Wells and is run by Mr. Hayward.

RICHARD GOLTY AND HIS TITHE ACCOUNT BOOK

Richard Golty was baptized in 1596, and in 1619 became a graduate of Pembroke Hall, Cambridge. He was rooted in High Church and royalist ideals, and on his appointment to St. Michael's,

Framlingham, was, at once experiencing at first hand the complaints of the Puritans in their Millenary Petition. In 1627, in spite of his background and beliefs, Richard Golty married Deborah Ward, the daughter of Samuel Ward, the Puritan Rector of Haverhill, and later the well-known Puritan preacher of Ipswich.

We learn many details of Richard Golty's troubled times as Rector of St. Michael's from his Tithe Account Book, which has survived, and which he kept, along with his 'grey book', from 1628 to 1678. when he died. This Tithe Account book may be approached with high hopes that a clear picture of the state of agriculture in the C17 and of the fluctuating prosperity of the inhabitants of the area will be revealed. Unfortunately, Richard Golty was not a methodical man, and without access to his grey book, which one imagines contained his day to day records, little of real comparative information may be gleaned. Even a cursory look at the analysis of the Tithe Account Book's pages shows that Richard Golty's summaries are not in chronological order, that he keeps to no set format, but rather uses the book as an *aide memoir*, recording the 'monies owing to him', or his costs and returns on the sale of corn, without, alas, recording the quantities of the crop being given. The chief benefit that may be noticed is his house-by-house listings, so that it is possible to discover, in many instances, who were the inhabitants of the various houses that can be identified today.

Evidence for the care of his parishioners does not shine forth - rather his anxiety to exact his dues; he allows debts to build up only from his wealthier parishioners, while referring the smaller debtors to the courts. One senses that he is often defending his right to tithes, and that few readily support his claim to them. He listed all his parishioners and set their tithes annually against their names, apart from the years 1650 to 1660, when he was sequestrated.

Richard Golty was 64 years old when he returned to Framlingham from his sequestration. He found a well-knit non conformist community that had been led by Henry Sampson in the Church, and Thomas Mills in Lincoln's Barn. One observes that the entries become spasmodic, and sometimes in another's hand, suggesting that he was in failing health.

RICHARD GREEN

Richard Green, 1788 - 1873, came to Framlingham from Islington and became chief clerk to Charles Clubbe, Solicitor. He married Miss Howlett of Bridge Street, Framlingham, and they had two daughters and one son, who died as a child. Richard Green bought the type from William King, an early, though small-scale, printer in Framlingham, and set up as a printer an the south side of the Market Hill. He became a bookseller with a stationery office and removed to the Regency House in Church Street. He is best known for his *'History of Framlingham'* published in 272 pages in 1833 by private subscription, and for his *'Stranger's Guide to Framlingham'* of 1860.

SIR ROBERT HITCHAM

Sir Robert Hitcham was born in Levington near Ipswich and was an undergraduate of Pembroke Hall, Cambridge. He became in 1596 an M.P. for West Looe in Cornwall, and in 1603 he was appointed Attorney-General to Queen Anne of Denmark. In 1616 he was made King James' senior Serjeant at Law and was knighted. From 1623 to 1628 he was an M.P. for Orford, and in about 1630 he bought and lived in Seckford House, Ipswich. He bought Framlingham Castle on 29th July 1635, and appointed Thomas Alexander of Framlingham as his chief steward. He died in 1636 leaving the castle and demesnes to Pembroke Hall Cambridge, with provision for a school and a poor house in Framlingham (See Chapter 3).

DR. JOHN KINNELL

Dr. John Kinnell lived in Double Street and in 1832 he gave a tea party to the town, served along Double Street. He was several times invited to be a guardian to fatherless children, and he bought two plots on the north side of the Saxmundham Road and had dwellings built for seven families.(See photograph).

Dr. John Kinnell's Houses

ROBERT LAMBERT J.P.

Robert Lambert produced his first *Almanack* in 1857 while he was working for Richard Green. He printed 500 copies of his sixteen-page *Almanack* which sold for one penny each. In 1858 he printed 750 copies of a twenty-four-page issue with sixteen pages of advertisements and offered small prizes to those who bought lucky numbers. This was considered to be gambling and he stopped his offers and reverted to producing at one penny per copy. In 1873 he bought the Regency House and used it for his business of bookseller and stationer.

By 1896, with copies of the *Almanack* still at one penny each the circulation had risen to 10,000. In that year Robert Lambert sold his printing works in 9 Double Street to H.B. Maulden & Sons who continued production until 1901, when the printing was removed to Arthur Fairweather of Woodbridge.

Robert Lambert was a County Councillor and a J.P. from 1908 until his death in 1911.

HORACE HAROLD LANMAN

Horace Harold Lanman should be remembered not only as an antique dealer in the town, but as the founder of the Lanman Museum which is now housed in the library wing of the castle. He also made the replica (now in the museum) of the Flodden helm which was used in the 1931 pageant.
(See Section 5.1).

JAMES LARNER

James Larner, a Wesleyan preacher and a national speaker against the drink curse, was a total abstainer himself, a guardian of the parish and a man who worked for the elevation of the working classes. His influence for temperance diminished and he died in 1871.

The people of Framlingham erected an 18 ft. high obelisk, with the following inscription 'The monument is erected in acknowledgment of his abundant labours as a preacher of righteousness, a teacher of temperance, and an advocate of civil rights and political freedom, by those who knew his private virtues and public work, and to whom his loss is irreparable and his memory dear !'

THE MAULDEN FAMILY

James Maulden was one of four people in a consortium who bought from John Cattermole 'a malting yard with a robust and sizeable structure upon it'. This was situated at the bottom of Bridge Street on the north side of the River Ore and was run as a maltings. It was somewhat overshadowed in the 1820s by George Brooke Keer's rival maltings, established in the heart of the town and supplying his 21 inns until the 1830s when bankruptcy caused the sale of all George Brooke Keer's assets. Demands were changing, the need for flour was increasing. In 1847 a corn hall was built in the Crown Inn yard where weekly sales were held and this ensured a ready supply of corn for milling. In 1864 in order to meet growing demand for flour and to recompense for the loss of two local mills, James Maulden junior, a maltster and miller, in cooperation with others in a consortium, converted part of the maltings into a steam rolling mill and in 1879 James Maulden paid £600 to became the sole owner and one of the largest employers in the town. From his advertisements, found in Robert Lambert's *Almanacks*, his trade included not only flour but also bran, pollards, meals etc, and he also dealt in coal, coke, and cake as well as corn.
(See Printing).

By 1885 he was established as a seed merchant and he bought extra storage property near to the railway station. In 1892 as his business flourished, he invested in one of the latest models of steam rolling mills from Whitmore and Binyon's works at Wickham Market, and his 1893 advertisement changed to supplier of 'the best roller flour at lowest market prices, having recently erected a complete roller flour plant, under the most modern and approved principle, capable of producing 20 sacks of flour per day'. His milling business was so successful that he dispensed with the coal and coke trade. In 1902 before his death in 1905 he bequeathed equally to his two sons James John and William Edmund the mills of Framlingham and Kelsale. W.E. Maulden, a miller, became the owner of the Framlingham mill which he ran until 1929 when he died intestate. His two sons, who were millers, shared the estate until 1955, when they sold it to E.P. Clarke, son of E.G. Clarke the successful grain distributor, who used it as extra storage space and also dismantled and disposed of the Whitmore & Binyon machinery.

WILLIAM MAYHEW

William Mayhew should not be forgotten as a benefactor to Framlingham for it was he to whom Thomas Mills left his business, the Garden House and Brook Farm. It was he, who as one of the first seven trustees, and as Treasurer for ten years to the Thomas Mills trust, was largely responsible for the expeditious building of the six Thomas Mills almshouses on Feak's pightle, and he gave and supported a further two Almshouses. It was he who by leaving money in his will of 1713, made it possible to build a Presbyterian chapel in Bridge Street in 1717, which later became the Unitarian Meeting House.

THOMAS MILLS

Thomas Mills, a local man, was by 1660 a man of influence, and shortly to be a man of wealth. He was most likely born in 1624/5, the son of a yeoman, John Mills of Bramford, where there was a Baptist colony. He was apprenticed to one of the two tailors in Grundisburgh, probably William Yorke, and he lived there for about two years, during which time he possibly knew, among many young people, Alice Briggs, a cousin of the Yorkes. In 1640, aged about 16 years, the approved age for wheelwright's apprentices, he came to Framlingham and was taken on by Edward Smith, whose wheelwright business was established in Brook Lane. Thomas Mills was already a responsible young man, and we learn that, unusually, he was dealing with the business accounts from 1641, within one year of his apprenticeship. From his early days in Framlingham he found his way to the Baptist meeting place in Lincoln's Barn.

Thomas Mills' master did not approve of his apprentice's Baptist leanings and religious studies. Encouraged by his wife Mary, he planned to confront Thomas Mills as he preached at the barn, and so placed himself directly under the pulpit. Instead of a confrontation, Edward Smith was so much impressed by the young man's words and sincerity that he vowed never again to say anything against his beliefs and practices. A friendship grew between the two men, and Thomas Mills accepted more and more of the responsibilities of the business. It was to him in 1656 that William Mayhew was apprenticed. Thomas Mills journeyed to neighbouring villages in search of suitable woods for the trade, and dealt, among others, with Edmund Groome and William Hammond of Ufford.

<< Tomb House - Garden House >>

Edward Smith was widowed in 1659 and died in 1660 without living issue. He left his Garden House, Brook Farm and his whole business to Thomas Mills. It was to Thomas Mills, already a respected and trusted member of society, known to be good at figures, that Alice Groome, née Briggs, appealed for help following the death of her husband Edmund Groome in 1658. Alice was the sole executrix to Edmund's will, and the beneficiary of his extensive properties in Pettistree, Woodbridge, Ufford and neighbouring villages. She was being worried by some of Edmund's relatives, who were questioning the will. The trust and friendship which grew between Thomas Mills and Alice Groome as he managed her affairs, resulted in their marriage in 1661. They lived for the most part at Pettistree, and bore the loss of their only child, a baby girl, with fortitude. Thomas Mills, nPow that he controlled acres of woodland, was finding that his role as timber merchant was developing fast; in addition to his requirements for his wheelwright's business, there was a growing demand for oak and other woods for ship-building, to satisfy the demands for merchant ships for trade with the Low Countries, and later for warships in case of war with Spain or the Netherlands. Timber waggons were required to transport the local woods to Snape bridge and Woodbridge for the ship-building centres of Woodbridge, Chatham and the Thames naval shipyards. Mills bought a warehouse at Wapping

Stairs in which to store his Suffolk wood near to the shipyards of the Thames. Often he and his wife stayed in London, leaving the wheelwright business in the care of William Mayhew, who was accepted as a friend to them both. After Alice's death in 1691, it is likely that Thomas Mills moved back from Pettistree to the Garden House in Framlingham, which he shared with William Mayhew.

The Act of Uniformity of 1661/2 necessitated Mills having to hide from the authorities, especially when it was known that there was a warrant out for his arrest as an Anabaptist and regular preacher who would not conform. He prepared for this by constructing a hidden room in the Garden House with access via the wainscoting, and by arranging to have ready access into part of his property in Ufford, which was in the name of his tenant. He was also given shelter in a remote cottage in Kettleburgh, and was never caught nor imprisoned. His acumen, diligence, industry and forthrightness brought him great wealth. He acquired much land, and owned 74 acres in Framlingham 37 acres in Parham 147 acres in Pettistree, 220 acres in Ufford, 45 acres in Dallinghoo, 23 acres in Dennington. Much of this had belonged to his wife.

This acreage brought him an annual income of about £643.10s.0d; additionally, he earned much money from the sale of timber, his wheelwright business, investments in New Consols and from cash on deposit at Gurney's Bank at Halesworth.

In his will, apart from the many individual gifts, he left this money in trust to provide six two-storeyed brick-built and tiled Almshouses for the poor of Framlingham, whether Dissenters or not, bread for the poor of several villages and money for the education of poor children. He was a man typical of Baptist leaders of his time in that he was an artisan with no university qualifications, much respected, and among the first of the Dissenters to provide Alsmhouses for the poor. Robert Hawes wrote comparing the Sir Robert Hitcham Alsmhouses with the Thomas Mills Almshouses: 'the wheelwright's almshouses as far exceed, the knight's in magnificence, as the knight exceeded the wheelwright in quality'. Thomas Mills' generosity included help for all the poor, including a free school for children, whether churchgoers or Dissenters, remarkable for one who had been hounded for not conforming. The memory of this generous benefactor lives on in Framlingham, for the comprehensive school established in 1974 is called Thomas Mills High School.

RICHARD PORTER

Richard Porter was a lawyer, a rich property owner, Steward of the Castle from 1689-1701 and a benefactor to Framlingham. He made provision for 18 2 lb. loaves to be given each week to the poor of Framlingham, which benefaction continued until this century. He had two surviving daughters, one of whom, Mary, married Waller Bacon and died shortly after her father in 1701; the other, Jane, married Thomas Kerridge and had one daughter, Cecilia, who was unmarried and left the estate to Folkes, a friend of her father, and a distinguished London lawyer, who put up the Roubiliac memorial to Richard Porter in St. Michael's Church.

ARTHUR GEORGE POTTER, J.P.

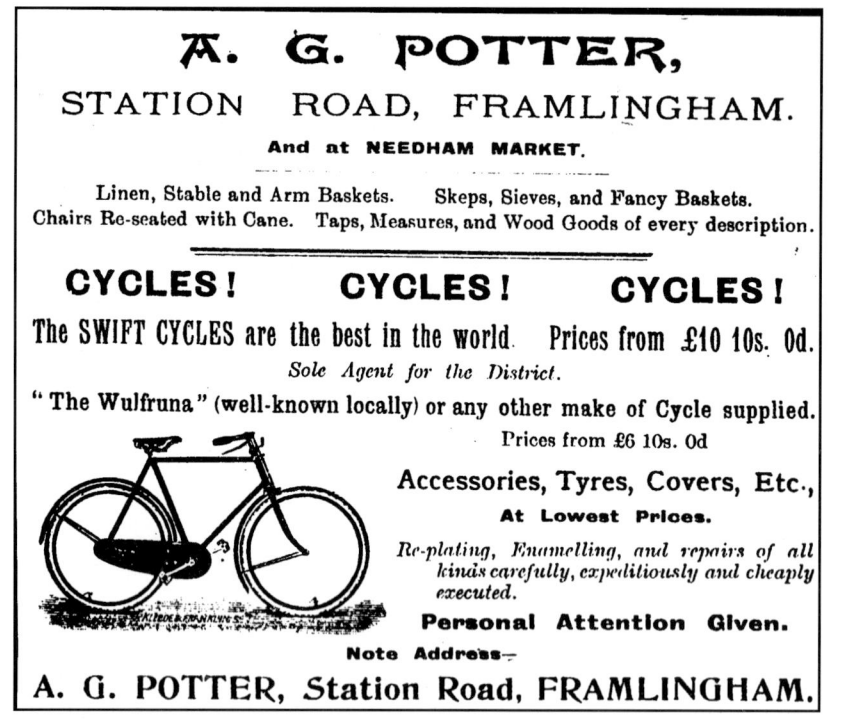

A. G. POTTER,
STATION ROAD, FRAMLINGHAM.
And at NEEDHAM MARKET.

Linen, Stable and Arm Baskets. Skeps, Sieves, and Fancy Baskets.
Chairs Re-seated with Cane. Taps, Measures, and Wood Goods of every description.

CYCLES! CYCLES! CYCLES!

The SWIFT CYCLES are the best in the world. Prices from £10 10s. 0d.
Sole Agent for the District.
"The Wulfruna" (well-known locally) or any other make of Cycle supplied.
Prices from £6 10s. 0d

Accessories, Tyres, Covers, Etc.,
At Lowest Prices.

Re-plating, Enamelling, and repairs of all kinds carefully, expeditiously and cheaply executed.

Personal Attention Given.

Note Address—
A. G. POTTER, Station Road, FRAMLINGHAM.

Advertisment for 'Cycles' - 1903

A.G. Potter as a young married man in 1898 came to Framlingham from Needham Market. He was trained as a blacksmith but set up his business as a basket-maker, with an agency to sell Swift bicycles and later the cheaper Wulfruna bicycles. In 1901 he bought Garden House (with the Mills, Mayhew tomb in the garden) and the old Reading Room once Mills' School in Brook Lane, which he adapted as his workshop. Gradually he became an agent for several makes of motor cars and in 1930 he bought the important Market Hill site from F. Barnes & Sons, with land reaching to the river. His employees erected a large workshop for the repair and maintenance of cars. He became the agent for Ford cars and opened a repair yard for heavy vehicles on the cinema site in New Road. He undertook his full share of the affairs of Framlingham, becoming a Parish Councillor, a County Councillor, a J.P., a school governor, a double-bass player and a special constable. He died aged 69 in 1942.

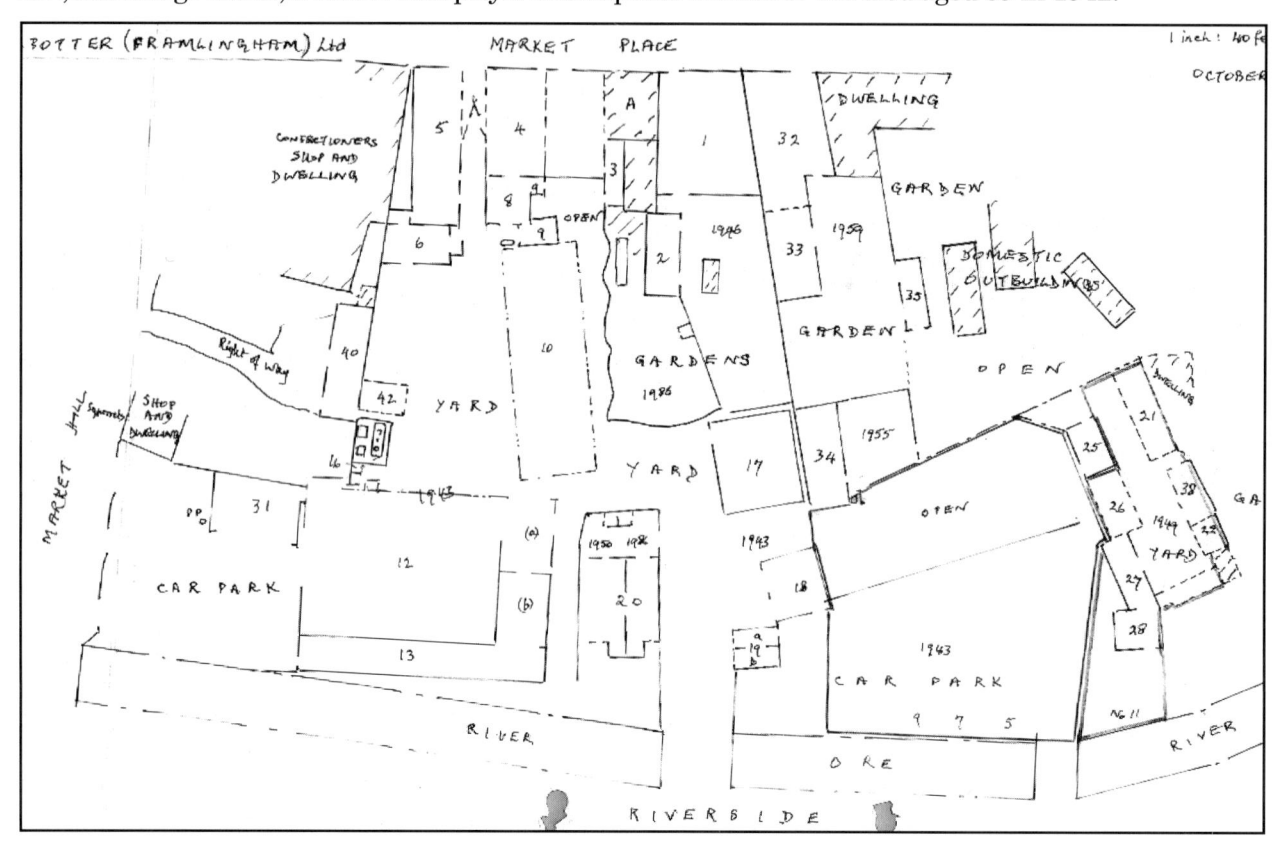

Plan of Potter's Garage Property

HENRY SAMPSON

Henry Sampson was born in 1629, son of William and Helen. William, a poet and a notable dramatist, died in 1636. Henry's mother was Helen Viccars, whose brother John was the renowned linguist and author of the *'Decapala in Psalmos'* drawn from sources in ten languages. Henry was himself an able linguist and scholar. He was educated in his step-father's grammar school at Atherston, and then at the Henry VIII Grammar School in Coventry, when his step-father, Obadiah Grew, moved to Coventry as a non-conformist minister. At 17 Henry became a pensioner (fee-paying student) of Pembroke Hall, and pupil of the nonconformist William Moses; in December 1646 he was elected to the Watts scholarship for the study of Greek.

Henry Sampson at the early age of 21 was made a Fellow of his College, and in 1650 was further rewarded by being appointed to St. Michael's, Framlingham, one of the richest and best livings in the gift of Pembroke Hall. He replaced Richard Golty, who had been sequestrated for refusing the Oath of Allegiance to the Commonwealth. In 1651 Pembroke Hall appointed Henry Sampson Lecturer in Greek, in 1652 Junior Bursar, and in 1653 Lecturer in Philosophy. Henry Sampson was also a well known Hebrew scholar - a man of much talent, a beloved teacher and preacher, and a writer - he wrote the '*golden epistle*', the Latin Preface to Thomas Parker's '*Methodus Gratiae Divinae*' (a copy of this book is in the Bodleian Library at Oxford).

He gave Foxe's *Book of Martyrs* to Framlingham Church. This outstanding man was in 1654 appointed one of the Commissioners for Suffolk. He introduced his brother-in-law, Jonathan Grew, a Pembroke graduate and strong non-conformist, to assist him in his care of the Parish of St. Michael's and to free him for his duties in Cambridge.

At the restoration of the monarchy in 1660, Henry refused to conform: he was deprived of his living in Framlingham and also lost his Fellowship of Pembroke Hall, though this was later restored to him by Royal Mandate. Henry Sampson at first chose to remain in Framlingham, where he had a large and devoted following. He preached in private houses, in the non-conformist chapel built in 1651 and in Lincoln's Barn with Thomas Mills.

In 1661 he married Margaret, daughter of Oliver Bromskill, Rector, during the Commonwealth, of Loughborough, Leicestershire, and they had a son, Nathaniel, who, with his Mother, died in 1662. In 1663 Henry Sampson wrote a short *History of Framlingham Castle* in which he described some of the buildings within the walls, which, in accordance with Sir Robert Hitcham's will, were demolished in 1656. Henry Sampson was never ordained, and shortly after his wife's death, deciding to become a medical doctor, he left Framlingham for Montpelier University, from which he transferred to Padua and then to Leiden, where he wrote his thesis and was awarded an M.D. He practised, mostly among the non-conformists, in London for 30 years, until his death in 1700. He was elected an Honorary Fellow of the College of Physicians in 1680.

JOHN SELF, J.P.

John Self, senior, took over the tailoring business run for 75 years in Well Close Square by Clodd & Larner. He was a Parish Councillor from 1896 to 1922 and a County Councillor from 1912. He moved into Henry Wells shop, where his wife ran a milliner's business above his tailoring business which provided ready made clothing, breeches, overcoats and ulsters in Melton, Beaver, tweed and worsted, with cord and velveteen vests (See advertisement). Both John Self senior and junior were photographers.

John Self junior married in, 1910 Mabel Lambert and in 1916 the shoe shop in Well Close Square was opened. John Self junior was a Parish Councillor from 1932 and Vice-chairman from 1937 to 1946 when he became Chairman until his death in 1958.

HENRY AND SIR HENRY THOMPSON

Henry Thompson's father, one of the five sons of Thomas Thompson, a curate at Mildenhall, came to Framlingham about 1755 and set up a grocery and drapery business which Henry Thompson inherited. Henry was a successful business man, a member of the Congregational Chapel, who married the daughter of the artist Samuel Medley, and they had one son Henry. It was assumed that he would, in turn, take over the business, but he elected to be apprenticed to a doctor in London, where he became a successful surgeon. Among his patients were Leopold the King of the Belgians, and later Napoleon III. He was appointed surgeon to Queen Victoria who created him a baronet. He was a talented artist recognised by the Royal Academy, and a photographer who developed a telescopic lens that was praised by officials at the Greenwich Observatory. He was instrumental in founding the temperance society in Framlingham in 1874, and the Cremation Society which was legalised in 1902 by Act of Parliament. In 1872 he presented Framlingham with a clock, accepted as the Parliamentary clock for the borough and positioned on the south side of the church tower.

HERBERT MANBY AND THE WALNE FAMILY

Herbert Manby came from Dennington in the 1890s, and set up his corn and coal business in Station Road, and from 1862 occupied Broadwater House, following the Corrance sale. On his retirement (in 1924/25) H.A. Walne from Kettleburgh became the owner, and his son Brian continued the corn business from 1969 until 1993. His brother, Mr. Leonard Walne in 1920 established the Riverside Garage and bought the Maulden Maltings from E.G. Clarke who had used the premises as a grain store. Additionally Leonard Walne bought and sold cars, and built a ramp so that these cars could be stored in the granary. His son Peter ran the business from 1952 to 1992. Sadly the main part of the granary building was burnt down in 1993, leaving the chimney as a reminder of its glory in former days.

SELECT BIBLIOGRAPHY

ALLEN, I. C.   Doctor on the Line

BOOTH, J.   Framlingham College, The first Sixty Years (1925)

CLAY, H.   A Guide to Framlingham (Harper, Halesworth)

GILLETT, L.   Framlingham College, The second Sixty Years (1992)

GRAY, S.   Framlingham Amateur Dramatic Society

GREEN, R.   A History of Framlingham, (London 1833)

GREEN, R.   The Stranger's Guide to Framlingham, (London, 1872)

HAWES & LODER   A History of Framlingham (Privately printed Woodbridge 1798)

JOHNSON, I.   Map of Townlands of Framlingham, 1797

KIRBY, J.   The Suffolk Traveller, 1735 (London 1764)

LAMBERT   Almanacks, 1873 - 1916 (Framlingham and Woodbridge)

SITWELL, O. R.   Framlingham Guide (Woodbridge, 1974)

DOMESDAY HERITAGE 1160

Index

A

Albert Memorial College 40, 42, 120
Almshouses 175
Anthony, Rev. Marcus 17, 116
Attwood, Rev. G. 32, 33, 34, 35, 43, 50, 111

B

Banking 82
Bibliography 180
Bickersteth, Rev. Edward 111
Bigod, Hugh, 4th earl of Norfolk (ob 1270) 8
Bigod, Roger, 5th earl of Norfolk (1245-1306) 9
Bigot, Hugh, created earl of Norfolk (1100-78) 4, 44
Bigot, Roger, 1st castle tenant 4, 44, 69, 123
Brickmaking 85
Brotherton, Thomas 123
Buckmaster, T.Twiddle 40, 49, 132
Buildings 87
    Castle 92
    Church, St. Michael's 100
    Corn Hall or Corn Exchange 88
    Court House 89
    Crown Inn 88
    Griffin Inn 89
    Guildhall 91
    Regency House or 7 Church Street 92
    The Ancient House 87

C

Chambers, Jemmy 45
Charitable benefaction 99
Charles I, king of England (1600-**25-49**) 133
Charles II, king of England (1630-**60-85**) 4, 22
Churchill, Winston 73, 76
Clarke E.G. 40, 123, 130, 178
Corrance, Frederick 40
Coucy le Château 81
Cover photograph (by courtesy of the East Anglian Daily Times) 7

D

Dale, Thomas 41
Danforth, Nicholas 16, 19, 133
Domesday 4
Duchess of Norfolk 10

Index

E

Edmund, St. king of East Angles (**841-870**) 4, 7
Education & Schools 116, 176
    East Suffolk Prize Scheme 116
Edward 'the Confessor', king of the English (**1042-1066**) 7
Edward I, king of England (1239-**72-1307**) 9
Edward II, king of England (1284-**1307-27**) 9
Edward III, king of England (1312-**27-77**) 9
Edward IV, king of England, (1442-**61-83**) 11
Edward V, king of England, (**1470-83**) 11
Edward VI, king of England (1537-**47-53**) 4, 20, 23, 44
Edward VII, king of England (1841-**1901-10**) 56, 57, 60
Edward VIII, king of England (1894-**1936-37**) 73
Elizabeth, queen of England (1533-**58-1603**) 13, 16, 104

F

Fairs 9, 123
Families 165
    Buckmaster 167
    Clarke 167
    Corrance 168
    Fruer 168
    Garrard 170
    Golty 170
    Green 171
    Hitcham 171
    Keer 165
    Kinnell 172
    Lambert 172
    Lanman 172
    Larner 172
    Manby/Walne 178
    Maulden 173
    Mills 174
    Porter 175
    Potter 176
    Sampson 177
    Self 177
    Thompson 178
Farming 123
Fire Service 58, 67, 73, 74, 76, 125
Flodden field 12, 15
Flodden Helm 71, 105, 172
Framlingham Castle 4, 6, 8, 9, 10, 11, 12, 13, 14, 15, 16, 20, 21, 33, 38, 39, 43, 45, 48, 51, 52, 54, 60, 62, 68, 76, 81, 88, 123, 125, 130, 171

Index

F

Framlingham Castle (cont'd)
    imprisonment of recusant Roman Catholics 14
    pond 78
    re-use of castle building materials 20
    Saxon castle 6
    workhouse 33
Framlingham College 32, 39, 40, 51, 55, 62, 75, 77, 85, 121, 146

G

George I, king of England (1660-**1714-27**) 23
George V, king of England (1865-**1910-36**) 60, 61, 72, 73
George VI, king of England (1895-**1937-52**) 73
Golty, Richard 15, 16, 18, 23, 105, 123, 133, 177
Green, Richard 41, 43, 116, 123, 135, 140, 146, 165, 172
Grey, lady Jane (1537-54) 4

H

Hart, Jonathan 41
Hawes, Robert 4, 21, 25, 99, 108, 153, 175
Henry I, king of England (1068-**1100-35**) 8
Henry II, king of England (1133-**54-89**) 8
Henry III, king of England (1207-**16-72**) 8, 9
Henry IV, king of England (1367-**99-1413**) 10
Henry V, king of England (1387-**1413-22**) 10
Henry VI, king of England (1421-**1422-1461**) 10
Henry VII, king of England (1457-**85-1509**) 11
Henry VIII, king of England (1491-**1509-47**) 12, 102, 104
Henry, earl of Surrey 101, 102, 104, 105
Hereford, duke of 10
Hitcham and Mills charities 48
Hitcham, Sir Robert (1576-1636) 5, 16, 17, 20, 23, 27, 32, 39, 43, 45, 48, 85, 99, 104, 105, 116, 121, 175, 177
Howard, Philip, son of 4th duke of Norfolk 14, 104
Howard, Thomas 104
Hoxne 7, 16

I

Inns 127

Index

J

James I, king of England (**1566-1625**) 14, 104
James I, king of England (**1566-1625**) 171
James II, king of England (1633-**85-88**-1701) 22
Jeaffreson pump 64, 139, 152
Jeaffreson, J.P., Dr. G.E. 53, 54, 57, 139
John, king of England (1167?-**99-1216**) 8, 44

K

Keer, George Brooke 28, 29, 34, 82, 85, 123, 130, 167, 173
Kerrison, Sir Edward 48, 51
Kinnell, Dr. John 29

L

Lambert, Robert 40, 41, 43, 45, 46, 53, 57, 60, 92, 135, 139, 140, 173
Lancaster, duke of 10
Lanchester, Rev. H.C.O. 64, 72, 112
Lanman 89
Larner, James 48, 51
Ludbrook, John 46

M

Magna Carta 9, 44
Maltings 5, 25, 41, 52, 61, 123, 130, 168, 173, 178
Mary, queen of England (1516-**53-58**) 4, 16, 20, 44, 78, 88, 104, 138
Mary, queen of Scots (**1542-87**) 4, 14
Matilda, the empress (**1102-67**) 8
Maulden, James 41, 52, 61, 123, 153
Maulden, James Jnr. 124, 130, 173
Mayhew, William (ob. 1715) 21, 43, 99, 134, 174, 175
Mills Girls Grammar School 67, 76, 121, 122
Mills Grammar School 123
Mills, Mayhew tomb 176
Mills, Thomas 32, 43, 48, 99, 113, 116, 121, 133, 134, 135, 171, 173, 174, 177
Moses, William 17

N

Non-conformity 133
Norfolk, John Howard, 1st duke of (2nd creation) (1430?-85) 11
Norfolk, John Mowbray (1406-34) 10
Norfolk, John Mowbray, 3rd duke of (1415-61) 10
Norfolk, Margaret, duchess of 10

Index

N

Norfolk, Roger de Bigod, 2nd earl of (ob. 1220) 5
Norfolk, Thomas de Brotherton, earl of (1300-38) 9, 10
Norfolk, Thomas Howard, 2nd duke of, earl of Surrey (1443-1524) 11, 15, 102, 104
Norfolk, Thomas Howard, 3rd duke of (1473-1554) 12, 16, 101, 102, 104, 105
Norfolk, Thomas Howard, 4th duke of (1536-72) 13, 23, 88, 101, 102, 104, 112
Norfolk, Thomas Mowbray, 1st duke of (1st creation) (1366?-99) 10
Northampton, Henry Howard, earl of (1540-1614) 14

P

Pageant 71
Parish Council 5, 52, 53, 57, 70, 89, 121, 122, 125, 126, 138, 151, 152, 167, 176, 177, 178
Peirson, Jasper 37, 40, 42, 51, 131, 168
Peirson, John 132, 135
Pembroke College 43, 45, 51, 60, 62, 64, 68, 69, 78, 79, 109
Pembroke Hall 5, 16, 23, 27, 33, 34, 99, 105, 116, 133, 170, 171, 177
Pembroke, William Marshal, earl of (1146-1219) 8
Pilkington, Rev. J.H. 62, 64, 111, 112
Plague 5, 9
Potter A.G. 40, 58, 62, 72, 78, 126
Prince Albert Memorial College for Boys 5
Printing 140
Public Houses 129

R

Raedwald, king of East Angles (?-**616-?**) 6
Railway 5, 37, 40, 52, 78, 145
Read, Francis 57, 60
Read, T.W. 138, 139
Richard I, 'Coeur de Lion', king of England (1157-**89-99**) 8
Richard II, king of England (1367-**77-99**-1400) 10
Richard III, king of England (1452-**83-5**) 11
Roads 146
Roman Catholicism 137
Roubiliac memorial 109, 175

S

Sampson, Henry 16, 133, 171, 177
Saxon castle 6, 7, 44
Saxon church 7
Self, John 51, 53, 57, 62, 69, 72, 127

Index

S

Services
- Lighting 151
- Sewage 151
- Telephone 152
- Water 152

St. Edmund 44, 78
St. Michael's Church 4, 15, 17, 23, 28, 34, 35, 39, 43, 51, 54, 60, 61, 64, 66, 92, 100, 101, 126, 134, 167, 170, 171, 175, 177
- bells 52, 65, 72, 76, 77, 114, 126, 135
- building of 11
- chancel improvements 12
- clock 41, 64, 77, 80
- dedication 43
- despoilation 105
- dimensions 43
- gallery 43
- gates 78
- income 25
- organ 43, 52, 109, 113
- re-opening 52

Stephen, king of England (1097?-**1135-54**) 8
Suffolk, Theophilus Howard, earl of 5, 14
Suffolk, William Ufford, earl of 9, 16
Surrey, Henry Howard, earl of (1517?-47) 12
Surrey, John Mowbray, earl of (1231?-1304) 11
Surrey, Thomas Howard, earl of (1443-1524) 11

T

Tanneries 153
Thompson, Abraham 27, 29, 36, 37, 40, 41
Thompson, Henry 40, 41, 42
Thompson, Sir Henry 41, 48
Toms, Samuel Say 29, 43, 88, 111, 134
Trades 154

U

U.S.A. 390th Bomber Group 5, 74, 75

V

Victoria, queen of England (1819-**37-1901**) 34, 39, 51, 54, 56, 178
Vines, Richard 17

Index

W

William I, 'The Conqueror', king of England (1027-**66-87**) 7, 8
William II, Rufus, king of England (**1087-1100**) 8
Windmill 5, 25, 124, 131
Wren, Christopher 109
Wren, Matthew 16, 17